POWER, CULTURE,
AND RELIGION
IN FRANCE
c.1350–c.1550

POWER, CULTURE, AND RELIGION IN FRANCE c.1350–c.1550

Edited by
Christopher Allmand

THE BOYDELL PRESS

© Contributors 1989

First published 1989 by The Boydell Press, Woodbridge

The Boydell Press is an imprint of Boydell & Brewer Ltd
PO Box 9, Woodbridge, Suffolk IP12 3DF
and of Boydell & Brewer Inc.
Wolfeboro, New Hampshire 03894–2069, USA

ISBN 0 85115 514 6

British Library Cataloguing in Publication Data

Power, culture, and religion in France c.1350–c.1550
1. France, 1328–1589
I. Allmand, C. T. (Christopher Thomas), 1936–
944′.025
ISBN 0–85115–514–6

Library of Congress Cataloging-in-Publication Data

Power, culture, and religion in France, c.1350–c.1550 /
edited by Christopher Allmand.
   p. cm.
Based on papers presented at a conference held at the
University of Liverpool in 1987.
Includes bibliographies.
ISBN 0–85115–514–6 (alk. paper)
  1. France – Civilization – 1328–1600 – Congresses.
  2. Politics and culture – France – History – Congresses.
  3. Reformation – France – Congresses. I. Allmand, C. T.
DC33.2.P68   1989
944 – dc19   88–7932
                                                       CIP

The paper used in this publication meets the
minimum requirements of American National Standard
for Information Sciences – Permanence of Paper for
Printed Library Materials, ANSI Z39.48–1984

Printed in Great Britain by
St Edmundsbury Press, Bury St Edmunds, Suffolk

12-11-90

CONTENTS

ILLUSTRATIONS

ACKNOWLEDGEMENTS

Our thanks are due to Mrs Janet Barlow (*née* Shirley) and the Oxford University Press for agreeing that short passages from the *Journal d'un Bourgeois de Paris, 1405–1449* should be taken from Mrs Barlow's translation, *A Parisian Journal, 1405–1449*, published by the Oxford University Press in 1968.

ABBREVIATIONS

A.D.	Archives Départementales
A.N.	Archives Nationales
BEC	*Bibliothèque de l'École des Chartes*
B.L.	British Library
B.N.	Bibliothèque Nationale
EHR	*English Historical Review*
ms. fr.	manuscrit français
ms. lat.	manuscrit latin
Nouv. acq. fr.	Nouvelle acquisition française
P.R.O.	Public Record Office, London
Rot. Parl.	*Rotuli Parliamentorum*
RS	Rolls Series
SHF	Société de l'Histoire de France

INTRODUCTION

England has never lacked historians interested in France and in her past.[1] Some periods, particularly those of the modern era, have had notable contributions made to them by British historians. Today (even today!) it is not unusual for a university department of History to have one or more specialists in the subject among its members. French historians will recognise that their British counterparts, both through works of synthesis and the more specialised, often localised, study, have made a not insignificant contribution to the history of France.

In addition to those works which have reached publishers' lists or the pages of academic periodicals there have been others, largely theses presented for higher degrees, whose contents and conclusions have remained unpublicised, their contribution to historical scholarship unrecognised. It was in the hope of bringing at least a few of these to light that it was decided to convene a small colloquium at Liverpool University in April 1987, to which were invited a number of scholars with interests in the history of late medieval and early modern France and, most welcome, a small number whose training was more literary than historical. The papers which make up this collection were presented on that occasion, some in a slightly different form from that in which they are offered here. Granted the backgrounds of the contributors, the papers deal with a diversity of subjects which, none the less, have certain things in common. As a group, they are based upon a wide variety of sources, literary, archival, and artistic, which, together, draw upon the evidence to be found in the main Parisian centres and in France's network of provincial libraries and archives.

Many of the papers carry wider implications than their titles and contents may seem to suggest. Dr Ditcham's contribution on French reactions to the presence of foreign, in particular of Scottish soldiers in France in the fifteenth century considers how soldiers, brought in to fight for the king, were regarded by the French upon whose land they made war, and whose properties and titles were granted to them as rewards.[2] In the context of the present collection it is almost as important to stress the dependence of the crown of France upon forces from Scotland, as it struggled to stem the advance of English and Burgundian armies in the early years of the reign of Charles VII. This contribution demonstrates how, *in extremis*, the

---

[1]   The recent foundation of a Society for the Study of French History, with its *Bulletin* and its annual conference, together with the decision to publish a periodical, *French History*, are but the most recent manifestations of that interest.

[2]   See also Bernard Chevalier, 'Les Écossais dans les armées de Charles VII jusqu' à la bataille de Verneuil', *Jeanne d'Arc, une époque, un rayonnement* (C.N.R.S., Paris, 1982), pp. 85–94.

practical exercise of royal power came to depend upon military aid brought in
from abroad. Furthermore, whatever help the Scots may be judged to have given
the French against the English (the point is debatable), their very presence may
have contributed in a rather unexpected way by helping to create a reaction
against the foreign 'saviour', thereby furthering the growth of a sense of 'Frenchness' developing in France as the country struggled against the effects of war and
invasion. The forming of the royal Guard, built around a rump of those Scots who
had come to serve the French crown, may be seen as rather more than the creation of a body of men engaged to defend the royal person, although it did just
that. Its presence in France, and in particular at the court, may have had an influence when, in the middle years of the century, the decision was taken to establish
a more permanent force to defend the country as a whole. But the new force was
not to be made up of foreign soldiers; by then, the king was sufficiently in control
of his country to be able to count on his own subjects. The employment of Scots
had been a sign of weakness. The change was to symbolize the crown's growing
strength and confidence.

It is generally recognized that the treaty of Troyes of 1420, far from uniting
France, deeply divided her, with some communities looking to one king, others to
the other. The city of Paris and the 'bourg' of Saint-Denis, which included the
ancient and prestigious Benedictine abbey of that name, followed different political allegiances, in spite of the fact that the distance between them could be
travelled in two hours on foot. As Dr Thompson reminds us, one of the points to
be emphasised is that the abbey of Saint-Denis was the spiritual centre of the
French monarchy which, while the English occupied Paris between 1420 and
1436, represented an outpost of loyalty to the Valois dynasty whose representative, the Dauphin, had been excluded from the throne by the terms of the
treaty of Troyes. The monks, guardians of the tombs of the kings of France and,
more recently, of those of two notable royal servants, Bertrand du Guesclin and
Louis de Sancerre, were also keepers of the sacred 'oriflamme', the standard of the
monarchy and the nation at war. Furthermore, the monastery was heir to a tradition in historical writing which made it a strong supporter of the legitimate Valois
kings as the defenders of the kingdom and its unity. The English, likewise, appreciated the role which the abbey could play in furthering their cause. To them,
'Monseigneur Saint Denis', the saint himself, represented, along with St George of
England, the notion of the two saints working together, as they appear to be doing
on the reredos of the chapel in Henry V's chantry in Westminster Abbey. Appro-
priately enough, it was at the burial of Charles VI at Saint-Denis in November
1422 that the Duke of Bedford claimed the kingdom for his young nephew, Henry
VI. To do this in the abbey itself, at the funeral of the last Valois king, was the
most effective way of underlining the English claim to the succession enshrined in
the treaty of Troyes, a claim which Bedford badly needed to stress. Saint-Denis
was a sacred place where each side in the dynastic struggle could see its claim receive legitimization. Its place in the war of ideas was thus a significant one.

The close link between culture and the exercise of power, and the ways in which political ideas and concepts could be expressed through cultural means, is one which, in recent years, has greatly interested historians of France, and not merely those of the Middle Ages.[3] It is scarcely surprising, therefore, to find over half the contributions to this collection dealing with aspects of that theme. In time of war, in particular one resulting from disputed legal rights, it was necessary to be assertive in reminding all, both friend and foe, that a claim being pursued by force was a rightful one. The importance of the visual symbol, by which even modern man, for all his sophistication, is still heavily influenced, is rightly emphasised by more than one contributor as having been of importance in this process. Wars could be fought with pictures as well as with arms. The figure on coin or seal, the emblem shown on tapestry (or, in time of financial stringency, in paint), the impact of formal ceremonial associated with a coronation or a royal Entry into a loyal town, all were ways in which the need to impress the senses provided opportunity for artistic imagination – as well as work for the artist himself, starved as he might be by conditions of war or economic depression of the chance of major commissions. In such circumstances the artist who came to court, where such wealth as there was might be found, could be employed for purposes which had a political end. Whether, as Miss Rosie shows, he used his skills to organize festivals of music and dance at the court of Savoy (at which painters, embroiderers, players of a variety of musical instruments, dancers, even cooks, were given ample opportunity of displaying their skills), or, as Mrs Richards demonstrates, he took part in the elaborate and expensive ceremonial deemed appropriate in a great city like Rouen to make an impression upon the young Francis I (by praising him for what he had already achieved, by hinting at glory to come, and by seeking favours for the city which entertained him in this way) the artist was helping to prepare what Dr Reynolds has justly termed 'functional imagery' for an overtly political purpose, whether that was the esteem in which the Savoyard court would be held by influential persons from outside the duchy who happened to visit it, or the personal reputation of a young king who had already won success in battle against his country's enemies.

Art might thus be used, for instance, to enhance the king's position through the image which it could help to create both of him as a person and of the position which he occupied as the leader of French society. This was done on the occasion of the king's visit to Rouen in August 1517; the lavish Entry organized on that occasion was intended to increase popular esteem for both the king himself and the

---

[3]   The best general work on this broad subject must be that of Bernard Guenée, *States and Rulers in Later Medieval Europe* (Oxford: New York, 1985); not the least important aspect of this book is its excellent bibliography. Four recent works may also be noted here: *Culture et idéologie dans la genèse de l'état moderne* (Collection de l'École Française de Rome, 82), Rome, 1985; Colette Beaune, *Naissance de la nation France* (Paris, 1985); *Idéologie et propagande en France* ed. Myriam Yardeni (Paris, 1987); and C. de Mérindol, *Le Roi René et la seconde maison d'Anjou. Emblématique, art, histoire* (Paris, 1987).

majesty of monarchy which he personified. Yet attempts to emphasise the role played by the king and the monarchy (seen as both ruling and representing a united France) were far from new in the early sixteenth century. As Dr Daly shows, the writing of history in France, undertaken in the previous century by a group of royal secretaries who, as servants of the crown, had access to its records and archives, encouraged the development of an historical and intellectual basis for monarchical authority which, since the early fourteenth century, had been challenged by a succession of English kings through means of propaganda, as Miss Danbury's paper shows. The recovery of France and of the Valois monarchy in the second half of the fifteenth century owes something to these writers who, using their art for political ends, stressed the assumption, derived from their particular reading of history, that France possessed a natural and ancient identity founded upon a strong monarchy whose power was further strengthened by the unity of the country based upon a common past and a common development and, by implication, a common destiny, too.

We are brought back once more to the functionalism of art, whether the creation of the painter with his brush or of the writer with his pen. Courts were centres of patronage; they were also centres of political power; and patronage, properly used, could be employed to develop that power. All over Europe at this time the artist was being called upon by the courts to help create political images, even political myths, through appeals to the senses, the emotions, and the intellect. That all this was necessary presupposes two developments to which reference must be made. The first was what we would today call 'public opinion' as an important 'growth-factor' in late medieval life. In an age when rulers were coming to depend more and more upon public support in their pursuit of particular political or military policies, art which could play a persuasive or didactic function in the growth of greater participation in the public life of France was worthy of encouragement. Secondly, we should not forget how such developments furthered the evolution of a wider group-consciousness, or nationalism, within France, not least by stressing that the French crown and its people were blessed and approved by God himself. The need to rebut English claims to France, and to show that the Valois were true kings of that country (surely proved, it was argued, by the length of the line from which they were descended) was a crucial aspect of the work of lawyers and compilers of histories who helped to create a greater sense of French nationhood around those already prestigious symbols of authority and power, the monarchy and royal family of France.

Finally, there is the link provided by humanism between the papers presented by Dr Daly and Mrs Richards on the one hand, and that of Dr Nicholls on the other. Humanism reflected a particularly intellectual approach to social and religious attitudes. If there was, in the works of the secretary-historians, and in the minds of those who prepared the elaborate Entry of Francis I into Rouen, an attempt to air the relationship between ruler and subject, the humanistic contribution to the Reformation was essentially one to the debate concerning the relationship between God and man. What was important was the very conscious attempt to intellectualize the approach to these relationships. Historically speaking, too, of no less significance were those persons responsible for such developments, and the milieux from which they sprang. Those who wrote history with the purpose of emphasising the role of the monarchy were almost all office-holders in its employ, most of them men with a legal background and training. Those who were to play a significant part in furthering the advance of reformed ideas in Tours, for example, were men of the same sort and background, educated bureaucrats, who held positions of (public) responsibility. These were the mainly educated people who reflected the progress which humanistic ideas had been making in France since the end of the fourteenth century (earlier than in England), progress which was to be seen later principally among those employed at court (to the benefit of the monarchy, whose powers they advocated) and others who, forming urban élites, were in a position to found new colleges in which some of the reformers were educated and where new approaches to religion and religious attitudes could be developed and taught. The links between the humanism of the fifteenth century and that of the sixteenth, which reflected the practical application of the intellectual developments of the period, need following up. In the meanwhile, something of the indivisibility of history, in spite of the remains of the traditional barriers between late medieval and early modern history which still exist, is again underlined in the papers which follow.

'Mutton Guzzlers and Wine Bags': Foreign Soldiers and Native Reactions in Fifteenth-Century France

BRIAN G. H. DITCHAM

In late August 1423, Charles VII wrote to his loyal subjects in Lyon. It was not the happiest of occasions. The royal army had just been defeated by the Burgundians at Cravant with heavy loss of life. To cheer up his audience he made the following comment on the battle and its consequences: 'Anyway, at the said siege there were very few nobles of our realm, almost none in fact, but only Scots, Spaniards and other foreigners who normally live off the land so the harm done was not so great.'[1]

This was a curious thing for Charles to be saying, since in earlier and subsequent morale-boosting missives to Lyon and other towns in his obedience he had made regular play of the arrival of foreign contingents to bolster his forces (and was not above inventing such contingents if the circumstances seemed to demand it).[2] At the time that he wrote the letter Charles was engaged in negotiations to ransom Stewart of Darnley, commander of the Scots he had so disparaged, and to that end he agreed not only to make a financial contribution of 500 *livres tournois* (which even appears to have been paid) but to exchange the Marshal of Burgundy who had been captured at La Bussière.[3] There is a contradiction here

---

[1] L. Caillet, *Étude sur les relations de la commune de Lyon avec Charles VII et Louis XI* (Paris: Lyon, 1909), pp.106–7: 'Tous voyes n'y avoit il au dit siege que tres peu et comme rien des nobles de nostre royaume, mais seulement Escoz, Espaignaulx et autres gens estrangiers qui avoient accoustume de vivre sur le pays et par quoy le dommage n'en est pas si grant.'

[2] For example, the mythical reinforcements under the Earl of Mar and the Marquis of Ferrara talked of after Verneuil (See G. du Fresne de Beaucourt, *Histoire de Charles VII* (6 vols., Paris, 1881–91), II, p. 79.

[3] On La Bussière, which was very much an Italian victory, see Gilles le Bouvier (dit Herault Berri), 'Chronique du feu roy Charles septième' *Histoire de Charles VII*, ed. D. Godefroy (Paris, 1661), p. 370; *Les Chroniques du roi Charles VII par Gilles le Bouvier, dit le Héraut Berry*, ed H. Courteault and L. Celier, with M.-H. Jullien de Pommerol (SHF, Paris, 1979), pp.113–14; and Guillaume Cousinot, *Chronique de la Pucelle*, ed. A. Vallet de Viriville (Paris, 1859), p. 221. On the payments to Darnley, see E. Cust, *Some Account of the Stuarts*

which it is the purpose of this paper to explore. How did the French, from the king down to a shoemaker in Dax, and passing through bishops, nobles, irate householders and peasants, react to the influx of foreigners from Spain, Italy and especially Scotland come to fight the wars of their monarch?

Officially, the highest mutual esteem was deemed to prevail. Alain Chartier was the spokesman for this attitude in the eulogy which he made of the valour of those Scots who had fought in France delivered at the Scottish court in 1436 when he formed part of the embassy which collected Margaret of Scotland to take her to her promised husband, the Dauphin·Louis. This resounded with phrases like 'grandis fiducia inter duos regnos Franciae et Scotiae',[4] and echoed his much earlier words in the *Quadrilogue Invectif* ('We see foreign allies of our realm who brave the dangers of the deep to come to our aid and share in our adversity and troubles' – though one should bear in mind that this exemplary behaviour was being stressed in order to throw the sloth of the French nobility into higher relief).[5] Traces of a similar attitude can be found in chronicle sources.[6] High office was distributed to foreigners without any obvious discrimination; the Earl of Buchan became Constable of France in 1421, the Earl of Douglas was named Duke of Touraine in 1424, the Italian Théaude de Valpergue served for many years as *bailli* of Lyon and was made mayor of the freshly-conquered town of Bayonne – the list is lengthy.[7] As late as the Estates General of 1484 complaints were being made about the number of foreigners in high office.[8] Most visible of all, there was the king's own Scottish Guard, a pampered body of men, though far from a purely ceremonial unit, as their exploits at Montlhéry showed.[9] We can still see them in

---

of Aubigny, in France, (1422–1672) (London, 1891), pp.10–11. Darnley was, however, still struggling to meet the costs of his ransom in Jan. 1427, when he wrote to the Lyonnais asking for help in repaying 6,000 écus borrowed from Tanguy du Chastel (Caillet, *Étude*, pp. 85–6).

4   B.N., ms.lat.8757, fo. 50.

5   Alain Chartier, *Le Quadrilogue Invectif*, ed. E. Droz (Paris, 1923), p. 51: 'nous voions les estrangiers alliez de nostre royaume qui passent les fortunes de mer pour venir a nostre secours et estre parçonniers de nostre adversité et de nostre paine.'

6   On Buchan and his men 'qui moult vaillament se portent en gardant leur loyauté au roy nostre sire', see *La Chronique du Mont-Saint-Michel*, ed. S. Luce (2 vols, Paris, 1879–83), I, p. 25.

7   For more detailed information about the recruitment and careers of the foreign units in the French forces during the fifteenth century, see B. Ditcham, 'The Employment of Foreign Mercenary Troops in the French Royal Armies, 1415–1470' (unpublished Edinburgh University Ph.D. thesis, 1979).

8   P. Contamine, *Guerre, état et societé à la fin du moyen âge; études sur les armées du roi de France, 1337–1494* (Paris: The Hague, 1972), p. 419.

9   They were recorded by Jean de Roye as having saved Louis XI's life there (*Journal de Jean de Roye, connu sous le nom de 'Chronique Scandaleuse'*, ed. B. de Mandrot (2 vols, SHF, Paris, 1894), I, pp. 66–7). The Guard's own muster rolls record the casualties of the day: Thomas Wild, Robert Ros, Jehan Keslin (or Herskin), Guille Edmonston, and David Crespin (See

Etienne Chevalier's Book of Hours, resplendent in their parade ground uniforms as they stand guard over Charles in his role as first of the magi.[10]

One can however cast doubts on the consistency and reliability of royal favour to foreigners. The very pattern of recruitment suggests that they were a necessary evil endured for lack of an alternative rather than warmly welcomed friends in need. In the 1420s any country with a tradition of alliance with France could expect to be pestered with embassies seeking military aid (Castile alone received four, all sent away empty handed – no doubt because the French expected them to fight at their own expense).[11] French emissaries bought armies 'off the shelf' in Scotland and Italy to plug the gaps left in the French ranks by Agincourt and the Burgundian defection. For a time in that decade it would have been hard for Charles to put any kind of army into the field without a substantial foreign contingent. With the turn of the tide, mass foreign recruitment ceased. The 6,000 men, whom the 1428 marriage agreement between Margaret and Louis had called upon to escort the bride on her passage to France and then enter French service,[12] were politely turned away on grounds of cost when they actually arrived in 1436.[13] At the individual level, royal generosity to foreigners had a distressing habit of being short-lived and unstable. After the earl's death at Verneuil, Douglas' wife and son (the latter, as Earl of Wigtown, had done much service himself in France) were rapidly pushed out of the estates granted to Douglas with little concern for legal niceties.[14]

Wigtown himself lost his lands at Dun-le-Roi in 1431 since he was not there to defend them, and they were needed to reward another, the Breton, Richemont.[15] It is hard to imagine that Charles could have been so high-handed with a native French family. In practice, royal gifts made in moments of desperation all too often turned out to be not worth the parchment they were written on, unless an heir was on hand to enforce his rights of inheritance. Those families, like the

---

W. Forbes-Leith, *The Scots Men-at-Arms and Lifeguards in France* (2 vols, Edinburgh, 1882), II, p. 36).

[10] Most recently illustrated on the dust jacket of M. G. A. Vale, *Charles VII* (London, 1974). The Guard was expensive; the royal stable accounts for the year Oct. 1463–Sept. 1464 alone record payments of over 3,620 *livres tournois*, mostly for uniforms (A.N., KK 65, fos 100–112v). During the 'Guerre du Bien Publique', the year's new issue of uniforms spent much time on the road between Tours and Paris, following a tortuous route to avoid rebel forces, only meeting up with their intended owners at Rouen early in 1466 (A.N., KK 65, fo. 236).

[11] B.N., ms.lat.6024, fos 12–16, gives an account of a failed mission in 1428. On recruitment in general, see Ditcham, 'Employment', ch. 5.

[12] A.N., J 678, nos 21–6.

[13] B.N., ms.fr. 17330, fo.123.

[14] For the grant of the lands, see A.N., X1a 8604, fos 69v–70v; for the Countess of Douglas' arguments for at least a share of the duchy, and Charles' disingenuous replies, see B.N., ms.lat.10187, fos 4–6v.

[15] A.N., X1a 8604, fos 109v–110.

Stewarts of Aubigny, which did manage to hold on to their gains, recognised this fact, and chose to settle in France on a permanent basis.[16] Even those who did this, however, might find themselves vulnerable to the shifts of royal policy; when Louis XI became reconciled with the Chabannes family, one of the incidental victims was a Scot who was deprived of lands he had been given some twenty years before for being the first man to enter Pontoise when it had been taken in 1441, and was now forced into an unequal exchange.[17] Foreigners had fewer close allies to help them play the patronage game and fight off royal encroachments than had the native French.

The fickleness of royal favour, however, may have been less apparent than its scale, at least in the 1420s when the pot of royal patronage was in any case distressingly poorly filled. Those who habitually dipped into it, the native French nobility, appear to have felt that foreigners were crowding them out of their rightful position as the prime benificiaries of royal favour, and resented them accordingly. The Scottish chroniclers who recorded the experiences of their compatriots in France wrote of the scorn and hostility of the French, who referred to their allies as mere 'mutton guzzlers and wine bags' and tried to steal all the glory of the victory at Baugé.[18] Hard though it is to prove, it seems likely that the appointment of Buchan as Constable was resented as much as that of the almost equally foreign Richemont was to be later. While the conflicting accounts of what happened at Verneuil cast an almost impenetrable fog around this particularly bloody battle, it looks very much as if any plans for a coordinated French attack foundered on differences between Buchan and the viscount of Narbonne, with the result that the French army went into battle in conditions of some confusion. One can easily see why French commanders could have resented foreign privileges. The status of the Army of Scotland (which existed as an entirely separate entity in the French forces, with its own command structure and administration, and whose commander was at least on certain occasions given the privilege of being paid for whatever number of men he cared to claim as being under his command) must have been a permanent irritation to French commanders struggling to obtain payment from an impecunious monarch.[19] In 1424 Charles was even reduced to the desperate expedient of disbanding most of his army on financial grounds; the Scottish and Italian units were among those exempted in another show of favour which cannot have endeared them to the native nobility.[20] This understandable irritation may have blinded them to certain facts. Many rewards were honorific rather than im-

[16] Though Darnley's widow had to go to law to keep her lands after his death (A.N., X1a 9199, fo.191).
[17] H. de Chabannes, *Histoire de la maison de Chabannes* (10 vols, Dijon, 1892–1901), II, pp.111–12.
[18] *Book of Pluscarden*, ed. F. Skene (Edinburgh, 1890), p. 354.
[19] A. Stuart, *A Genealogical History of the Stewarts* (London, 1798), p.129, which uses documentation now destroyed.
[20] B.N., Fonds Doat, 9, p. 279.

mediately profitable to their recipients: for example Darnley's right to quarter the royal arms of France with his own, or the gift of the county of Evreux made to him while it was entirely in English hands; nor is there evidence that he benefited from the royal right to buy it back for 50,000 *livres*.[21] Foreign commanders appear to have had as much trouble as anybody in ensuring that they were actually paid in those bad days, and many ended deep in debt incurred in the royal service.[22]

When things improved for the monarchy from the 1430s onward, the growing size of the cake of royal patronage seems to have stilled resentment at the size of the slices coming into foreign hands, despite the spectacular way in which the Italian, Théaude de Valpergue, and his clan, or the Scot, Pettilot, could milk the system for their own profit,[23] although complaining voices could still be heard. In this period noble resentment against foreigners, where it can be detected, focussed on other aspects of their role in France. Antoine de Chabannes (admittedly a doubtful witness since he was under interrogation for his own plots against Charles VII) told of the Dauphin, Louis, pointing to a member of the Scots Guard and saying 'There goes one of those who keep the kingdom of France in subjection', and going on to refer cryptically to people who would behave differently if the Guard were not there.[24] This would appear to point to a clear and resented political role for the foreign units in the French army and ties in with Kiernan's emphasis on the role of mercenaries as the pillars of absolutism in early modern Europe.[25] There is some evidence to this effect: for instance, the slaughter of the Genoese crossbowmen in the streets of Paris when the Burgundians took the city in 1418, since they were seen as the mainstay of the detested Armagnac regime; [26] or Richemont's allegation, when out of favour in 1425, that his court enemies were recruiting foreigners to serve against him.[27] No doubt the continued loyalty of the Guard was a vital factor in keeping court faction under control, but it would, I think, be exaggerating to read into this one *ex parte* statement that the Scots were widely resented by the nobility as a whole as the upholders of a detested royal tyranny. Louis' main complaint was no doubt that the Guard was too loyal to Charles to permit him to seize power for himself. The Guard was certainly a highly political unit, as the purges associated with the arrest of its captain, Cunningham, on trumped-up treason charges in 1455, and those which followed

[21] A.N., J 216, no. 20; K 168, no. 682; X1a 8604, fo.100v; Stuart, *Genealogical History*, p.144.

[22] For the financial problems of foreign mercenaries, see Ditcham, 'Employment', pp. 202–07.

[23] *Ibid.*, pp. 213–17.

[24] B.N., ms.fr. 20427, fo. 3.

[25] V. Kiernan, 'Foreign Mercenaries and Absolute Monarchy', *Past & Present*, no.11 (1957), 66–86.

[26] Jean Juvénal des Ursins, *Chronique de Charles VI*, ed. Michaud et Poujoulet (Paris, 1836), p. 541.

[27] Caillet, *Étude*, p. 92.

the accession of Louis XI to the throne, clearly show.[28] For the same reason, however, the Guard was itself a crucial part of the patronage system, and thus inte-
grally involved in court intrigue, rather than standing above or outside it. There is
clear evidence that this was as true of the foreign units in the *compagnies d'ordonnance* as of the Guard or of the French units in the army. During the 'Guerre du
Bien Publique', an anonymous correspondent wrote to Louis XI from the Auvergne to tell him that the Scottish company under the same Cunningham who had
once commanded the Guard (and who was very much Louis' man) had, in effect,
been neutralised by the action of the rebels in sending Patrick Folcart (the co-
mander of the Guard who had been purged by Louis and who now served his
brother, Charles of France) around the company's billets to appeal to the men.
Since many had been victims of the purge of the Guard, the unit had split between Louis' supporters, Folcart's men, and a group who intended to sit tight and
see who won.[29] By the 1460s, at least, foreign troops were too well integrated into
the factions contending for power at court to make them any more reliable props
for despotism than their French equivalents. Nor did the French monarchy take
any positive steps to prevent this integration from happening, whether by ensuring a steady supply of fresh foreign soldiers or by seeking to insulate those whom it
had already raised from French society.

If the political role of foreign soldiers was less significant than may at first sight
appear, what did account for the fears and hatred which at times hung round
them? One clue may be found in the account of the battle of Verneuil given in
Thomas Basin's chronicle of the reign of Charles VII. After starting his account of
the battle with praise of the Scots (good soldiers, if over confident) he closed by
enumerating the Scottish dead and remarking in tones reminiscent of Charles
himself that their death was not the disaster it might have appeared since they
had plotted to take over much of central France for themselves.[30] One might dis-
count this very late account if the reaction of the city council in Tours (one of the
areas supposedly earmarked for Scottish control, and already in Douglas' territorial
endowment) did not suggest similar fears. Relations between Douglas and the city
had been stormy during his brief residence there, and one can almost detect a sigh
of relief in the council minutes when he marched out. After his death, the councillors acted swiftly and decisively to rid themselves of the Scottish presence. The
civic militia placed the remaining Scottish garrison under blockade in order to

---

[28] For the proceedings involving Cunningham, which dragged on from 1455 to 1457 and
strained diplomatic relations between France and Scotland, see Ditcham, 'Employment',
pp.136–40; while the 1457 purge in the Guard, which was presumably associated with
them, can be traced in Forbes-Leith, *The Scots Men-at-Arms*, II, pp. 21–3. For the purge at
Louis XI's accession, which involved about half the strength of the Guard, see Ditcham,
'Employment', pp.143–4, and Forbes-Leith, *The Scots Men-at-Arms*, II, pp. 25–40.

[29] B.N., ms.fr. 6971, fo.161.

[30] Thomas Basin, *Histoire de Charles VII*, ed. and trans. C. Samaran (2 vols, Paris, 1933), I,
p. 99.

prevent it from linking with other Scots in the countryside. An agreement was eventually reached whereby it was paid to evacuate the city, and similar agreements were subsequently entered into with other Scottish garrisons in the area.[31] Despite this success, the good bourgeois of Tours were haunted by the fear of a Scottish takeover (perhaps in the name of Douglas' heirs). When Isabelle of Anjou, Queen of Sicily and new lady of Tours, approached the walls in 1425 along with Richemont, there was a panic because her forces contained 'many foreign men-at-arms and archers such as Scots, Lombards and others who could do much damage to the city and country around if they were allowed to enter it'. That the real fear concerned the Scots is clear from the measures taken to cope with the emergency; the guard on the gates was reinforced and all Scots within the walls were expelled. A list of some eighteen names survives including women, men married to local women, and a Dominican friar.[32] Whether they were readmitted later is unclear: as so often, the evidence is ambiguous. Up to that moment most had presumably managed to live on reasonable terms with their neighbours, and the same entry in the council minutes shows that Scottish pillagers, like the Lord of Poloc (who persecuted the city intermittently during the 1420s and 1430s), had a house there. Tours however remained extremely wary of Scots. In 1435 one Pierre Caigne was paid compensation for a hat lost in a scuffle with a group of Scots trying to force an entry at one of the gates, and in the following year the city militia was called out to ensure that the men of Guille Stewart were kept a safe six leagues away from the city.[33] While the council might sometimes enter into formal protection agreements like that made in July 1433 with 'We, James Stewart, Bastard of Scotland',[34] its general view was that the best Scot was, if not a dead Scot, at least one far away from Tours.

Not all cities shared Tours' near paranoia (which was not entirely unjustified after the misfortune of falling into the hands of the Earl of Douglas, whose hunger for money was matched only by his military incompetence). Orléans had excellent relations with Darnley who had, at one point, promised to support the citizens in any dispute with the king 'as if they were of his own country'.[35] The anonymous author of the mystery play about the siege gives him a magnificent epitaph ('The most valiant on earth . . . who was so prudent in war'),[36] words

---

[31] A.D., Indre-et-Loire, BB 22, entries for 19 and 22 Aug. 1424; CC 21, fo. 95v.
[32] A.D., Indre-et-Loire, BB 23, fo. 37v: 'grant numbre de gens darmes et de trait estranges [comme] escossays, lombars et autres qui pourroient faire moult de maulx en ladite ville, si ilz entroient ou pais denviron.'
[33] A.D., Indre-et-Loire, CC 26, fos 47v, 112.
[34] A.D., Indre-et-Loire, BB 25, fos 172v–173.
[35] A.D., Loiret, CC 549, fo.17.
[36] Le Mistère du siège d'Orléans, ed. F. Guessard and E. de Certain (Paris, 1862), p. 342:

> 'Le plus vaillant dessus la terre . . .
> Qui estoit tant prudent en guerre
> On ne pourroit son bruit exquerre
> Tant estoit vaillant et hardi'.

spoken by Dunois, himself one of the central heroes of the story. Indeed his fame spread as far as Catalonia, where he could be presented as a model of chivalry.[37] In the 1430s his son was assured of a splendid reception in Orléans, while wounded Scottish veterans of the siege were still receiving municipal charity as late as 1443.[38] Orléans had a Scottish bishop and a university with a significant Scottish element and more reasons than most to be grateful to foreign soldiers. But in this it was perhaps hardly typical. Lyon may have been more so than either Tours or Orléans in the mixed nature of its relations with foreign soldiers: bad with its Italian *bailli*, Théaude de Valpergue, who meddled in its municipal government to an unacceptable extent; ambivalent with the Spanish *écorcheur*, Rodrigo de Villandrando, who might be given a torchlight reception and gifts of sugar, but who equally inspired fear at his approach; and cordial with the Italian, Caqueran, who invested money there and was helpful in its dealings with the king in the 1420s.[39]

Below the level of the nobility and the constituted authorities of the towns and the regional estates (which seem to have dealt with foreign companies in much the same way as they did with French ones, assessing them by the likelihood that they would offer effective protection in return for the money they extorted, to judge from the behaviour of the estates of Rouergue which were quite prepared to accept Villandrando's protection in 1438 in place of that of the House of Armagnac until the latter bestirred itself)[40] we enter a much more difficult world. In considering the attitudes of the mass of the population to foreigners, we have to face up to additional conceptual problems. Who, for instance, was a foreigner? Richemont's Bretons or Armagnac's southerners could appear as foreign as a Scot or an Italian to a peasant in the Champagne region. Furthermore, when we encounter apparent spasms of hatred of foreign troops, how far can one tell whether that hatred was aimed at the foreigner rather than the soldier, since it was almost axiomatic that all soldiers were detested by those who had close contact with them in late medieval France? If we find a peasant killing, say, a Scotsman who had just raped his wife, we can be reasonably sure that the Scottishness of his target was at most a secondary consideration nerving his arm as he drove the pitchfork home.

[37] Joannot Martorell and Marti Joan de Galba, *Tirant lo Blanc*, trans D. H. Rosenthal (London, 1984), p. 48, where 'Sir John Stuart of Darnley' is linked with Skanderbeg and an apparently mythical figure, called the Duke of Exeter, as one of the 'knights of our own time' worthy of honour.

[38] A.D., Loiret, CC 657, fo. 22v; CC 654, fo. 9.

[39] *Registres consulaires de la ville de Lyon; Recueil de délibérations du conseil de la commune*, ed. M.-C. Guigue (Lyon, 1882), pp.171, 352–3, 411, 416, 446, etc.; J. Quicherat, *Rodrigue de Villandrando* (Paris, 1879), pp. 247–8, 255–6. One of the complex financial affairs involving Lyon, into which both Valpergue and Caqueran were drawn, is recounted in detail by P. S. Lewis, 'The Centre, the Periphery, and the Problem of Power Distribution in later medieval France', *The Crown and Local Communities in England and France in the Fifteenth Century*, ed. J. R. L. Highfield and R. Jeffs (Gloucester, 1981), pp. 37–9; in this case Valpergue was in a helpful mood.

[40] A. Thomas, 'Rodrigo de Villandrando en Rouergue', *Annales du Midi*, ii (1896), 215.

Other cases are less clear cut. There is, it must be admitted, no entirely satisfactory solution to these problems. The best one can do is explore certain approaches which may bring us closer to the mind of the ordinary Frenchman and woman of the age.

The anonymous 'Complaint of the Poor Labourers of France' (not, of ocurse, written by a poor labourer) reproached the royal government for allowing the 'Rodrigois', that is, the international train of plunderers who followed Rodrigo de Villandrando, and the Scots to do as they pleased.[41] Whether foreign troops were really more undisciplined than Frenchmen is doubtful, given the record of French écorcheur commanders in the 1430s. In any case, the evidence which might permit us to come to a conclusion is lacking, since a full series of letters of remission does not begin until well into the 1440s and, while some issued in those years refer back to the preceding decade, they are not numerous enough to give the full picture. After 1445 one is dealing with the army of the compagnies d'ordonnance. While the changes which the establishment of this force made to the discipline of the royal forces can be greatly exaggerated (the bulk of the rank and file came from the écorcheur companies and had not changed their habits) it did, perhaps, focus trouble on the towns in a way which had not happened before.[42] In this context foreign troops are well represented among those petitioning for pardons (or as victims of those so doing). Contamine counts fifty-four out of 200 letters concerning soldiers in the post-1445 period as relating to foreigners, which would mean that they were heavily over-represented; on the other hand it is not entirely clear that he had counted all cases in which soldiers were the victims, and foreigners may have felt more inclined to purchase a pardon as a result, for instance, of social isolation.[43] Any figures relating to letters of remission should be treated with great caution. The evidence which they provide does, however, if used carefully throw an interesting light on what might happen at local level. Foreign companies do seem to have got into quarrels with the local population with considerable ease. The Scots had something of a reputation for quarrelsomeness and brawling, if one is to judge from the petition of a Norman soldier who heard a riot in the street outside his billet and assumed that the troublemakers were Scots (as it happened, he was wrong).[44] More generally, the impression which comes over is of a kind of touchy defensiveness easily tipped over into violence, and thriving in a fundamentally hostile environment: witness the Scot who, petitioning for pardon after killing an inhabitant of Aurillac, specifically mentioned his fear of the anger

---

[41] Quicherat, Rodrigue de Villandrando, pp. 38–9:

> 'Car s'ilz pensoient bien en Rodigues
> Et Escoçois, et leurs complisses'.

[42] Ditcham, 'Employment', passim, esp. pp. 252–60, for problems of discipline in ordonnance companies.
[43] Contamine, Guerre, p. 457.
[44] A.N., JJ 179, no.164.

of the people; or the Spaniards from Garcia's company who fled directly into sanc-
tuary after killing a man in the Saintonge.[45]

In these cases, one could argue that the environment had something to be hostile about; yet the basic problem went deeper. No town welcomed a garrison; the
privileged orders fell over themselves to obtain exemption from having to put up
soldiers and councils tended to dump them on the inn-keepers. They, in turn, did
not rejoice at the prospect of having their rooms filled by rowdy soldiers who
drove normal trade away.[46] There was a deeper conceptual problem as well. How
could one reconcile the noble status theoretically conferred upon soldiers by the
profession of arms with the reality of a group of effectively unemployed layabouts,
exempted from taxation, who spent their time drinking, dicing, and whoring in a
quite ignoble way. Foreign soldiers were even more vulnerable on this score since
they belonged to what was effectively a part-time army, were less likely to have
homes to go back to between musters, and were therefore more apt to remain
among the doubtful pleasures of the garrison town. The professional soldier's life-
style was significantly closer to that of the marginal elements of society described
by Geremek in a Parisian context than that of the noble or even the ordinary artisan.[47] Hence the venom of quarrels over payment for goods and services (foreign
soldiers were convinced that all those around were out to cheat them) and,
maybe, the full significance of the cry of a shoemaker from Dax uttered in the
course of an ultimately fatal quarrel: 'Damned Scots villain, I'm as well-born (gentil) a man as you are.'[48]

It is easy to find evidence of hostility between foreign soldiers and their French
hosts. The problem is to determine how far the criminal records of the age give a
fair picture of this relationship. Peaceful integration into French society shows up
less well in the material available; yet it clearly happened. Even the letters of remission let us see cases such as that of the Scot, apparently happily married and
settled in a village community, who came to the attention of the law for a typical
piece of village mayhem, and was able to count on the support of his neighbours
when seeking a pardon.[49] The letters also underline just how long some foreigners
had been in France (Wastre Arthus, of the Guard, could look back with pride on a
career of over thirty years in French service)[50] and permit us to infer how few at-
tachments with home some may have had to start with (Peter Forrest joined

[45] A.N., JJ 179, no. 318; JJ 190, no.167.
[46] For the practical problems caused by billeting, see Ditcham, 'Employment', pp. 274–7;
P. D. Solon, 'Popular Response to Standing Military Forces in Fifteenth-Century France',
Studies in the Renaissance, xix (1972).
[47] B. Geremek, Les Marginaux parisiens aux XIVe et XVe siècles, trans. D. Beauvois (Paris,
1976); Ditcham, 'Employment', ch. 8, esp. pp. 283–8.
[48] A.N., JJ 188, no. 180: 'Villain rigault Escossois, je suis aussi gentil homme que tu es.'
[49] A.N., JJ 180, no. 93.
[50] A.N., JJ 190, no. 125.

Darnley's army at the age of fifteen before being captured at Cravant).[51] In time, many have come to regard France as their real home. It is noticeable how few Guard members appear to have returned to Scotland after being mustered out, and how few Scots dispatched their profits to Scotland; there was no Scottish Sir John Fastolf.[52] Instead, like their commanders, those who had done well sought to build up a patrimony in France itself; I have been able to trace the land acquisitions of one member of the Guard round Azay-le-Rideau which left him the possessor of three houses and, as a consequence, a modestly significant local property owner.[53] Some sought to settle near their old commanders, like the Marshall from Aubigny-sur-Nère who is to be found in a letter of remission of the 1470s (it is not clear whether he was a native Scot or the child of a Scottish colony formed around the Stewart household).[54] This was sensible in a society dominated by patronage where it was useful to remain firmly in the eye of one's patron – even if the latter might find the burden of supporting old retainers a heavy one (witness the description of the multi-lingual throng around the household of Antoine de Chabannes at the end of his career).[55]

In the long run, many appear to have naturalised themselves as French and sunk quietly into the surrounding population. Foreign troops appear to have picked up the French language fairly rapidly; the author of the chronicle known as the 'Livre des Trahisons', who appears to have fought on the Burgundian side at Cravant, records the Scots swearing at the Italians 'in bad French such as they commonly speak' as the latter ran for their horses.[56] There were exceptions: Michel Ambleton, beneficiary of a miracle said to have been wrought at the intercession of St Katherine de Fierboys, must have told his story through an interpreter since it emerges that he had to communicate in sign language with the abbess of the convent in which he was cared for after his miraculous rescue from hanging.[57] It is also sadly true that mutual linguistic comprehension did not necessarily lead to greater harmony, as the evidence of the letters of remission

---

[51] A.N., JJ 179, no. 136.
[52] In the years 1467–68, when the accounts give reasons for men leaving the Guard (and ignoring transfers between the various sub-units of that body), only one man is stated to have returned to Scotland as against two who retired on grounds of age, one who died, one who transferred to the Scottish *ordonnance* company, and one who was invalided out (Forbes-Leith, *The Scots Men-at-Arms*, II, pp. 40–2).
[53] A.D., Indre-et-Loire, E 1055, 1069.
[54] A.N., JJ 197, no. 279.
[55] Contamine, *Guerre*, pp. 445–6.
[56] 'Livre des trahisons de France envers la maison de Bourgogne', *Chroniques relatives à l'histoire de la Belgique sous la domination des ducs de Bourgogne*, ed. K. de Lettenhove (3 vols, Brussels, 1870–76), II. pp.169–70: 'la povoit on ouyr les Escochois en leur mauvais franchois tel que communement le surent parler'.
[57] 'Livres des miracles de Sainte Katherine de Fierboys, 1375–1470', ed. Y. Chauvin, *Archives Historiques de Poitou*, LX (Paris: Poitiers, 1976), pp. 57–60, no.105. The story as told, however, bears a remarkable resemblance to a *topos* familiar to hagiographers concern-

shows; many fights were started by insults given and received by both Frenchman and foreigner. Nevertheless, the basic ability to communicate was established. In addition, there does not appear to have been any prejudice against marrying foreign soldiers on the part of Frenchwomen (indeed a member of the Guard could be a distinct catch in financial terms)[58] and little evidence that wives were imported from Scotland or elsewhere.[59] On a business level, Scottish soldiers were able to establish trading relationships with inhabitants of the towns in which they were billeted, as the Toulouse notarial archives show.[60] In the long run, all the pressures were for assimilation.

The process was inevitably uneven. The son of so notorious an adventurer as the Spaniard, Jean de Salazar, could become archbishop of Sens, but Commynes could still refer to Béraud Stewart of Aubigny as a Scottish gentleman even though his family had lived in France from the 1420s.[61] Although the Spanish and Italian companies faded away and ceased to be distinct units with a national character in the 1480s, the Scottish one remained distinctly Scottish (at least judging by the names of its members, even if they were in fact French-born) into the period of the Italian wars. The Guard remained Scots-speaking into the sixteenth century (judging by the graffiti left by its members on the chapel wall at Chenonceaux) though by that stage it was recruiting in Scotland, and Franco-Scottish links were as close in the period 1540–60 as they were ever to be.[62] On the whole, however, the majority of the foreign soldiers in French service came to integrate themselves into French society at all levels, including the criminal underworld.[63] All the pressures were in that direction, and there were few counterbalancing forces to block the process.

That is, perhaps, the main conclusion to be drawn from the evidence. Attitudes towards foreign soldiers were mixed, with a tendency towards the negative. While no French military theoretician suggested that the misfortunes of the realm would be cured by the establishment of a purely native army (their prescriptions were more basic: the army should be regularly paid, firmly disciplined, and sub-

---

ing a hanged thief saved after hanging for three days, which suggests that the person taking down the story had 'normalised' it into a familar pattern. For a history of the story, see R. Chartier, 'La Pendue miraculeusement sauvée – Étude d'un occasional', Les Usages de l'imprimé, ed. R. Chartier (Paris, 1987).

[58] Jehan Simple received 700 livres tournois as a wedding gift (B.N., ms.fr. 2886, fo. 13v).

[59] The only evidence of Scots bringing brides with them is in a letter of remission involving a girl who came from Scotland to marry (A.N., JJ 199, no. 362); it is not clear whether her intended husband was a soldier or a merchant. See also A.N., JJ 198, no. 322, for a Scot clearly married to a French wife.

[60] P. Wolff, Commerces et marchands de Toulouse (vers 1350–vers 1450) (Paris, 1954), pp. 126–7, 458; A.D., Haute-Garonne, 3E 1449, fo. 4v; 3E 4468, fo. 7.

[61] Philippe de Commynes, Mémoires, ed. J. Calmette and G. Durville (3 vols, Paris, 1924–25), III, p.136.

[62] For the later history of the foreign units, see Ditcham, 'Employment', pp.157–61.

[63] De Roye, Journal, I, pp. 325–6.

jected to the kind of moral order which Joan of Arc sought to impose),[64] chroniclers were apt to blame French reverses on foreigners (for instance, Cousinot's
clearly ridiculous allegation that the Italians at Verneuil ran away without striking
a blow),[65] and there was a feeling that it was better not to have to rely on them.
Henri Baude's eulogy for Charles VII, written in 1484, stated falsely that by the
end of his reign that king had dispensed with all foreign troops apart from the
Guard; this represented a view less of how things had actually been in the past
than a suggestion as to how they should be in the future.[66] At times, the heavy reliance on foreign troops caused the native nobility to resent the favour shown to
them. Disaffected potentates muttered about the role of the Guard in blocking
their political designs. Royal favour was fickle. Suspicion and hostility in town
and country alike could easily turn to hatred. On the other hand, if the foreign
soldier as an individual chose to stay in France and to become a part of French society, there were no insuperable barriers to him attaining this end. Being a foreign
soldier in the France of Charles VII and Louis XI was in a sense a transitory condition. It was hard to maintain a real sense of separate identity in an all-male world
relatively open to intermarriage with local women, and without a regular 'topping
up' of mass recruitment from the homeland. Within a lifetime most foreign soldiers who had survived the wars and the equal dangers of peace had become
Frenchmen, too.

[64] See, for instance, the suggestions for improving military affairs in the anonymous
chronicle, B.N., ms.fr. 5059, fos 53v–55v.
[65] Cousinot, *Chronique*, pp.197–8, 225.
[66] Baude's eulogy can be found in Jean Chartier, *Chronique de Charles VII, roi de France*, ed.
A. Vallet de Viriville (3 vols, Paris, 1858), III, pp.130–5.

'Monseigneur Saint Denis', his Abbey, and his Town, under the English Occupation, 1420–1436

GUY THOMPSON

On or about 10 August 1419 Henry V's brother Thomas, duke of Clarence, presented himself before the town of Saint-Denis-en-France and asked to be allowed to perform his devotions at the abbey of the glorious martyr. His manner was peaceful but the circumstances were not propitious; with the fall of Pontoise to the English on the last day of July 1419 Clarence felt that the key to Paris itself had been secured and he had set out to give a display of force to the inhabitants of the Île-de-France. Charles VI and Queen Isabella had only just left the abbey, concerned to find that they were so close to the advancing enemy, and the monks no doubt acted correctly in refusing Clarence's request on the basis that he had not obtained the prior permission of the king of France. Clarence was furious; he would obtain what he wanted another time whether the monks liked it or not.[1] In this way the English came within shouting distance of one of the spiritual centres of the French monarchy and, as if to prove their strength not only to the monks but to the Parisians, Clarence led his expedition as far as Saint-Laurent – a few hundred yards from Paris's porte Saint-Martin – and his men camped for a night at Saint-Ouen and other villages around Saint-Denis before returning to Pontoise.[2] But the invaders made no effort to wrest the town from the French by force; although Henry V, more diplomatic than his brother, spent the night of 8 May 1420 at the abbey on his way to the peace negotiations at Troyes, it was by virtue of the treaty of Troyes that Saint-Denis came within the scope of Lancastrian France and it was never deemed to be included in the so-called *pays de conquête*.[3]

---

[1]   *Chronique du Religieux de Saint-Denis, contenant le règne de Charles VI, de 1380 à 1422*, ed. L.-F. Bellaguet (6 vols, Documents inédits sur l'histoire de France, Paris, 1839–52), VI, p. 354; M. Félibien, *Histoire de l'abbaye royale de Saint-Denis* (Paris, 1706), p. 340; Jean Juvénal des Ursins, *Histoire de Charles VI, Roy de France*, ed. D. Godefroy (Paris, 1653), p. 368.

[2]   *Journal de Clément de Fauquembergue, greffier du Parlement de Paris, 1417–1435*, ed. A. Tuetey and H. Lacaille (3 vols, SHF, Paris, 1903–15), I, p. 312 (10–11 Aug. 1419).

[3]   *Journal d'un Bourgeois de Paris (1405–1449)*, ed A. Tuetey (Société de l'Histoire de Paris

The town of Saint-Denis was, like Paris, a place at the ideological heart of the French state. According to the official legend, the gospel had been brought to the Gauls by St Dionysius the Areopagite, one of the members of the court of Areopagus addressed by St Paul on his visit to Athens, a man wrongly identified as a third century bishop of Corinth, conflated with the fifth-century pseudo-Dionysius, author of the *De Hierarchia*, and in turn confused with the papal missionary, first bishop of Paris, who was executed with his companions, Rusticus and Eleutherius, outside Paris.[4] Here was a legend that, for the people of the Île-de-France above all, had an immediacy and political importance that transcended its perceptibly fragile factual basis. The landscape of the capital was crowded with reminders: in the capital itself the little church of Saint-Denis-de-la-Chartre (allegedly the site of the saint's imprisonment) nestled next to the cathedral of Notre-Dame; the hill of Montmartre, by false etymology identified as the place of execution of St Denis and his companions, overshadowed Paris to the north; at the entrance to the town of Saint-Denis the church of Saint-Denis-de-l'Estrée marked what, in some versions of the legend, was the first burial place of the saint at the end of his walk from Montmartre to Saint-Denis, after his execution and carrying his head.[5] Most important of all, however, was the abbey founded by Dagobert and said to have been consecrated by Christ himself.[6] To rule over a part of France that included Saint-Denis gave added weight to the English claim to the French throne, similar to recognition by the *Parlement* of Paris, the University, and the chapter of Notre-Dame.

The abbey and the town had grown in step with the legend of St Denis. Many – though not all – of the traditions had been elaborated in the abbey, and the abbey controlled the town. By the thirteenth century, building on the intellectual constructions of Abbot Hilduin in the eighth century and the more recent material developments of Abbot Suger, and with increasingly enthusiastic royal patronage, the abbey had become a massively wealthy institution, unrivalled throughout the kingdom. Land-holdings were centred on the Île-de-France where, apart from the town of Saint-Denis, there were twelve other *châtellenies* or *prévôtés*, mostly to the north and west of Paris; some of these were vast, and a few had their own fortified castles.[7] By the early fifteenth century the great days were past: the monetary

et de l'Île-de-France, Paris, 1881), p.139. For approximate boundaries to the *pays de conquête*, see J. H. Wylie and W. T. Waugh, *The Reign of Henry the Fifth* (3 vols, Cambridge, 1914–29), III, pp. 235–7.

4 C. Beaune, *Naissance de la nation France* (Paris, 1985), pp. 84–5.

5 R. Bossuat, 'Traditions populaires relatives au martyre et à la sépulture de Saint Denis', *Le Moyen Age*, 1xii (1956), 489–91, 505–6.

6 See the version of the legend of the consecration recounted by Antonio Astesano, 'Éloge descriptif de la ville de Paris et des principales villes de France en 1451', ed. A. Le Roux de Lincy and L.-M. Tisserand, *Paris et ses historiens aux XIVe et XVe siècles*, (Histoire générale de Paris, Paris, 1867), pp. 546–8.

7 G. Fourquin, *Les Campagnes de la région parisienne à la fin du Moyen Age* (Paris, 1964), pp.134–6, 149–51.

changes of the first half of the fourteenth century, which halved the purchasing power of domaine receipts, the Black Death, and a consequent shortage of man-power on the estates, had taken their toll.[8] But the legends lived on, and the town of Saint-Denis was itself very well established, having perhaps nearly 10,000 in-habitants in 1328 (a little larger than Pontoise), with an important role in the cloth trade both through manufacturing in the town and – through the fair of the Lendit just outside – as a trading centre.[9] The wealth and influence of the monks were reflected in the prosperity of the fair. The tax revenues from the Lendit were greater than for any part of the *prévôté* of Paris except for the capital, ahead even of the town of Saint-Denis itself and of Corbeil, the other principal contributor from the region.[10] Always, however, the abbey dominated the town. Only in the mid-fourteenth century did the monks concede the right of the people of Saint-Denis to rent out properties without their consent; none the less they retained full administrative and judicial control over the town, with the paraphernalia of audi-tories and officers expected of the owners of full judicial rights.[11]

This, then, was the abbey and town which, like Paris, came under English con-trol by treaty and not by force. The history of Saint-Denis was, however, to be very different from that of the capital. While Paris remained staunchly 'Burgun-dian', and thus securely under English control throughout the period of the Anglo-Burgundian alliance, 1420–1435, Saint-Denis followed a far less even course. 'Burgundian' in 1418, menaced but not attacked by the English in 1419, the place where the duke of Bedford first laid claim to the regency of France in 1422, it opened its doors to the newly-crowned Charles VII in August 1429 before reverting to the English when Charles left the Île-de-France the following month. Pillaged by the French in March 1430 and recaptured by them in the small hours of 1 June 1435, it then suffered one of the most bitter sieges of the war in the Île-de-France before the 'Armagnacs' left on 4 October 1435, only to return in April 1436 immediately prior to the recapture of Paris.[12]

The town emerged from this period in a sorry state. The description by Charles of Orléans' Italian secretary, Antonio Astesano, of what he found in 1451 is in marked contrast to his description of the capital nearby: what had been regarded by the French as their leading small town (*burgus*) was still largely in ruins fifteen years after the departure of the invaders.[13] Even allowing for his hearty detestation of the English – perhaps understandable in an employee of duke Charles, who had

---

[8]   Ibid., pp. 204, 265–6, 274–9.
[9]   G. Fourquin, 'Premier apogée, premières difficultés (vers 1300 – vers 1345)', *Histoire de l'Île-de-France et de Paris*, ed. M. Mollat (Toulouse, 1971), p.133; Fourquin, *Campagnes*, pp.115–16.
[10] Fourquin, *Campagnes*, p. 589.
[11] Ibid., p.179; Félibien, *Histoire*, pp. 337–8; A.N., LL 1209, pp. 25–31.
[12] *Bourgeois*, pp.104, 180, 243, 246, 251, 305–8, 314.
[13] Astesano, 'Éloge', p. 552. For Astesano, cf. P. Champion, *Vie de Charles d'Orléans (1394–1465)* (Paris, 1911), pp. 366–70, 414.

spent a quarter of a century in captivity in England – it is still striking that he should have been so decisive in attributing the condition of the town to them when he made no such complaint at the condition of Paris, which can, indeed, be shown to have largely recovered from the troubles of the occupation. Had the invaders been brutal with Saint-Denis in a way that they had not been with Paris? If so can it be that the town – or perhaps the abbey and its monks – followed a political line that was different from that of the solidly Burgundian capital?

Saint-Denis, in our own day the firmly pro-communist buckle in the ragged 'red belt' to the north of Paris, has never been afraid to be out of phase with its capital. At the end of the Middle Ages the dispute between the bishop of Paris and the abbot of Saint-Denis as to who should pronounce the blessing at the opening ceremony at the Lendit was almost as traditional as the fair itself, while the chapter of Notre-Dame had for two hundred years cast doubt on the authenticity of the skull of the saint possessed by his abbey by insisting that they possessed the top of his skull.[14] The major law suit of 1410 over this bitterly contested subject ended inconclusively but, as the arguments had identified, there were even two rival iconographies of the saint depicting the appropriate cranial mutilation; the minority 'Parisian' vision of the missing top of the skull had received tacit royal approval in the representation of the saint prepared in the reign of King John II for the nave of the chapel of St Michael in the courtyard of the royal palace.[15]

Perhaps we can see in the fluctuating fortunes of the town of Saint-Denis in the early fifteenth century another example of diverging attitudes. For Guy Fourquin, the bourg was 'sans doubte continuellement loyaliste', as was apparently evidenced by the readiness of the inhabitants to welcome Charles VII in 1429, while the capital rallied behind its Burgundian and municipal captains to repel the assault of Joan of Arc.[16] And yet the period was a crucial one for the decline of the cult of St Denis at the expense, above all, of St Michael, archangel and saintly warrior, whose Norman abbey was a stronghold for the dauphinists. In the words of another leading authority, the patron saint of France had in effect become 'le protecteur de la double monarchie', fêted by the English and offering his blessing to their enterprises.[17] Such a view, making of the apostle to the French a celestial Marshal Pétain in the face of the de Gaulle of St Michael, would set 'Monseigneur

---

[14] H.-F. Delaborde, 'Le Procès du chef de Saint Denis en 1410', *Mémoires de la Société de l'Histoire de Paris et de l'Île-de-France*, xi (1884), 297–409. Cf. B.N., ms. fr. 20851, fo. 257, for some early disputes over the Lendit.

[15] Reproduced in B. de Montfaucon, *Les Monumens de la monarchie françoise* (5 vols, Paris, 1729–33), II, plate lv, no. 5.

[16] G. Fourquin, 'Un siècle de calamités (du milieu de XIVe siècle au milieu du XVe siècle)', *Histoire de l'Île-de-France et de Paris*, p.164.

[17] Beaune, *Naissance*, p. 81.

Saint Denis' not only against his own people but also against his town and, perhaps, his abbey as well.

To look at the role of the saint before that of the abbey or the town; although it may be attractive to imagine the saints as marshals or generals in the propaganda war, they were, in reality, simple conscripts in the battle of ideas. Since the saints have always been intercessors and comforters for the people of God, countries and regions of this world have had their particular allies in heaven. With a special intensity, however, the factions of the early fifteenth century had rallied the heavenly host to their own ends. When an Armagnac sash was hung on the statue of St Andrew, the patron saint of Burgundy, in the church of Saint-Eustache in Les Halles in Paris, as the chronicler of Saint-Denis recorded, then that was a calculated insult to the devotees of St Andrew and to the Burgundian party; a few years later another author was to write in astonishment at seeing the sashes of the count of Armagnac hanging on the statues of the kings and images of the saints in the churches of Paris.[18] These deliberately inflammatory gestures were the product of bitter rivalry; when the English had come to the Île-de-France they had done so as a result of the treaty of Troyes, and thus in relative calm. For them there was no real question of abusing the role of the saints; they were lawfully entitled to the throne of France, and St Denis was the symbol of the country. Evidently, then, he was the symbol of the 'French' component in the alliance and the subsequent dual monarchy of Henry VI; there was no need for him to be more than that. Thus when St Denis stood behind Queen Catherine and St George behind Henry V in the image presented to the chapter of Notre Dame by Bedford in 1422, St Denis was doing no more than supporting the French partner in the alliance.[19] The three scenes from the life of St Denis presented to young King Henry at his entry into Paris were similarly part of a comprehensive presentation of entertainments aimed at the English and drawing attention to the needs of Paris and France: it was certainly not a 'dual monarchy' presentation.[20] The 'Bourgeois de Paris' regarded the failure of the Armagnacs' ill-conceived attempt to enter Paris on Saint-Denis' day 1433 as evidence of the saint's care for Paris, while the peaceful manner in which the English were later expelled was similar evidence of his intercession.[21] When the abbot of Saint-Denis referred to Bedford's devotion to the saint, it was to St Denis as 'totius Gallie protector' ['protector of the whole of France'] not, obviously, protector of the dual monarchy as such.[22] To regard St Denis as protector of the dual monarchy is to miss the point of what the English and their continental allies were attempting to achieve.

---

[18] G. Ll. Thompson, 'The Anglo-Burgundian Régime in Paris, 1420–1436' (D. Phil thesis, University of Oxford, 1985), pp. 276–8.

[19] Ibid., p. 277.

[20] Ibid., p. 324.

[21] Bourgeois, pp. 297, 317.

[22] A.N., LL 1212, fo.16; cf. p. 26, below.

The monks of Saint-Denis were, then, custodians of a proudly and coherently French tradition, and it is not at all easy to divine their attitude. Arguably, their experiences in the 1410s had left them with an understandable suspicion of both sides. In 1411, at the outset of the civil war, the abbey had been captured first by the Armagnacs (who left the abbey 'toute desimée et despoullée') ['decimated and ransacked'] then by the Burgundians (who imprisoned the abbot).[23] It may well be, however, that the concern of the Burgundians that the abbey harboured men who were in their eyes 'Armagnacs' was in some measure justified. There were few Parisian families more resolutely Armagnac than that of the Genciens. Pierre Gencien, general master of the mint and *prévôt des marchands*, had been ousted from the Hôtel de Ville by the Cabochiens and had returned with their defeat; his nephews, Pierre and Bureau Boucher, had important roles to play in the kingdom of Bourges. Pierre Gencien's brother, the celebrated Benoît Gencien, master in theology at the University of Paris and monk of Saint-Denis, had delivered the address of 30 January 1413 that – on the eve of the Cabochien uprising – had brought the deep-seated divisions of Parisian society to the fore; he was not to be forgotten, and in 1418 was one of those who fell victim in the anti-Armagnac massacres.[24] In that year most of the monks were perhaps safely out of reach of the Burgundian backlash, although the abbot, Philippe de Villette – theologian, ecclesiastical politician, gifted administrator and, according to the 'Bourgeois', 'tres faulx papelart' ['a thorough humbug'] – was imprisoned (as in 1411) by the Burgundians. This time he came close to death in the prisons of Saint-Eloi before being rescued by Jean de Villiers, lord of L'Isle-Adam, he who had led the Burgundian entry but had also showed his other face in saving the house of Benoît Gencien's sister, Jeanne, from being ransacked.[25]

Other Armagnacs included Pierre de Versailles, another eminent academic; and when Henry V took Meaux in 1422 he captured three monks of Saint-Denis who displayed their loyalties in a different manner, by fighting on the dauphinist side.[26] They were led by Philippe de Gamaches, originally of Saint-Denis and one day to be abbot there, although at the time abbot of Saint-Faron. Philippe, like his brother Guillaume, captain of Compiègne in 1422, was firmly tied into the Armagnac camp, and he was to benefit from the patronage of Charles VII as a result. No doubt one could multiply the examples if more detailed records survived. Michel Pintoin, precentor of Saint-Denis and author of the chronicle of the reign of Charles VI to the end of 1420, was scarcely an enthusiastic Burgundian, however much he avoided sensitive comments; as much could be said for the man who

---

23 A.N., L 830, no.1; *Bourgeois*, p. 93, n. 3.

24 For the Gencien family, see A. Coville, *Les Cabochiens et l'Ordonnance de 1413* (Paris, 1888), pp.166–7, 178; F. Autrand, *Naissance d'un grand corps de l'État: les gens du Parlement de Paris 1345–1454* (Paris, 1981), pp. 76–83, 196, 238, 290–1, 320.

25 Félibien, *Histoire*, pp. 336–8; *Bourgeois*, p. 93; *Religieux*, VI, p. 273; Autrand, *Naissance*, pp.196, 320–1.

26 Félibien, *Histoire*, p. 339; Juvénal des Ursins, *Histoire*, p. 388.

completed the work, Jean Chartier, who was eventually to be appointed official historiographer to Charles VII.[27]

None the less, there is a limit to what can be deduced from examples of that type. One could counter with men such as Jean de Bourbon (of whom much more below), who was appointed abbot on the initiative of the duke of Burgundy in September 1418, when Philippe de Villette finally expired at the Château de l'Isle-Adam; like Benoît Gencien, he had a politically significant family, for his brother was the Burgundian captain, Girart de Bourbon. But the position of the town and the relationship between the town and the monks certainly gave scope for the development of attitudes independent of those that prevailed in Paris.

Like all the leading institutions of France, the royal abbey accorded great importance to maintaining its freedoms, its privileges, and its rights. As they were not slow to point out, the monks of Saint-Denis had all justice and lordship in their town, subject only to the king and the *Parlement*. In particular, the *prévôt* of Paris, whose *prévôté* certainly encompassed Saint-Denis geographically, was said to have no authority there whatsoever, the monks and their subjects being exempt from his control. Difficulties could hardly be avoided even though the monks farmed out the administration of their own *prévôté* to persons whom they thought likely to be able to enforce their rule of law; with a reforming central government, such as that of the Anglo-Burgundian régime in Paris, it was frustrating to have a largely independent enclave within walking distance of the capital. Some of the problems were typical of many seigneurial administrations. In 1421 the monks appointed Jean Le Maire, a professional and pro-Burgundian soldier, to the post of *prévôt* of Saint-Denis because, as he said, the times were so 'perilleux et dangereux'. But his commission came to an abrupt end when Le Maire assaulted the Breton *procureur* of the abbey with an axe by mistake and, after exchanging blows in the street and insults in the *Parlement*, he had to be sacked by the one court of law that the monks did recognize.[28]

Elsewhere in the region, the daily round of pursuing criminals and, in times of civil war, political opponents was the responsibility of the *prévôt* of Paris. The enthusiasm of the monks for their own rights and liberties clearly made his tasks extremely difficult, particularly since Saint-Denis formed the nearest haven for those seeking to avoid royal justice. In the summer of 1422, guards at the gates of Paris arrested two men on their way out of the capital with supplies that – they suspected – were destined for the enemy. Put to the question, the prisoners were forced to confirm the suspicions of the guards: they were two of a three-man team from hostile territory. The third man was nowhere to be found, but his servant was

---

[27] For the authorship of the *Chronique d'un religieux*, see C. Samaran, *La Chronique latine inédite de Jean Chartier* (Paris, 1928), pp.17–22, and N. Grévy-Pons and E. Ornato, 'Qui est l'auteur de la chronique latine de Charles VI, dite du Religieux de Saint-Denis', BEC, cxxxiv (1976), 85–102.

[28] A.N., X1a 4793, fos 30, 35 (Feb.–Mar. 1421).

traced to Saint-Denis. The monks went so far as to arrest him, but he was forcibly removed from their prisons by an agent of the *prévôt*. In the predictable litigation that followed the *procureur du roi* was forced to play his ideological trump card, 'le roy est empereur en son royaume', if he was to have any chance of resisting the grievances of the monks. The king, he claimed, had all justice in the *prévôté*, and no one but his *prévôt* could be responsible for crimes of *lèse-majesté* or treason.[29] (This was a credible-enough claim, although, in fact, the monks could have looked to concessions dating back to the time of King Louis VI 'le Gros' to prove the opposite if they had consulted the cartulary commissioned in 1411 by Philippe de Villette.)[30]

Because we have to rely on disputes finding their way to the *Parlement* on appeal we are inevitably short of information on this type of incident, but it is certain that there were remarkably few well-known Burgundian supporters in the town. The most notorious was the former Cabochien, Jean Bertrand, who declared himself captain of Saint-Denis when the Burgundians took Paris in 1418.[31] Interestingly, he was a butcher, and we know that the principal officers of the *Grande Boucherie* of Saint-Denis in 1434 were members of the Bertrand family.[32] Echoes here of the Saint-Yon and Le Gois dynasties of master-butchers in Paris, leading supporters of the Burgundians and the English, but our captain of 1418 was in fact murdered within a few weeks of placing himself in office, and there is no evidence that any of his kinsmen followed him into transient celebrity on the political stage. If any substantial Burgundian party had developed from his leadership, whether centred on the butchers' trade or otherwise, we would expect to find at least some information about it.

Thus, while evidence of political attitudes in Saint-Denis is slight, the conclusion must be that there was no automatic pro-Burgundian support in either the abbey or the town. And the first effort to remedy that led to a dispute which dominated the civilian affairs of the abbey throughout the 1420s.

The death of Abbot Philippe de Villette in 1418 shortly after, and no doubt partly as a consequence of, the Burgundian *coup* in Paris had provided an opportunity to correct the perceived Armagnac bias at the abbey. The duke of Burgundy brought pressure to bear on the monks to elect as their new abbot someone with the correct political attitudes, and in accordance with the duke's wishes they chose Jean de Bourbon, one of their number but from Burgundy and with a brother, Girart, sire de Montperroux, whose own efforts in the Burgundian cause dated back at least to May 1399, when he had been sent by duke Philip the Bold

---

[29] A.N., X1a 4793, fo.195v.
[30] A.N., LL 1209, p. 25; Félibien, *Histoire*, p. 337.
[31] *Bourgeois*, p.105; A.N., JJ 171, nos 115–17.
[32] A.N., LL 1212, fos 42v–43v: on 26 May 1434 the leaders of the *Grande Boucherie* at Saint-Denis (including Jean Bertran, *maître des bouchers*, and Jaquet Bertran, *doyen*) agreed to the abbot appointing a new butcher because so many members of the trade had died in the '*grant mortalité*' the previous year.

as an ambassador to the king of the Romans.[33] Jean de Bourbon was abbot of Saint-Denis from 1418 to 1430, and it is not unjust to describe the period of his administration as disastrous. In November 1423, little more than five years after his election, the *Parlement* was obliged to strip him of his right to administer the temporality, which was placed in the hands of a committee of principal officers of the abbey, under the supervision of three councillors from the *Parlement.*[34]

The motive for this action was primarily concern over the fate of a large part of the abbey's priceless treasury. When Jean de Bourbon was elected, he commissioned his brother, Girart, to organize his confirmation as abbot before the court of Rome. This was always an expensive operation, and it is likely that – as Girart claimed – he was given some authority, probably from the monks as well as from his brother, to raise money for this purpose. Exactly what he was permitted to do was obscure, but by the time the *Parlement* removed the temporality of the abbey from the control of his brother there was little dispute about the fact that a large number of jewels from Saint-Denis had found their way to Burgundy. On the fall of Pontoise, part of the treasury was taken to Paris for safe keeping in the Collège Saint-Denis, where it was properly inventoried, but many more jewels and reliquaries were taken to the Hôtel Saint-Eloi, where the abbot kept a key to the box. It was from this collection that – it was claimed – a large number had been removed by Girart de Bourbon.[35]

In February 1424 the jewels which Girart acknowledged that he had had were brought to the *Parlement* and inventoried under the expert eye of Jean Sac, the influential Italian banker and merchant.[36] There were long arguments not only over the extent of Girart's authority, but also involving those people who had lent him money for the purposes of the abbey and believed that they had done so on the security of the jewels in his possession.[37] However, the most interesting matters concern the jewels themselves. The inventory, which recorded about 100 items brought to the *Parlement* in February 1424, included a few pieces of very considerable value; but – said the monks – it was not complete. The most significant omission which they identified was the royal sceptre but, leaving that particularly sensitive matter on one side, the *Parlement* gave Girart a deadline to produce detailed accounts and allowed the monks custody of the angels and other pieces from the reliquary of St Denis, which were amongst the most striking of the items taken to Burgundy by the abbot's brother.[38] Meanwhile, the abbot was manoeuvring to regain control of the abbey, and on 5 June 1424 produced royal letters passed in the *Grand Conseil* lifting the royal hand from the temporality which

---

[33] Fourquin, *Campagnes*, p. 311; R. Vaughan, *Philip the Bold: the Formation of the Burgundian State* (London, 1962), p.108.

[34] Félibien, *Histoire*, p. 343; *Fauquembergue*, II, p.112.

[35] A.N., X1a 4793, fos 379v, 380v.

[36] *Fauquembergue*, II, pp.115–16.

[37] A.N., X1a 4793, fos 350, 383.

[38] A.N., X1a 4793, fo. 380v; 1480, fos 289v, 292v.

was to be entrusted to an unlikely committee including the abbot, his brother, and a monk of Saint-Denis, brother André Pelerin, of whom more was to be heard. The *procureur du roi*, understandably suspicious, asked for the chance to study these letters, and the *Parlement* ultimately resolved to send the First President to remonstrate before the duke of Bedford and put forward a compromise proposal, which involved adding the abbot to the committee previously put in place by the *Parlement*, but otherwise leaving matters as they were.[39]

When the dispute revived in 1427, the arguments centred around André Pelerin, who had been appointed Grand Prior by Abbot Jean de Bourbon. The debate was even more acrimonious than it had been three years before: the monks complained that it was notorious that the abbot administered everything so badly that all was falling in ruins outside and inside the town; as for the church itself, so much rain had come in lately that one could have used a boat inside the abbey for it leaked everywhere; nothing was paid for, while debts increased and jewels, reliquaries, ornaments, and books were sold or alienated. As for Pelerin himself, the abbot's placeman if the monks were to be believed, he was neither suitable nor adequate, was ignorant of Latin, and it was general knowledge that he kept a young woman, whom he called his cousin, with him in his room; her hearty singing could easily be heard in the abbey.[40]

In the face of these charges Pelerin understandably tried to distance himself from the abbot and to stress his competence and moral probity. But when last heard of his case had been considered by Bedford in person in the *Requêtes de l'Hôtel* and Pelerin was to be interrogated on the outstanding charges.[41] The abbot himself went on the offensive: matters had not got worse during his time in office, and the monks were as well fed as any others in the region; to the claim that he was saying nothing about the royal sceptre, he countered that the monks were themselves keeping quiet about the Holy Nail, the Crown of Thorns, and a beautiful gold collar.[42] The taunts about the Holy Nail and the Crown of Thorns were particularly apposite: these spent several years in safety in the Sainte-Chapelle in Bourges, only returning to Saint-Denis in 1445; at first sight it appears likely that they would have been taken by Charles VII on his return from the Île-de-France in 1429.[43] But this comment, suggesting that they were already missing in 1427, bears out the claim of the 'Bourgeois de Paris' that they had been taken to Bourges by a monk of Saint-Denis. If so, then the fact that so little mention was made of the absence of some of the abbey's most precious relics is another hint of continuing support for Charles VII. We are reminded of the story, heard by Antonio Astesano while visiting Saint-Denis, of how the most valuable items from the treasury were buried during the occupation to protect them from looting (in this

[39] *Fauquembergue*, II, pp.130–1.
[40] A.N., X1a 4795, fos 89–89v, 92v–93, 105–105v (6–13 May, 3 June 1427).
[41] A.N., X1a 4795, fo.111v; *Fauquembergue*, II, p. 274.
[42] A.N., X1a 4795, fos 111v–112v.
[43] As Beaune, *Naissance*, p.117, assumes.

version an English soldier was struck blind while prodding in the earth in an effort to locate them).[44]

The long-running dispute between Jean de Bourbon and his abbey was settled on 29 April 1428: two monks (a master of theology from the University and the third-prior) were to join the abbot in the government of the temporality, while a new commander was commissioned at the same time. The monks reserved the right to proceed against André Pelerin and Girart de Bourbon. By separate letters issued on the same day as this settlement was reached, a new fixed allowance was granted to the abbot and a restricted food and clothing allowance was granted to the monks.[45]

Obviously the affair of Jean de Bourbon can have done nothing to assist the development of the English cause in Saint-Denis. But the invaders showed in other ways that they recognized the importance of the abbey within their territory and made some effort to win its support. Like all effective rulers in *ancien régime* France, they overruled privileges when they had to, but respected traditions that reflected well on themselves. Henry V stayed at, or passed through, Saint-Denis at least three times in the years 1420–22; after his death his body was brought directly from Vincennes to the abbey to lie in state for a day on its way back to England.[46] In Henry's passage by Saint-Denis we see a shadow perhaps of the practices at the burial of a king of France, and certainly, like a French monarch, Henry took care to ensure that the royal abbey had a tangible memorial of his passing. In the last codicil to his will Henry bequeathed to the abbey a set of red vestments and a silver gilt cross, as was noted by Jean Chartier and Juvénal des Ursins; these were delivered by Master Robert Gilbert, dean of the late king's chapel, on behalf of Henry's executors by 28 June 1425.[47]

When King Charles VI himself died a few weeks later he was, almost inevitably, buried at Saint-Denis with his ancestors.[48] This was a ceremony fraught with practical difficulties on account of the unprecedented political situation: what was virtually an interregnum was only resolved by the appearance of Bedford in Paris to make a decisive claim to the throne for his young nephew and to accompany the late king on his last journey to Saint-Denis. It was an extraordinary ceremony in some ways, with Bedford the only layman of note from either England or France to be present, and with the graveside acclamation of the new king, being made in honour of an English-born child, still expressly rooted in the traditions of the French monarchy. Indeed the ceremony is particularly well recorded because it

---

[44] Astesano, 'Éloge', p. 548; *Bourgeois*, pp. 377–8.

[45] Félibien, *Histoire*, p. 344; A.N., LL 1212, fos 4–5v, 11v–12v; L 830, nos 2, 3.

[46] *Bourgeois*, pp.139, 154, 174, n.4, 176; Félibien, *Histoire*, p. 341.

[47] *Religieux*, VI, pp. 482–4; Juvénal des Ursins, *Histoire*, p. 395; P. and F. Strong, 'The Last Will and Codicils of Henry V', *EHR*, xcvi (1981), 79–102; T. Rymer, *Foedera, Conventiones, Literae, et Cujuscunque Generis Acta Publica* (20 vols, London, 1704–35), X, p. 346.

[48] Félibien, *Histoire*, p. 342; Juvénal des Ursins, *Histoire*, p. 397; *Religieux*, VI, pp. 490–8; *Bourgeois*, p.180.

had been many decades since the last burial of a king of France, and it was believed it would set a precedent for the future.[49] The abbey was provided with sumptuous ornaments not only for the funeral ceremony but also for the anniversaries of the king's death in 1423 and 1424. On 16 October 1423 the commissioners for the king's funeral rites ordered that a carpet in the French royal colours of azure with gold fleurs-de-lis be supplied for the chapel where the king's body lay. On the same date in the following year they stipulated that the chapel be provided with a valuable set of church vestments and hangings in the same design (though with the crowned 'KK' motif of Charles V, to whom they had once belonged).[50]

Bedford saw to it that gifts in honour of the late kings of England and France were handed over, and he himself presented a set of vestments ('ecclesiastica indumenta') to Saint-Denis. These were, or included, a set of copes preserved in the abbey long after the departure of the English and known as 'les Beddefordz'. Items given by Bedford were still to be seen in the abbey two hundred years later. The regent's reward was to be granted an annual mass on the eve of St Denis' day (9 October) in perpetuity as a founder and benefactor of the abbey, a grant itself made on the saint's feast day in 1426, while Bedford was in England.[51] Even if Bedford did indeed make or authorize the presentation, it is conceivable that these vestments formed part of one of the chapel sets that had come into his hands after the death of Charles VI. Perhaps the regent had a fairly robust view of what should belong to the abbey; we know, for example, that he had carried the royal sword 'Joyeuse' before him when he returned to Paris after the funeral of Charles VI (it is uncertain when it was returned), and it is possible that he had also taken the 'Oriflamme', the sacred banner of the French state.[52]

Up to the end of 1429 isolated presentations, coupled with limited interference on political or administrative grounds, seem to have been all that the Lancastrians

[49] R. E. Giesey, The Royal Funeral Ceremony in Renaissance France (Geneva, 1960), pp.129, n.11, 198.

[50] J. Guiffrey, 'Inventaire des tapisseries du roi Charles VI vendues par les Anglais en 1422', BEC, xlviii (1887), 396, 398, 400; A.N., KK 38, fo. 63–63v; cf. Inventaire du mobilier de Charles V, roi de France, ed. J. Labarte (Documents inédits sur l'histoire de France, Paris, 1879), p.143, no.1092.

[51] J. Doublet, Histoire de l'abbaye de S. Denys en France (Paris, 1625), p.1077; A.N., LL 1212, fo.16; printed in B. de Montesquiou-Fezensac and D. Gaborit-Chopin, Le Trésor de Saint-Denis: inventaire de 1634 (3 vols, Paris, 1973–7), II, 253), and Doublet, Histoire, pp.1077–8. The heading, in a later hand, refers to 'les chappes qu'on appelle les Beddefordz'.

[52] Bourgeois, p.180. For the 'Oriflamme', see Article A 165 ('pro recuperalzone unius reliquie vocate auriflambe') in J. Stratford, Three Inventories of the Goods of John, Duke of Bedford (d. 1435) [Society of Antiquaries of London, forthcoming]. I am indebted to Mrs Stratford for this reference, and for her assistance with this part of my paper. I understand from her that a few chapel sets delivered to Bedford cannot be traced to England by the 1430s, although all the copes can be so traced.

trians thought necessary with regard to Saint-Denis. In particular, they made no effort to mount a substantial garrison there. After the English had taken Pontoise, the Burgundians had, for several months, installed a garrison remembered principally for ransacking the abbey, destroying the crops of the peasants, and installing girls in those of the monks' cells that had been commandeered.[53] However, Henry V seems to have had no interest in placing his own men in charge there when he took over the other strongholds of the Île-de-France after the treaty of Troyes.[54] Perhaps out of deference to the monks, the town of Saint-Denis was left virtually undefended.

The year 1429, however, saw the relief of Orléans and the consecration and coronation of Charles VII at Reims. Many towns had fallen to the Valois forces on the ride to Reims, and the next step for Charles (if he were truly following precedent) would have been for him to make his entry into Paris, leaving for his capital from (it need hardly be said) Saint-Denis. Charles' troops arrived in the town on 24 or 25 August 1429, meeting no resistance whatsoever; the king arrived a few days later, to be crowned in the abbey, if we are to believe Thomas Basin for whom the ceremony in Reims had simply been a consecration.[55] The French troops went on to take Montjoye (near Saint-Germain-en-Laye and once a possession of the abbey, although since the early thirteenth century a lay fief) and thus managed to make communications between Paris and Normandy extremely difficult.[56] Yet there was no sustained assault on the capital itself. Perhaps this was due as much to faulty intelligence as to the strength of the English in the capital, but more particularly it was a result of the fact that the Parisian people showed not the slightest inclination to follow the path of non-resistance taken by their neighbours in Saint-Denis, nor to yield to the display of force that was offered to them.[57] When Bedford's relief force for Paris began to march decisively on Paris, Charles retreated from Saint-Denis; he left the count of Vendôme and the admiral of France behind, but when they had reflected on the relative weakness of the town they, too, retreated and took the road for Senlis and safer regions.[58]

Thus Burgundian Paris was to prove impervious to the charisma of Joan of Arc,

[53] Juvénal des Ursins, Histoire, pp. 368–9; Religieux, VI, pp. 356–8.

[54] Cf. Thompson, 'Anglo-Burgundian Régime', p.176, for the appointments at the Bastille, the Louvre, the Pont de Charenton, and Vincennes, in 1420, to add to Saint-Germain-en-Laye (taken in 1419).

[55] Beaune, Naissance, p.117. Bourgeois, p. 243, states that the French entered Saint-Denis on the 25th; according to Perceval de Cagny, Joan of Arc and the duke of Alençon arrived on the 26th (Procès de condemnation et de réhabilitation de Jeanne d'Arc, ed. J. Quicherat, (5 vols, SHF, Paris, 1841–9), IV, p. 25).

[56] B.N., ms. fr. 4488, pp. 769–70: payment for a guide taking a messenger from Mantes to Saint-Cloud (just outside Paris) on foot 'pour eschever les perilz des Armignacs qui estoient a Saint-Denis et en la tour de Montjoye'.

[57] See, for example, Bourgeois, pp. 244–6.

[58] Chronique de la Pucelle ou chronique de Cousinot, ed. A. Vallet de Viriville (Paris, 1859), pp. 335–6.

but Saint-Denis fell easily to the French. There was room for a wide variety of interpretations of what had happened. Waurin described how most of the leading bourgeois had evacuated the town on the approach of the Valois, leaving the place virtually deserted.[59] There is no evidence that either the English or the Burgundians made any effort to protect the town, and the limited fortification meant that there would be little likelihood of the inhabitants mounting any resistance on their own initiative; instead when the enemies had approached Saint-Denis, the authorities in Paris had ordered that they should bring their possessions to the capital.[60] Obviously this presented people with homes in both towns with serious problems: the Saint-Dionysian Pierre de Linières, who was married to a Parisian widow, elected to stay in his home town with the inevitable result that possessions in the capital were confiscated to help pay for the emergency garrisons there, although the guardian of the de Linières' stepchildren opposed this, claiming they had known nothing of the order that property be brought to Paris. Whether or not one believes that, there is certainly a ring of truth in the claim that when the inhabitants of Saint-Denis had demanded protection and a garrison, they had simply been told they would have to manage the best they could.[61] Some arrived in Saint-Denis because, like the secretary, Michel de la Tillaye, they had been expelled from Paris where their allegedly Armagnac views made them into security risks.[62] Others, like Michelette, the widow of Guyot Le Bossu, certainly made their way to Saint-Denis of their own volition: her story was that she had left Paris with her aged mother about mid-July 1429 to live at Longchamp, and had only gone to the enemy at Saint-Denis in early September to obtain permission to harvest her vines. This may have satisfied the duke of Bedford, who approved her letters of remission, but there is no need for us to be deceived. Michelette's supposedly blameless life included the period during which she had organized the distribution of letters from the kingdom of Bourges to the Parisians; her aged mother was probably the widow of the leading Armagnac, Guillaume d'Auxerre; and she was herself only fairly recently returned from exile in Bourges with the benefit of equally misleading letters of remission.[63]

Whatever interpretation was placed upon the temporary loss of Saint-Denis, the rulers in Paris were understandably concerned at the ease with which the town had fallen to the dauphinists. The duke of Bedford, Simon Morhier, *prévôt* of Paris, and the leaders of the municipality imposed heavy fines on the townsmen as

---

[59] Jehan de Waurin, *Recueil des croniques et anchiennes istories de la Grant Bretaigne à present nommé Engleterre, 1422–1431*, ed. W. and E. L. P. Hardy (RS, London, 1879), p. 338.

[60] A.N., X1a 4796, fo. 228.

[61] A.N., X1a 4796, fo. 239v.

[62] A.N., X1a 4796, fo.102v.

[63] *Paris pendant la domination anglaise (1420–1436)*, ed. A. Longnon, (Société de l'Histoire de Paris et de l'Île-de-France, Paris, 1878), pp. 298–9. For the previous history of Michelette d'Auxerre, widow of Guyot Le Bossu, see A.N., X2a 16, fo. 453, and for Jeanne, widow of Guillaume d'Auxerre, see *Domination anglaise*, p. 266.

punishment for their failure to resist the French and as a composition by which they avoided having all their property confiscated.[64] When the duke of Burgundy became governor of the Île-de-France on 13 October 1429 he placed a garrison in Saint-Denis, but this failed to stop the French scaling the walls the following March, killing the townsmen who were on watch and a large number of Picard soldiers.[65] We know that in July 1430 the *prévôt*, plainly overriding the privileges of the abbey, had installed his own token force in the town of one man-at-arms and five archers[66] but, while the Armagnacs may have been kept at bay for some years, the administrative problems had not been solved. The monks brought Pierre de Cheruel, self-styled captain of Saint-Denis, before the *Parlement* in 1433 for infringing their jurisdiction. He explained how, far from denying the authority of the abbey, he had gathered together eighty men to capture an Englishman who had killed a woman near the porte de Pontoise and had then handed him over to the justice of the monks, whose own officers had not dared to apprehend him. Notwithstanding these heroics, de Cheruel's case fell to pieces when on closer inspection his letters of 'capitainerie' showed him only guard of one gate and not captain of the town at all.[67]

While efforts to reform the defences of Saint-Denis moved forward slowly, the abbey and the town struggled with the hardships imposed by war and a decade of poor administration. The receipts of the abbey, as Guy Fourquin has shown, were far below peacetime levels.[68] This was scarcely surprising, given the dependence of the monks on rents from vulnerable agricultural land. But the dislocation brought by the war went further than that. One might have thought that the Anglo-French dual monarchy would have signalled the end to the troubles that the monks of Saint-Denis had had in controlling their English estates. While forgeries in the archives at Saint-Denis (and now in the Archives Nationales) would have traced their English interests back to the eighth century, the possessions which the monks may have had in Sussex (at Rotherfield, where the church is still dedicated to St Denis, Pevensey, and Hastings) had long since been lost. Elsewhere their title was better: since the reign of Edward the Confessor they had possessed the priory of Deerhurst in Gloucestershire, with extensive lands.[69] But the relationship between abbey and priory was never easy as poor communications, dis-

64 *Bourgeois*, pp. 246–7; A.N., XIa 4796, fo. 239v.
65 Waurin, *Recueil . . . 1422–1431*, p. 345; *Bourgeois*, p. 251.
66 A. Vallet de Viriville, 'Sépultures de Blanche de Popincourt, femme de Simon Morhier, prévôt de Paris, et de Jean Pluyette . . . ', *Mémoires de la Société Impériale des Antiquaires de France*, xxv (1862), 280.
67 A.N., XIa 4797, fos 61v, 65.
68 Fourquin, *Campagnes*, pp. 352–3.
69 *Victoria History of England: County of Gloucestershire*, II, p.103, VIII, pp. 26–7; A.N., L 844, nos 6, 37. For the Sussex forgeries, see L 844, no. 2 and, for other references, P. H. Sawyer, *Anglo-Saxon Charters: an Annotated List and Bibliography* (Royal Historical Society, London, 1968), pp.105, 149, 227, 349.

putes over presentations, and the periodic hostility of the English crown to alien priories left a troubled background that could only be further disturbed by war. When, in 1424, the abbot of Saint-Denis agreed to a settlement of the arrears of the due remittance of 120 marcs sterling and a reduction for the future, he could have expected a steady, if reduced, income from the one part of his possessions untouched by fighting.[70] In fact, however, the priory was soon to resume its independent way, and while a *procureur* was specially appointed in 1430 to travel to England armed with stern letters reminding the prior of his obligations, there is no reason to believe that he met with any success;[71] in fact one ruse after another was to keep Saint-Denis at arm's length right up to the Reformation.[72]

Nearer to home a new abbot, Guillaume de Farréchal, was to have to contend with a deepening crisis. Like Jean de Bourbon he was a native of Burgundy, but he was a more experienced and authoritative administrator. Having begun his religious life at the abbey of Saint-Ouen in Rouen, where he rose to the rank of almoner, he had since spent thirty years as abbot of Saint-Wandrille before exchanging that post with Jean de Bourbon.[73] When he took on the far more challenging position at Saint-Denis in 1430, the evidence of decline in the countryside, the town, and the abbey was plain to see. The historian is no doubt entitled to be sceptical of the complaints of the religious houses of France in the face of the war but, where inhabitants of Saint-Denis were trying to show their inability to pay their rent charges on their houses, it was in the interests of the monks – who were perfectly capable of driving a hard bargain when they chose – to minimize the difficulties. So when they were prepared to forgo part of their entitlement to rents on houses in Saint-Denis in return for what they hoped would be greater security for the rest, there is every reason to believe descriptions such as 'demolly et venu en petite valleur', 'en friche et de nulle valeur', 'en ruine et de nulle valeur', 'grant ruine', 'grant ruine et desolation', 'en grant ruine et en grant desollacion', or 'en masure' ['demolished and of minimal value', 'waste ground of no value', decayed and of no value', 'completely decayed', 'completely decayed and desolated', 'completely decayed and completely desolated', 'in ruins'].[74] Such scenes were the indirect consequence of the war, or sometimes the direct result, as one man who took a new *ferme* at Easter 1429 discovered. Almost immediately afterwards came 'la fortune de guerre et gens d'armes; pons, pors, passages, chastealx, fortresses, et bonnes villes prinses . . . ainsy que ung chascun scet' ['the fortune of war and men at arms, bridges, landing places, paths, castles, fortresses, and large towns captured . . . just as everybody knows']. No better off was Phelipot Oger, who described his

---

[70] A.N., L 844, no. 38
[71] A.N., LL 1212, fos 17v–18.
[72] Félibien, Histoire, pp. 311–12.
[73] Ibid., pp. 346, 575.
[74] A.N., LL 1212, fos 2v, 3v, 6v, 13, 15, 17, 23.

house at Saint-Denis in 1434 in these terms: knocked down by the English, the Armagnacs, and the Picards, each had knocked down their bit as they went by.[75]

Where there was anything to be recovered by the monks in the way of rent charges a standard fifty per cent reduction was given on condition that the owners kept their houses in good repair, so that what was left of the income could be better assured. Compromise was essential, and it was in this way that the monks tried to keep the deficits and difficulties within bounds. Thus Jean Chartier, *prévôt* of La Garenne in the early 1430s, and more concerned at the time with supplies of peas and soup than with writing history, had to go back to his brethren annually for permission to provide more meagre rations to the abbey than he should have done as administrator of one of their most important *prévôtés*.[76] With the demolition of the choir library to make room for the tombs of King Charles and Queen Isabella, the king's executors had paid the prior 28 gold nobles for a replacement; in June 1432 Abbot Guillaume felt obliged to take the money for more urgent works both in the church and the vineyards, promising to restore the funds when the church's finances had convalesced.[77] The sale of part of the shrine of St Cucuphat, four silver 'burettes' and three gilded and enamelled chalices, was only partially compensated for by the fact that the abbot finally succeeded in obtaining the definitive restitution of the jewels handed over to the *Parlement* by Girart de Bourbon eight years before, and was able to arrange for a verbatim transcription of Clément de Fauquembergue's inventory into the abbey's own register.[78]

Clearly, then, the difficulties faced by the abbey and the town had much in common with the problems confronted by the Parisian institutions dependent on their estate income and on rents which dwindled with the contraction of the population. If, as seems likely, the problems were greater in Saint-Denis, it must be that the smaller town had much more limited resources on which to rely; there was no question of one district compensating for another in a little town as it could in Paris, and the great size of the Parisian population – even when assailed by divisions and confiscations – gave an aura of near invulnerability to the capital that could never be attained by a smaller place. Thus, when French troops slipped into Saint-Denis early in the morning of 1 June 1435, even if the inhabitants had been minded to resist (which seems unlikely) there was little that could be done in the absence of support from a professional garrison which, as always, seems to have been lacking.[79] So began nearly four months which, coinciding with the

---

[75] A.N., LL 1242, fo. 372; X1a 4797, fo.191v.

[76] A.N., LL 1212, fos 7, 19, 30.

[77] A.N., LL 1212, fos 31v–32, printed in C. Samaran, 'Études sandionysiennes: (i) notes sur la bibliothèque de Saint-Denis au XVᵉ siècle' *BEC*, civ (1943), 12.

[78] Samaran, 'Études', 9, n.1; Félibien, *Histoire*, p. 347; for the transcript, see A.N., LL 1212, fos 28v–29.

[79] *Bourgeois*, p. 306. The French put to death 'aulcuns Anglois quy dedans estoient en petit nombre' (Waurin, *Recueil . . . 1431–1447*, p. 66).

peace negotiations at the Congress of Arras, underlined the vulnerability of Parisian supplies because, even though Saint-Denis is not on the river Seine itself, it was certainly near enough to make river communications between Paris and Normandy impossible.

When it became apparent that this time the Armagnacs were not simply in Saint-Denis for a brief stay, a major effort to remove them was required. We have narratives written from the perspectives of both the besiegers and the besieged to describe the siege which, if it was not one of the longest of the war, was certainly conducted with as much ferocity as any other.[80] The Anglo-Picard offensive began in earnest in the last week in August under the leadership of l'Isle-Adam and, for the English contingent, Lords Willoughby, Scales, and Stafford, while the chancellor, Louis of Luxembourg, went once or twice a week to supervise operations from a fortress on the Île-Saint-Denis.[81] The French in the town could rely on a variety of artillery (including culverines which the 'Bourgeois de Paris' seems to have regarded as particularly lethal novelties). The assailants concentrated on weakening the town's defences, which were battered with siege engines until the English captains felt that the town would fall, and on the day following the feast of the Nativity of the Virgin, 9 September 1435, a major assault was undertaken. There were heroics on both sides as the attackers waded through the moats with water up to their necks carrying siege ladders; but finally the besiegers had to retreat after about eighty lives had been lost in the moats or on the walls, including that of Sir Robert Harling, Sir John Fastolf's long-serving nephew.[82]

The English were to return once more to Saint-Denis as victors, for what they had failed to attain by force they were to achieve by a combination of negotiation and cutting off the town's water supply.[83] The Armagnacs marched out defiantly on 4 October, which meant that Queen Isabella, who had died five days before, could at least be buried in the abbey alongside her husband, even if her body had to be brought to Saint-Denis by river for better security.[84] But the invaders' grip on the royal town was now feeble, and although they did place a garrison of some 400 men in Saint-Denis, the fact that they had completely destroyed what was left of the fortifications and had pillaged the town suggests that they had neither any expectation of holding the place for very much longer nor much desire to nurture

---

[80] The most detailed account is in the Latin version of Jean Chartier's chronicle (Samaran, Chronique latine, pp. 65–72), but the Bourgeois and Jean de Waurin in particular provide important information from the other side of the walls.

[81] Bourgeois, pp. 307, 309.

[82] Waurin, Recueil . . . 1431–1447, pp. 90–1; A Parisian Journal, 1405–1449, trans. J. Shirley (Oxford, 1968), p. 297, n.1. Sir Robert's tomb is in the church of St Peter and St Paul, East Harling, Norfolk, rebuilt by his daughter Anne (perhaps out of profits sent home by her father from France).

[83] Samaran, Chronique latine, p. 71; Bourgeois, p. 308

[84] Bourgeois, p. 310.

the loyalty of the inhabitants. The Picard soldiers, with their commander, l'Isle-Adam, obtained permission to go home.[85]

As support for the English crumbled in the Île-de-France during Holy Week 1436, Saint-Denis was on the itinerary of the night raiders sent out from Paris to pillage the towns and villages between the capital and Pontoise. The story was told of how one of the soldiers tore the chalice out of the hands of the celebrant in the middle of the Mass.[86] Obviously Saint-Denis was no longer a place where the Lancastrians could expect any possibility of loyalty and, despite fierce resistance from the English garrison when l'Isle-Adam (now on the 'French' side) and the Constable de Richemont returned to the Île-de-France under the joint instructions of Charles VII and the duke of Burgundy, the French were easily able to secure the town. They drove the garrison into one of the few remaining strongholds, the 'tour du Velin' or 'du Salut' adjoining the abbey. Leading the men in the tower was the lord of Brichanteau, nephew of the *prévôt* of Paris; attempting to escape on a mule sent to him by his uncle, he fell into the hands of a group of peasants and some of the less disciplined of Richemont's men (who had been refused entry into Paris) and was murdered.[87] Perhaps it is too much to say that this represents a final reaction by the more humble servants of the abbey of Saint-Denis against the intrusions of the pro-English, pro-Parisian, authorities. Yet the possibility can in no way be dismissed. The death of Brichanteau, whose body was exposed for a day in front of the abbey before burial, certainly symbolizes the rout of the Lancastrian cause and of the *prévôt* of Paris, the 'sceleratissimus' or 'wickedest' Simon Morhier, as Jean Chartier was to call him.[88] It was, as Antonio Astesano predicted, many years before the scars of the occupation were healed. Competent and forceful administrators at the abbey were not enough by themselves. Nor could Saint-Denis by itself generate its own revival; dependent on trade and on stability, it was much more vulnerable than its giant neighbour to the fluctuations of the 1440s and later. But whereas Paris remained under Charles VII's deepest suspicion, the town that had received him with something approaching enthusiasm in 1429 was treated far more favourably. In 1438, in order to raise money for a garrison at Saint-Denis to protect the inhabitants, taxes were levied in Paris on the wealthiest residents of the capital.[89] This time, Paris had to pay heavily to secure Saint-Denis; both the monks and the inhabitants of Saint-Denis, on the other hand, were exempted from royal levies, the town was declared a *ville d'arrêt* with the privileges of the other towns with that status in the kingdom, and the

---

85 *Bourgeois*, p. 309; Waurin, *Recueil . . . 1431–1447*, p. 93.
86 *Bourgeois*, pp. 313–14.
87 Waurin, *Recueil . . . 1431–1447*, pp.138–9; *Bourgeois*, p. 314; Félibien, *Histoire*, p. 351; *Chronique d'Arthur de Richemont . . . par Guillaume Gruel*, ed. A. Le Vavasseur (SHF, Paris, 1890), pp.116, 121–2.
88 Samaran, *Chronique latine*, p. 75.
89 *Bourgeois*, p. 332; J. Favier, *Les Contribuables parisiens à la fin de la guerre de Cent Ans* (Geneva: Paris, 1970), pp. 268–84.

exemption of the abbey from tolls was confirmed.[90] The king, whose reluctance to visit his capital was notorious, seems to have been quite happy to spend three weeks in Saint-Denis during the siege of Pontoise, and his confidence in the town can only have been increased by the election of Philippe de Gamaches, the fighting monk of Meaux, as abbot of Saint-Denis in 1441.[91] When, at the end of the decade, Charles finally entered Rouen in triumph, he restored to the monks all their lands in Normandy which had been occupied by the English and given to others.[92]

It is certainly true that the French monarchy in the fifteenth century developed a loyalty to St Michael and to other saints who appeared to have been stronger in the Valois cause that the predominantly Parisian St Louis and St Denis. But Charles VII's patronage of the abbey, and his support for the return of the Holy Nail and the Crown of Thorns from Bourges, suggest that the old loyalties had not been abandoned.[93] During his reign the 'oriflamme', the sacred banner of France, was never raised, and there were probably doubts about its worth after the failures of the 1410s; possibly, too, the flag that had been in the abbey at the time of the occupation had been taken by Bedford. But his secretaries retained the details of the consecration of a new banner ready for use when required.[94] The 'oriflamme' would be raised again within a few years of the death of the 'roi très-victorieux'.

Our verdict on the loyalty of 'Monseigneur Saint Denis', his abbey, and his town, is probably not far from that of their Valois king. Their commitment to the cause of Charles VII could have been more explicit and better sustained; indeed, it often seems that the pretensions of the Parisians were as offensive as those of the English. St Denis was first and foremost the protector of the French people, not only of their leaders; yet, for the people of Saint-Denis, who had grown up with the traditions and shadow of the past around them, there must surely have been a tendency to side with the Valois. How much more so was this true for the monks whose abbey contained the tombs of the kings and whose library contained the reference works on state ceremonial and history, and – not least – the first text of the Salic Law to be used for purposes of anti-English propaganda.[95] The more that the evolution of the French state can be seen as dependent on the elaboration of its intellectual sub-structure, the more one sees how the majority of scholars, lecturers, and secretaries were part of the development of a system that would not be

---

90 Félibien, Histoire, p. 352.
91 Bourgeois, p. 362; Félibien, Histoire, pp. 352–3.
92 Doublet, Histoire, pp.1094–5 (letters of 18 Nov. 1449).
93 Bourgeois, p. 378; Félibien, Histoire, p. 354.
94 The procedure set out in the formulary B.N., ms.fr. 14371, fo. 316, which dates from Charles VII's reign, in fact contains details not included with the late fourteenth-century prayer of blessing set out in B.L., Add. ms. 32069, fo.160v.
95 Beaune, Naissance, p. 269.

Where the monks of Saint-Denis stood in this, it may be impossible to prove: but many may have known the works of Abbot Suger, who had built the church in which they spent so much of their lives. For Suger, writing on the eve of the great three-hundred-year struggle between the English and French monarchies, it was contrary to natural law for the French to be subject to the English or the English to the French.[96] Perhaps his spiritual descendants, living through the final chapter of that long story, would secretly have agreed.

[96] Suger, *Vie de Louis VI le Gros*, ed. H. Waquet (Paris, 1929), p.10.

'Les Angloys, de leur droicte nature, veullent touzjours guerreer': Evidence for Painting in Paris and Normandy, c.1420–1450

CATHERINE REYNOLDS

Under the year 1436 the so-called 'Bourgeois de Paris' wrote:

> Les Angloys furent moult long temps gouverneurs de Paris, mais je cuide en ma conscience que oncques nulz ne fist semer ne blé ne advoyne, ne faire une cheminée en hostel qui y fust, ce ne fut le regent duc de Bedfort, lequel faisoit touzjours maçonner, en quelque pais qu'il fust, et estoit sa nature toute contraire aux Angloys, car il ne vouloit avoir guerre à quelque personne, et les Angloys, de leur droicte nature, veullent touzjours guerreer leurs voisins sans cause.

> [The English ruled Paris for a very long time, but I do honestly think that never any one of them had any corn or oats sown or as much as a fireplace built in a house – except the Regent, the Duke of Bedford. He was always building, wherever he was; his nature was quite un-English, for he never wanted to make war on anybody, whereas the English, essentially, are always wanting to make war on their neighbours without cause.][1]

If the bellicose pre-occupations of the English had interfered with the sowing of corn and the building of fireplaces, it is reasonable to assume that the painting of pictures had suffered likewise. Building of any consequence would, in itself, lead to the employment of painters for symbolic as well as purely decorative ornamentation. The Duke of Bedford, for instance, among his additions to, and alterations of, the Hôtel des Tournelles in Paris built a gallery in 1432 which came to be called the Galerie des Courges from its painted decoration which also displayed the duke's arms.[2]

---

[1] *Journal d'un Bourgeois de Paris, 1405–1449*, ed. A. Tuetey (Société de l'Histoire de Paris, Paris, 1881), p. 320.
[2] H. Sauval, *Histoire et recherches des antiquités de Paris* (Paris, 1724), II, p. 281.

The un-Englishness of the Duke of Bedford can be demonstrated from his patronage not only of architecture but of illuminated manuscripts, metalwork, embroideries and music, on a scale to place him beyond the scope of this paper.[3] Of all the English in France, Bedford alone went some way to match the luxurious levels of patronage established by the sons of John the Good and their descendants, for whom Paris had acted as the chief market-place for art and artists, often supplied from far afield.[4] As captain of Paris and regent of France, the duke had a settled establishment at the Hôtel des Tournelles of a sort which no other English magnate, despite grants of French lands, lordships, and Parisian hôtels seems to have emulated. In France principally to fight, English lords had little opportunity to enjoy their new residences, which were regarded more as investments than as residences.[5] On the whole, English settlement was by gentry and tradesmen, and then rather in Normandy which was further from the fighting and the centre of the English administration and its colonising efforts.[6]

The earlier presence in Paris of the royal court, with its princely and noble satellites, was normally recognised in preambles to legislation as one of the factors which had led to the city's exceptional growth and prosperity. Under the English, the causes of greatness often preface attempts to arrest decline, as in the ordinance of 1424 to regulate property, in which the law, 'the frequent presence of lords of our blood and lineage, and, with them, that of many noblemen, knights and other notable persons', the university, and merchants from all parts were said to have made Paris 'moult renommée, habitée de notables peuples et garnie tres abondamment de richesses et marchandises' ['very famous, lived in by persons of position, reflecting great wealth and commercial prosperity'].[7] Sensitivity about the absence of the king may underlie the words given to the young Henry VI, when he confirmed the privileges of Paris in 1431, mentioning 'la residence que faisoient en icele noz predecesseurs roys de France, qui y avoient, comme encores nous y avons, maison royal et demeure principal' ['the residence which our predecessors

[3] See J. Stratford, *Three Inventories of the Goods of John, Duke of Bedford (d. 1435)* [Society of Antiquaries of London, forthcoming]; J. J. G. Alexander, 'Painting and manuscript illumination for royal patrons in the later middle ages', *English Court Culture in the Later Middle Ages*, ed. V. J. Scattergood and J. W. Sherborne (London, 1983), esp. pp.150–1; J. Stratford, 'The Manuscripts of John, Duke of Bedford: Library and Chapel', *England in the Fifteenth Century: Proceedings of the 1986 Harlaxton Symposium*, ed. D. Williams (Woodbridge, 1987), pp. 329–50. Jenny Stratford has been most generous in sharing with me her knowledge of Bedford's patronage.
[4] J. Favier, 'Une Ville entre deux vocations: la place d'affaires de Paris au XVe siècle', *Annales*, xxviii (1973), 1245–79.
[5] Sauval, *Histoire*, II, p. 320.
[6] C. T. Allmand, *Lancastrian Normandy, 1415–1450. The History of a Medieval Occupation* (Oxford, 1983), pp. 53–6.
[7] M. Félibien, *Histoire de la ville de Paris*, ed. G.-A. Lobineau (Paris, 1725), Preuves, III, pp. 549-50.

as kings of France used to keep there, since they had, as we still have, a royal palace and principal place of abode there'].[8]

Henry VI's one, brief stay in Paris for his coronation at the end of 1431 only highlighted the failure of the treaty of Troyes to gain the adherence of the French nobility. Those who did not recognise the young king's sovereignty no longer had direct access to the capital and its markets, and could no longer contribute to its economic and artistic well-being. Nor, of course, could those captured or killed at Agincourt or, more recently, exiled by the Burgundians. Of the French of high rank who remained, the queen, Isabella of Bavaria, lived on at the Hôtel St Pol where, according to the 'Bourgeois', although kept short of money, she none the less 'kept her position as a widowed woman should'.[9] When she drew up her will in 1431, it is unlikely that any of the 'tableaux d'or et d'argent . . . livres et heures . . . chambres de tapisserie' ['images done in gold or silver . . . books or books of hours . . . or tapestries for hanging'] left to her daughter, Mary, a nun at Poissy,[10] were recent acquisitions. Isabella was still actively concerned in one artistic project: the rich *chapelle* of cloth of gold, which included an altar hanging embroidered with scenes from the life of Christ, together with Charles VI, Isabella herself and their patron saints, being made for the abbey of Saint-Denis at the time of her death.[11] This prestigious commission was, however, being executed at Avignon, although it is possible that a painter had drawn the cartoons at a place more accessible to both the queen and the abbey.

It was for a painter to design embroideries and for the embroiderers that Philip the Good returned to Paris in 1425 when preparing for his abortive judicial duel with Duke Humfrey of Gloucester.[12] The city still had something to offer which the Netherlands could not match, for a messenger was sent specially to bring Thierry du Châtel, embroiderer, and Hans of Constance, painter, to Bruges where Hans was to 'faire patrons et aultres choses de son art', cartoons from which the other was to work. His designs were carried out by a large team of embroiderers and painters drawn from all over the Netherlands. Later, Hans returned to Paris, but nothing further is known of his activities. In 1432 and 1435, Philip was deal-

---

8　*Paris pendant la domination anglaise (1420–1436). Documents extraits des registres de la chancellerie de France*, ed. A. Longnon (Société de l'Histoire de Paris, Paris, 1878), p. 334.
9　*Bourgeois*, pp.193, 202.
10　Félibien, *Histoire de la ville de Paris*, Preuves, III, p. 554. Mary of France's property seems to have passed to Poissy since it was from the convent that Marie Juvénal des Ursins bought the Belleville breviary which the Duke of Berry had given to his niece (V. Leroquais, *Les Bréviaires manuscrits des bibliothèques publiques de France* (Paris, 1934), III, p. 997).
11　Jean Chartier, *Chronique de Charles VII*, ed. A. Vallet de Viriville (3 vols, Paris, 1858), I, pp. 210–11; B. de Montesquiou-Fezensac and D. Gaborit-Chopin, *Le Trésor de Saint-Denis. Documents divers* (Paris, 1977), II, pp. 251–2, 493–6.
12　J. Duverger and J. Versyp, 'Schilders en borduurwerkers aan de arbeid voor een voorstenduel te Brugge in 1425', *Artes Textiles*, xi (1955), 3–17.

ing with the Parisian merchant, Guillaume Sanguin, for precious metalwork,[13] while in 1436 Guillebert de Metz thought it appropriate to dedicate his *Description de la ville de Paris* to the duke.[14] Through his agents, Philip was responsible for winding up the estate of his sister, Anne, Duchess of Bedford, and for her tomb in the church of the Celestines in Paris.[15] Yet the Burgundian-led administration sensed his increasing lack of interest in the capital, and bewailed the growing infrequency of his visits, as, for instance, in the appeal made to him during his stay in 1429.[16]

Neither the treaty of Arras (1435) nor the surrender of Paris to Artur de Richemont (1436) brought Philip back. Further, while Charles VII restored the city's judicial and administrative supremacy, he failed to make Paris his personal capital. According to Basin, Charles disliked large towns and Paris in particular,[17] so that it was left to Richemont and, more often, to his wife, Margaret of Burgundy, to maintain some kind of royal presence.[18] Margaret has been suggested as the original owner of the luxuriously illuminated Sobieski Hours (Royal Library, Windsor Castle);[19] her will provided for a tomb effigy, but no paintings or manuscripts, other than the missals of her chapel, were specified.[20] Charles VII's return was one of the first requests of the *Parlement* of Paris in 1436,[21] and his failure to take up residence continued to attract the criticism of the 'Bourgeois'.[22]

That observer, however, had reacted far from favourably to Henry VI's stay in Paris. He considered that no king had ever been so honoured by the city (taking the times into account), yet the English had failed to reciprocate:

> mais, pour certain, maintes foys on a veu à Paris enfans de bourgoys, que quant ilz se marioient, tous mestiers, comme orfebvres, orbateurs, brief gens de tous joieux mestiers en amendoient plus que ilz n'ont fait du sacre du roy et de ses joustes et de tous ses Angloys.
>
> [really, many a time a Paris citizen marrying his child has done more for

---

[13] A. Le Roux de Lincy and L.-M. Tisserand, *Paris et ses historiens aux XIVe et XVe siècles* (Histoire générale de Paris, Paris, 1867), p. 345.

[14] *Ibid.*, pp.131–236.

[15] J. Chipps Smith, 'The Tomb of Anne of Burgundy, Duchess of Bedford, in the Musée du Louvre', *Gesta*, International Center of Medieval Art, xxiii (1984), 39–50 (with some inaccuracies).

[16] Enguerran de Monstrelet, *Chronique*, ed. L. Douet d'Arcq (6 vols, SHF, Paris, 1857–62), IV, pp. 361–2.

[17] Thomas Basin, *Histoire de Charles VII*, ed. and trans. C. Samaran (2nd edn, Paris, 1964), II, p. 306.

[18] E. Cosneau, *Le Connétable de Richemont (Artur de Bretagne, 1393–1458)* (Paris, 1886), p. 330.

[19] E. P. Spencer, *The Sobieski Hours. A Manuscript in the Royal Library at Windsor Castle*, presented by R. Mackworth-Young (Roxburghe Club Publication 239, London, 1977).

[20] Cosneau, *Connétable de Richemont*, pp. 586–96.

[21] Félibien, *Histoire de la ville de Paris*, V, p. 269.

[22] *Bourgeois*, p. 327; see also pp. 369–70 for similar complaints in 1444.

tradespeople, for goldsmiths, goldbeaters, all the luxury trades, than the King's consecration now did, or his tournament or all his Englishmen.][23]

As in the comment under 1436, the 'Bourgeois' was not complaining of aesthetic opportunities lost, but of economic ones. It was the state of the artisan that he lamented, not the state of the arts. Paris had certainly provided a lavish show of pageantry for Henry's Entry, which the 'Bourgeois' described in some detail: the nine *Preux* and *Preuses*, the mermaid, the wildmen, the scenes from the infancy of Christ, the execution of St Denis, the stag hunt through the cemetery of the Innocents, the overt symbolism of the *lit de justice*, all required expenditure on costumes, properties and settings, although not, for such ephemeral entertainments, on commissions for the goldsmiths, goldbeaters and luxury traders.[24] Instead the painters' ability to imitate more costly materials and processes could be given full rein. Political insecurity or economic hardship might serve to increase the demand for painting as a substitute for arts requiring greater outlay in materials and labour, as well as longer periods of time for their accomplishment. Even in 1464, for Louis XI's Entry into Tournai, the three children presenting gifts to the king wore painted costumes, presumably mimicking woven or embroidered designs, whereas the magistrates wore robes with real embroidery for which they had to be advanced significant sums.[25] Painters were, of course, employed in more creative roles in such festivities: Jean Prévot, for example, designed a Jesse Tree for Louis XI's Entry into Lyon in 1476, as well as helping to make a lion out of calf skin.[26]

Henry VI's Entry and coronation must have benefited artists, even though the luxury traders felt their legitimate expectations had been disappointed. But at least the goldsmiths and goldbeaters had survived to complain, in marked contrast to the tapestry-makers, whose luxury industry had been flourishing at the turn of the century, but which appears to have disappeared initially under Armagnac-Burgundian feuding and then English occupation.[27] Theirs was an art which required expensive materials, skilled labour, and a considerable investment of time as well as capital. The taste for tapestry remained, however, and dealing continued in existing pieces. Charles VI's *Garde des tapisseries* had to be pardoned for selling part of his charge for his own profit, a good one even after he had paid for the tapestry to be washed and repaired.[28] The bulk of the royal collection was gradually absorbed by the Duke of Bedford, who began modestly in 1423 by hav-

---

23 *Ibid.*, p. 279.

24 *Ibid.*, pp. 274–6.

25 B. Guenée and F. Lehoux, *Les Entrées royales françaises de 1328 à 1515* (Paris, 1968), p.198.

26 *Ibid.*, pp. 204–05, 231, 238.

27 Exhibition catalogue, *Chefs-d'oeuvre de la tapisserie du XIVe au XVIe siècle*, Grand Palais, Paris, Oct. 1973 – Jan. 1974 (Paris, 1973), p.17; on the decline of weaving and the cloth trade in general in Paris, see J. Favier, *Paris au XVe siècle, 1380–1500* (Nouvelle Histoire de Paris, Paris, 1974), pp. 313–17.

28 *Domination anglaise*, ed. Longnon, pp. 30–2.

ing an old *banquier* made into cushions for Anne of Burgundy's *chariot*, but by 1432 he was being handed such famous sets as the *Jousts of St Denis*.[29]

In addition to their involvement in the tapestry industry as the designers and executors of cartoons, painters were also employed to produce painted cloths which could be hung instead of tapestries, and at much less cost. Their lower status and more fragile materials mean that few survive from the fifteenth century, the collection at Reims being a notable exception.[30] Inventories show them to have used similar subject matter to the tapestries which they replaced. Clément de Fauquembergue, *greffier* of the *Parlement* and a canon of Notre Dame, owned ten painted cloths when he died in 1438; four depicted religious scenes (the Three Kings of Cologne; St Gontier; the *mauvais riche*, probably Dives and Lazarus; and the Judgement), three were allegorical (the Virtues and Vices; Loyalty; and the Wheel of Fortune), while three were decorative 'non-subjects' (a morisco; one with people and corn stooks; and one with people and trees).He also owned two Turkey carpets, but no figured woven tapestries.[31] The Judgement, specified as small, could have been a fictive panel painting rather than fictive tapestry.[32] Such a collection may or may not have been typical, and could have been made from local products since the Parisian guild regulations of 1391 had envisaged painting on cloth,[33] or from imports from the Netherlands, where Bruges, with a separate division of the painters' guild for cloth painters, specialised in this kind of work.[34]

The one well documented work of painting which attracted comment in English-ruled Paris was the Danse Macabre, or Dance of Death, painted on a section of the cloisters at the cemetery of the Innocents. The 'Bourgeois' would seem to have been an interested observer of its making:

> l'an mil cccc xxiiii fut faicte la Danse Macabre aux Innocens, et fut commencée environ le moys d'aoust et achevée au karesme ensuivant.

---

[29] J. Guiffrey, 'Inventaire des tapisseries du roi Charles VI vendues par les Anglais en 1422', BEC, xlviii (1887), 59–110, 396–444.

[30] L. Paris, *Toiles peintes et tapisseries de la ville de Reims* (Paris, 1843); F. Pomarede, 'Les toiles peintes du Musée de Reims', *Mémoires de la société d'agriculture, commerce, sciences et arts du département de la Marne*, xci (1976), 229–42.

[31] *Journal de Clément de Fauquembergue*, ed. A. Tuetey (3 vols, SHF, Paris, 1903–15), III, pp.lxxii-lxxix).

[32] A surviving French example of the Virgin and Child with angels is on loan to the Staatliche Museen, Berlin-Dahlem (M. Meiss, *French Painting in the Time of Jean de Berry. The Limbourgs and their Contemporaries* (London, 1974), pl. 642). The difference between these and simulated tapestries is stressed by P. Vandenbroeck, 'Laatmiddeleeuwse doekschilderkunst in de zuidelijke Nederlanden: Repertorium der nog bewaarde werken', *Koninklijke Museum voor Schone Kunsten Antwerpen, Jaarboek*, XIV (1982), pp. 29–59.

[33] J. Leber, *Collections des meilleurs dissertations, notices et traités particuliers relatifs à l'histoire de France* (Paris, 1826–38), XIX, clause 15.

[34] D. Wolfthal, 'Early Netherlandish Canvases: Documentary Evidence', *Université Libre de Bruxelles: Annales d'Histoire de l'art et d'archéologie*, viii (1986), 19–41.

[In this year 1424 the Dance Macabre was made at the Innocents. It was begun about August and finished in the following Lent.][35]

In 1429 he used 'l'androit de la Dance Macabre' to indicate exactly where Frère Richard preached.[36] Guillebert de Metz noted at the Innocents 'paintures notables de la Danse Macabre et autres avec escriptures pour esmouvoir les gens a devotion' ['notable paintings of the Dance of Death and others with inscriptions to move people to devotion'].[37] The combination of image with text was common in tapestries and may have been equally so in painting, for Guillebert also recorded that the first *salle* in the house of Jacquet Duchie in Paris was decorated with 'divers tableaux et escriptures d'enseignement attachés et pendus aux parois' ['many pictures and inscriptions attached to or hanging from the wall, all of them intended to convey a message'.][38]

John Lydgate was in Paris in 1426, and there he saw the Dance of Death 'depicte / ones on a walle / Ful notably . . . I toke on me / to translaten al / Owte of the frensshe / Macabrees daunce' as portrayed at the Innocents.[39] The verses accompanied paintings in the Pardon Churchyard of St Paul's in London, which may have been equally dependent on the Parisian model.[40] Both the Pardon Churchyard and the cemetery of the Innocents have been demolished along with their murals; in a sixteenth-century painting of the Innocents, attributed to Jacob Grimmer, a few skeletal and human figures can be made out on a wall of the cloister.[41] The earliest derivations from the cycle come in two books of hours in which the Dance of Death winds through the marginal decoration.[42] Guyot Marchant published the verses in 1485 with woodcut illustrations, the figures in which are dressed in the fashion of that year and do not follow the original murals in more than the format of death figures whirling representatives of the different ranks of society into the Dance.[43]

The continuing popularity of the theme is shown by Marchant's subsequent editions. In 1486 he added to the Dance of Death the *Trois Vifs et Trois Morts*, with prints which might be loosely based on the famed relief carvings on the portal of the church of the Innocents.[44] These were explained in verses attributed

---

35 *Bourgeois*, p. 203.
36 *Ibid.*, p. 234.
37 Le Roux de Lincy and Tisserand, *Paris et ses historiens*, p. 283.
38 *Ibid.*, p.191.
39 John Lydgate, *The Dance of Death*, ed. F. Warren and B. White (Early English Text Society, original series 181 London, 1931), pp. 2–4.
40 J. Stow, *A Survey of London* (London, 1598), p. 264.
41 Paris, Musée Carnavalet, Inv. P620.
42 New York, Pierpont Morgan Library, ms. M. 359; see also J. Plummer, *The Last Flowering: French Painting in Manuscripts, 1420–1530, from American Collections* (New York, 1982), pp. 3–4, no. 4; Paris, B. N., ms. Rothschild 2535, fos 108v–109.
43 Reproduced by Le Roux de Lincy and Tisserand, *Paris et ses historiens*, pp. 291–7.
44 *Ibid.*, pp. 276–81.

to the characters and in a rhymed dedication which proclaimed the Duke of Berry as donor.[45] No evidence survives to indicate the patron of the Dance Macabre. By 1597, it was being attributed to the generosity of Charles V,[46] indicating that by that date, at least, there was no permanent or comprehensible record of the dona-tion. While it is tempting to credit the Duke of Bedford with this emulation of Berry's example, Lydgate would have had no reason not to point this out, even if French authors preferred to remain silent. The necessary funds could have been raised in some corporate way, or by a citizen like Guillaume Sanguin who, with his brother, Jean, founded a chapel of St Michael in the church of the Innocents, where he was buried in 1441.[47]

Exceptionally, the Dance Macabre is mentioned by three contemporary wri-ters. Other memorials of the dead have disappeared without trace, those painted rather than carved being particularly vulnerable. Of the wills published from the reign of Charles VI, four refer to painted commemorative images. In 1410, Pierre d'Auxon wanted to be buried at Pontaubert, where a picture was to be placed in the church to show, on the one side, the Virgin and himself, dressed in his robes as a doctor of medicine with his titles and degrees written below, and, on the other, St John with his brother and sisters.[48] In 1420, Nicolas l'Espoisse, greffier in the Parlement, asked to have made, 'de bonne painture', images of himself, his late wife and his children before the Virgin 'en parois' in the chapel of SS Michael and James in the Carmelite church in Paris, or in the cloister against the wall of the church.[49] In 1400 a mural painting had been the choice of Guillaume de Chambord, écuyer de corps du roi, to be made above his tomb in the church of the Celestines at Ternes:

> Une ymage de Nostre Dame qui sera painte dedans le mur, laquel image sera belle et bien faicte tenant Nostre Seigneur, son enfant, entre ses bras, et aura devant ladicte ymage une representacion de sa personne faicte en paincture dedans le mur à l'endroit de sa tombe ou il sera à ge-noulx, armé de ses armes, à mains joinctes, et sera presenté de deux ym-ages, l'une de Saint Jehan Baptiste et l'autre de Saint Guillaume.

> [A picture of Our Lady which shall be painted on the wall, the said pic-ture to be beautifully executed, and shall show her holding Our Lord, her child, in her arms; and in the front of the picture will be a portrait (of the donor) painted on the wall by his tomb, in which he will be depicted on

[45] J. du Breul, Le Théâtre des antiquités de Paris (Paris, 1639), pp. 621–2.
[46] Noel du Fail, Contes et discours d'Eutrapel (Rennes, 1597), cited by Le Roux de Lincy and Tisserand, Paris et ses historiens, p. 284.
[47] Le Roux de Lincy and Tisserand, Paris et ses historiens, p. 346.
[48] Testaments enregistrés au Parlement de Paris sous le règne de Charles VI ed. A. Tuetey (Paris, 1880), p. 510.
[49] Ibid., p. 614.

his knees, bearing his arms, hands joined; and there shall also be painted two figures, one St John the Baptist, the other St William].[50]

In 1411 Denis du Mouroy, the royal *procureur général* in the *Parlement*, had wanted to be buried with his family in the graveyard at Coulommiers:

> que on face faire a Paris une belle croix de bois, painte et ordenée comme celles qui sont ou cymetiere St Innocent . . . et que en l'un des costés soit le crucifiement, et de l'autre costé la Vierge Marie tenant son enfant, et au dessoubz du crucifiement deux prians ou representacions de deux bourgeois, et au dessoubz de Nostre Dame un homme, une femme, et des enfans.
>
> [let there be made in Paris a fine cross of wood, painted and prepared like those at the cemetery of the Innocents . . . and on one side shall be the Crucifixion, on the other the Virgin Mary holding her child; and beneath the crucifix two figures praying, or the representation of two bourgeois, and, beneath Our Lady, a man, a woman, and some children.][51]

Judging by the complexity of the imagery and the failure to specify sculpture, as is done in other details, this would seem to have been a flat, painted cross, not a polychromed relief.

For Guillaume de Chambord, a mural was part of an elaborate ensemble. The other three were not specially rich or important men, and for them painting can again be seen as providing a cheaper alternative, in this case to sculpture. It can only have been cost which led du Mouroy to specify plaster, instead of stone, for his family tomb. Within Paris under English rule, the need for economy must have been pressing; yet established funerary customs are unlikely to have lapsed completely, particularly the production of a type of cross sufficiently well known at the Innocents to serve as a definition in a will. Miniatures of graveyards frequently show large, sheltering ridges over crosses, indicating a painted image in need of protection, although illuminators did not attempt to differentiate between polychromed relief and flat painting.[52]

Polychromy led even the rich who could afford sculpture to employ painters. A surviving coloured tomb effigy from Paris is that of Philippe de Morvilliers in his red 'robe parlementaire', taken from the chapel which he founded in the Parisian church of St-Martin-des-Champs.[53] The lost effigy of his wife was recorded by Gaignières, who also had drawings of the polychromed standing figures of the

50 *Ibid.*, p. 297.
51 *Ibid.*, p. 542.
52 For example, Paris, Bibliothèque Mazarine, ms. 469; and Berlin-Dahlem, Staatliche Museen, Kupferstichkabinett, ms. 78 C 4, fo. 128v, reproduced in M. Meiss, *French Painting in the Time of Jean de Berry. The Boucicaut Master* (London, 1968), figs 164 and 152.
53 Paris, Musée du Louvre, Inv. L. P. 433; M. Aubert and M. Beaulieu, *Musée national du Louvre. Description raisonnée des sculptures du moyen âge, de la Renaissance et des temps modernes. I: Moyen Age* (Paris, 1950), pp.195–6, no. 283.

couple.[54] The foundation deed required them to furnish the chapel with 'calice, livres et autres ornemens' ['chalice, books, and other ornaments']55 which may not have been newly made but which demonstrate how commemoration of the dead could involve far more work for artists than the straightforward manufacture of a tomb.

Gold, good pigments and skilled labour could make the colouring of sculpture a luxury in itself: Charles VI paid François d'Orléans 4 livres parisis per figure for painting the statues of the apostles erected by Charles V in the chapel of the Hôtel St Pol.[56] The published accounts of the Hôpital St-Jacques-aux-Pèlerins show that statues needed frequent retouching and cleaning,[57] and the guild regulations of 1391 suggest that wooden statues were being repainted to hide defective materials. Standards were also set for the repainting of altarpieces and murals, as though both were commonplace.[58] Murals were certainly vulnerable to damp, and without careful maintenance the Dance Macabre could never have survived into the seventeenth century. Paintings in churches, like the Last Judgement at the Celestines, admired by Guillebert de Metz and possibly the work which Antonio Astesano thought worthy of Apelles in the middle of the fifteenth century,[59] were protected from the weather but were also exposed to soot and candle grease.

Troubled times did not leave the painters dependent on repair-work alone, for adversity encouraged religious observance with rituals formulated around images and artefacts. The realisation of peace within France and the prosperity of the city of Paris and all its inhabitants was one of the main petitions of the confraternity founded by the money-changers of the Grand- Pont in 1427 at the church of St Barthélemy; but neither did they forget to pray, too, for the souls of Charles VI and his queen, Isabella.[60] Although, unlike the prestigious Morvilliers foundation, no furnishings are referred to, books, altar vessels and an identifying image are likely to have been required.

Such items were too much a part of everyday life to attract comment from writers like the 'Bourgeois', who, apart from the Dance Macabre, mentions only one set of paintings: the anti-English pictures of 1438. In May of that year there were hung at each of the four gates of Paris

---

[54] H. Bouchot, Inventaires des dessins executés pour Roger de Gaignières (Paris, 1891), II, p. 99, nos 4482 and 4486; J. Adhémar, 'Les Tombeaux de la collection Gaignières, dessins d'archéologie du XVIe siècle', Gazette des Beaux-Arts, 6e période, lxxxviii (1976), 6, nos 1106 and 1107.

[55] Domination anglaise, ed. Longnon, p. 234.

[56] Sauval, Histoire, II, p. 281.

[57] F. Baron, 'Le Décor sculpté et peint de l'hôpital St-Jacques-aux-Pèlerins', Bulletin Monumental, cxxxiii (1975), 29–72.

[58] Leber, Collections, clauses, 8, 9, and 14.

[59] Le Roux de Lincy and Tisserand, Paris et ses historiens, pp.191, 541.

[60] Domination anglaise, ed. Longnon, doc. CXXVIII.

iii pieces de toile tres bien peintes de tres laides histoires; car en chascune avoit painct ung chevalier des grans signeurs d'Angleterre, icelluy chevallier estoit pendu par les piez à un gibet, les esperons chausseés; tout armé senon la teste, et a chascun costé un diable qui l'enchaînoit, et ii corbeaux laidz et hideux qui estoient en bas en son visage, qui luy arrachoient les yeux de la teste par semblant.

[three pieces of cloth very well painted with very unpleasant pictures; for on each had been painted a knight, one of the great English lords, hanging by his feet on a gallows, his spurs on, completely armed except for his head, at each side a devil binding him with chains and at the bottom of the picture two foul, ugly crows made to look as if they were picking out his eyes.][61]

The English lords were the Earl of Suffolk, Lord Willoughby and Sir Thomas Blount. While they may have been depicted with great skill, it is unlikely that expensive materials were used. Twenty *sous parisis* was the price paid per *drapelet* of the Prince of Orange, hanging by the heel, for display at the Hôtel de Ville, Palais and Châtelet in 1481,[62] the painter, Jean Fourbault, having been a resident on the Pont Notre-Dame for at least the year 1473–74.[63] Attacking the absent through effigy doubtless brought emotional satisfaction and ensured that the identity of the villain and the enormity of his crimes would be well publicised. When Dunois besieged the castle of Harcourt in 1449, he had its captain, Richard Frognall, 'pendu par les pieds en peinture à la porte' ['hung by the feet in a painting by the gate'] because he had broken his oath by taking up arms against the French, and so was 'fort deshonnoré'.[64] Hanging by the heels indicated that the offender had not yet received his just deserts.[65]

While the English, in these instances, were the provokers rather than the commissioners of paintings, they, too, were ready to use visual imagery in the wars. At the battle of Castillon, in 1453, the English leader, Talbot, carried

huict bannieres . . . tant du roy d'Angleterre que de St Georges, de la Trinité et dudit Talbot, avecques plusieurs estendars sciemment malicieusement pourpenséz et inventéz, chargéz d'inscriptions et devises injurieuses aux mespris et desdain de bons Francois.

[61] *Bourgeois*, p. 340.
[62] Sauval, *Histoire*, II, p. 442. The prince was also hung in effigy at Dijon and Bourges (B. Prost, 'Quelques documents sur l'histoire des arts en France', *Gazette des Beaux-Arts*, 2e période, xxxv (1887), 330), at Tours (E. Giraudet, *Les Artistes tourangeaux* (Tours, 1885), p.163), and at Evreux (L. de Laborde, *La Renaissance des arts à la cour de France* (2 vols, Paris, 1850–55), I, pp. 50–1).
[63] A. Vidier, L. Legrand, P. Dupieux, *Comptes du domaine de la ville de Paris* (Paris, 1948), II, col. 330.
[64] Chartier, *Chronique*, II, pp.115–16.
[65] See details of the paintings by Botticelli of the Pazzi conspirators on the Bargello in 1478 (H. Horne, *Botticelli, Painter of Florence* (repr. Princeton, 1980), pp. 63, 66).

[eight banners . . . of the king of England and St George, as well as of the Trinity and of Talbot himself, with several standards knowingly and deliberately made false and deceptive, carrying inscriptions and devices intended to be insulting and disdainful to good Frenchmen.][66]

While most of the trappings of war must have been prepared at base, it is possible that, as at Harcourt, men serving with the armies were able to respond more immediately. A Scot, often assumed to be one of the archers, could produce a picture of Joan of Arc kneeling to hand a letter to Charles VII, a composition of some complexity, although Joan gave no opinion on its competence.[67]

Visual symbols with which to attack and identify the foe complemented those which rallied and identified friends. The red cross on white of St George marked the English, as the St Andrew's cross the Burgundians, and the white sash the Armagnacs. Cheaply reproduced metal badges were made to fasten to clothes, but the full force of St George's cross required colour, whether stitched, woven or painted, as in such creations as the white bands all covered with small red crosses worn by the governors of Paris in 1436.[68] The situation in France demanded new imagery; at the battle of Verneuil in August 1424, the Duke of Bedford emphasised his alliance with Burgundy by carrying banners which combined the crosses of SS. George and Andrew.[69] New seals and coins bore images of new sources of authority,[70] and the English propaganda effort extended beyond such fundamentals of government. Warfare and political instability worked against the production of luxury art, yet provided the very conditions to encourage more functional imagery. It was a commonplace that images were necessary to inform the illiterate, and also that they had more force than verbal communications. People were more moved by what they saw, and remembered it for longer.[71] The 'Bourgeois' included several anecdotes indicative of the seriousness with which people regarded the visual image: the man who had his hand cut off for removing the white sash from a statue of St Andrew; the tearing of the dragon banner in the Burgundian riots of 1418; and the murmuring at the two mantles carried before Catherine of France in 1422.[72]

The Duke of Bedford linked verbal and visual information when he commis-

---

[66] Chartier, Chronique, III, p. 5.

[67] P. Champion, Procès de condemnation de Jeanne d'Arc (repr. Geneva, 1976), I, p. 75.

[68] Bourgeois, p. 313.

[69] Jehan de Waurin, Recueil des croniques et anchiennes istories de la Grant Bretaigne à present nommé Engleterre, 1422–1431, ed. W. and E. L. P. Hardy, (R S, London, 1879), pp.101, 103.

[70] See J. W. McKenna, 'Henry VI of England and the Dual Monarchy: Aspects of Royal Political Propaganda, 1422–32', Journal of the Warburg and Courtauld Institutes, xxviii (1965), 145–62.

[71] For example, John of Genoa, Catholicon, cited by M. Baxendall, Painting and Experience in Fifteenth-Century Italy (Oxford, 1972), pp. 40–1.

[72] Bourgeois, pp. 56, 110, 174.

sioned Laurence Calot's poem on the genealogy of the kings of England and France with its accompanying table, probably reflected in the family tree of the Shrewsbury Book presented to Margaret of Anjou in 1445. Like the outraged Burgundian who had lost a hand, a canon of Rouen defaced a copy of the genealogy hanging publicly in that city and had to pay for two replacements, indicating that they were widely disseminated.[73] Justification of Henry VI's claim to the French throne had to be matched by a reassuring maintenance of French traditions. If the 'Bourgeois' was not alone in being offended by the lack of French tradition in Henry VI's coronation in Paris,[74] greater care had been taken to follow French precedent for the funeral of Charles VI, although the body of his queen, Isabella, who died at a very low point in English fortunes, was to have a more hurried journey to burial at Saint-Denis by water.[75] Funerary pomp inevitably involved painters. Large numbers of coats of arms were supplied by François d'Orléans and others for the obsequies of Charles VI. The effigy carried on a decorated litter in the procession was probably based on the death mask which was taken, and which may have served for the tomb-figure sculpted by Pierre de Thury, now returned to Saint-Denis with that of Isabella.[76] The same artist also provided a polychromed statue of Charles to bring up to date the series of kings of France at the Palais.[77]

At a more routine level, all significant branches of government needed painters. In 1434, when Paris was rightly alarmed at the progress of the war, Mahiet Biterne was paid for painting the *grand grenier* of the artillery at the Hôtel de Ville with *fleurs de lis* and *rosiers* intertwined, together with the arms of France and Paris.[78] Such paintings cannot be classed as 'luxury'; their purpose was clearly political, the maintenance of morale and prestige.

Yet this was not a good time for painters. At least one gave up to earn a less precarious living as a *sergent* at the *Châtelet*,[79] while the great Parisian workshop producing illuminations in the style of the Boucicaut Hours seems to have disappeared about 1420.[80] The only paintings to survive in any quantity are those in books, some the product of the need or desire of men to ingratiate themselves with the new English authorities. The Norman cleric, Jean Galopes, dedicated his translation of the *Meditations on the Life of Christ* to Henry V, and carefully

[73] B. J. H. Rowe, 'King Henry VI's Claim to France: in Picture and Poem', *The Library*, 4th series, xiii (1932), 77–88; for Lydgate's translation, see V. J. Scattergood, *Politics and Poetry in the Fifteenth Century* (London, 1971), pp. 71–4.

[74] *Bourgeois*, pp. 277–9.

[75] *Ibid.*, pp.177–81, 309–10.

[76] Y. Grandeau, 'La Mort et les obsèques de Charles VI', *Bulletin philologique et historique du comité des travaux historiques et scientifiques, 1970. Philologie et Histoire jusqu'à 1610* (Paris, 1974), pp.176–7.

[77] B. Prost, 'Quelques Documents sur l'histoire des arts en France', *Gazette des Beaux-Arts*, 2e période, xxxvi (1888), 241.

[78] Sauval, *Histoire*, II, p. 483.

[79] Favier, 'Une Ville', 1254.

[80] Meiss, *Boucicaut Master*, esp. pp. 62, 73–4.

pointed out that his benefice was in the county of Harcourt held by the king's uncle, the Duke of Exeter. Royal ms. 20 B IV in the British Library may have been intended as the presentation copy, if one is to judge by the number and novelty of its illustrations, proved, perhaps, by the small marginal sketches which were never erased.[81] Of Galope's Latin prose version of the *Pèlerinage de l'Âme*, dedicated to and paid for by the Duke of Bedford, it would seem that only later copies survive.[82] The original must have been illustrated, for presentation miniatures are repeated, as in Lambeth Palace Library ms. 326.[83]

The book-trade and the illuminators had sufficient middle-range support to weather the removal of the French court and the luxury end of the market. In Paris, the university and the educated men of the church, administration and trades provided a continuing demand for books in which illumination was bound to play some part. As vital contributors to book production, the illuminators could come under university control, as did the scribes, *libraires* and *stationnaires*.[84] The university founded by the English at Caen had two illuminators, as well as parchment-makers, *libraires* and book binders, by the middle of the century.[85]

One Parisian bibliophile is known to have taken a special interest in illumination and the technique of illustration. Jean le Bègue advanced in the financial administration as a Burgundian protegé, and was restored to office in the general pardon of 1437. He owned at least fourteen books,[86] compiled a collection of scribes' and painters' recipes and techniques gathered from the workshops of Paris,[87] devised a programme of illustrations for Sallust's *Pro Jugurtha*,[88] and himself translated Leonardo Bruni's paraphrase of the *Punic War* into French, a work which he dedicated to Charles VII. Illustrated copies survive in some numbers, but with insufficient evidence to reconstruct the original programme which le Bègue surely devised.[89] There is a manuscript of the Sallust which follows his instructions for the pictures 'qu'on peut raisonnablement faire', the word 'raison-

[81]   G. F. Warner and J. Gilson, *Catalogue of Western Manuscripts in the old Royal and King's Collections* (London, 1921), II, pp. 360–1; IV, pl. 14. For comment on the sketches, see M. Meiss, *French Painting in the Time of Jean de Berry: the Late Fourteenth Century and the Patronage of the Duke* (London, 1967), p.12 and fig. 316.

[82]   Stratford, 'Manuscripts', p. 348.

[83]   M. R. James, *A Descriptive Catalogue of the Manuscripts in Lambeth Palace Library: The Medieval Manuscripts* (Cambridge, 1932), pp. 427–30.

[84]   See P. Delalain, *Étude sur le libraire parisien du XIIIe au XVe siècle* (Paris, 1891).

[85]   Allmand, *Lancastrian Normandy*, p.116, n.133.

[86]   J. Porcher, 'Un Amateur de peinture sous Charles VII: Jean Lebègue', *Mélanges d'histoire du livre et des bibliothèques offerts à M. Frantz Calot* (Paris, 1960), pp. 35–41.

[87]   Published by Mrs Merrifield, *Original Treatises on the Art of Painting* (London, 1849).

[88]   J. Porcher, *Jean Lebègue: les histoires que l'on peut raisonnablement faire sur les livres de Salluste* (Société des bibliophiles français, Paris, 1962).

[89]   For example, Paris, Bibliothèque de l'Arsenal, ms. 5086.

nablement' probably indicating some irritation at the more mindless repetitions of the painters' shops.[90]

Jean le Bègue may only have been exceptional in giving written expression to his interest in painting and illumination. The English shared the French taste for books, and Talbot expected Margaret of Anjou not only to read the Shrewsbury Book but also to be impressed by its miniatures 'qui bien sont dignes de memoire', memorable in every way.[91] References in wills and inventories to the property of Englishmen or English adherents are seldom precise about origin. Where did Thomas Beaufort, Duke of Exeter, obtain the copy of Tristram bequeathed to his sister Joan, Countess of Westmorland in 1426,[92] or Louis of Luxembourg the two books of song for his chapel, given after his death in 1443 by Henry VI to Gilles of Brittany?[93] Where provenance is listed or coats of arms recorded, it is more likely to be for metalwork. In his will, the Duke of Bedford distinguished one item by the name of its maker; the gold chalice which he had had made at the Hôtel des Tournelles by his goldsmith, Estienne.[94] But although a careful record was made in the Bedford Hours of the book's presentation to Henry VI, no mention was included of where it had been purchased or who had worked on it.[95]

Like other manuscripts possessed by English patrons who had neither the time nor the money to order specially commissioned books, the Bedford Hours was probably only adapted for the Duke and Duchess. The failure to complete the two manuscripts which Bedford had commissioned, the Salisbury Breviary and the lost so-called Pontifical, demonstrates the advantages in taking over an already completed book.[96] The full-page miniatures of Old Testament scenes could have been added to the Bedford Hours to make it more attractive to the young Henry VI,[97] just as the full-page scenes of monks and nuns reciting the office may have been added to an early fifteenth-century psalter to make it an acceptable present for the infant king. Certainly the arms of a Dauphin of France, worn by the psalter's original owner, were overpainted for Henry, so that he took over both manuscript and imagery very directly.[98]

[90] Geneva, Bibliothèque publique et universitaire, ms. lat. 54; miniatures reproduced by Porcher, Jean Lebègue . . . Salluste.

[91] B. L., Royal ms. 15 E VI, fo. 2v.

[92] J. Nichols, A Collection of all the Wills now known to be extant of the Kings and Queens of England (London, 1780), p. 254.

[93] Letters and Papers illustrative of the Wars of the English in France during the Reign of Henry the Sixth, King of England, ed. J. Stevenson (2 vols in 3, RS, London, 1861–64), I, p. 439.

[94] Both wills to be published by Stratford, Inventories.

[95] E. P. Spencer, 'The Master of the Duke of Bedford: the Bedford Hours', The Burlington Magazine, cvii (1965), 495–502.

[96] See Stratford, 'Manuscripts', pp. 344–6.

[97] Spencer, 'Bedford Hours', 496–7.

[98] B. L., Cotton ms. Domitian A XVII. See also J. Porcher, Les Belles Heures de Jean de France, duc de Berry (Paris, 1953), pp. 27, 48; Meiss, Limbourgs, p. 405; A. Farber, A Study of the Secondary Decoration of the Belles Heures and related Manuscripts, Cornell University

For a member or members of the Neville family, miniatures and prayers were added to a book of hours originally decorated in the Boucicaut style.[99] The miniature of the first owner (perhaps a scribe or academic, judging by the prominence given to his pencase and inkwell) was left untouched, but two new prayers were added, each headed by a devotional image to which pray, from flanking inserted leaves, the Neville sons with three daughters ranged behind Ralph, Earl of Westmorland, on one leaf, and, on the other, the daughters behind his second countess, Joan Beaufort. Robert Neville's episcopal robes date the miniatures to after his consecration as bishop of Salisbury in 1427. Family images of this kind are most unusual in books of hours, but are standard for painted epitaphs or votive panels such as that made for the Juvénal des Ursins family between 1444 and 1449 for their funerary chapel in Notre-Dame[100] which, despite the difference in scale and technique, shows some stylistic correspondence with the Neville miniatures. Perhaps their commissioner, presumably one of Joan's children, wanted a record of family achievement in a suitably devotional context which could be executed more quickly, and carried to England more conveniently, than a painted panel.

The Bedford and Neville Hours, and the psalter of Henry VI, are all of the Use of Paris, and therefore less likely to have appealed to their new English owners for their texts than for their decoration. How much people cared about the precise nature of the texts of their illustrated devotional books is debatable. The contents of some are clearly very idiosyncratic and personal, yet, on the other hand, the book of hours in particular had become almost as much a fashionable necessity as an aid to piety. Already, in the fourteenth century, Eustache Deschamps had referred to the would-be smart bourgeoise taking her book of hours to church,[101] while the 'Ménagier de Paris' instructed his wife to keep her eyes closely on her book.[102] That a book could be judged not for its contents but for its general effect as an object is demonstrated by the Parisian *femme amoureuse* who, in 1459, lost not only her over-rich chain and belt but also her book of hours for infringing the sumptuary laws.[103]

Ph.D. thesis (Ann Arbor, 1983), pp. 69–70, 112–19, who dates the added miniatures rather earlier, to about 1420.

[99] B. N., ms. lat. 1158. See C. Couderc, *Les Enluminures des manuscrits du moyen âge (du VIe au XV siècles) de la Bibliothèque Nationale* (Paris, 1927)), pp. 86–8, and pls LVII and LVIII; V. Leroquais, *Les Livres d'heures manuscrits de la Bibliothèque Nationale* (Paris, 1927), I, pp. 72–5.

[100] Paris, Musée du Louvre, currently exhibited at the Musée de Cluny. See C. Sterling et al., *Musée national du Louvre. Peintures: École française, XIVe, XVe et XVIe siècles* (Paris, 1965), no.15, pls LII-LVI. This was possibly the picture envisaged in the foundation deed which allowed for them to 'peindre à leur plaisir' on the wall adjoining the tomb (D. Godefroy, *Histoire de Charles VI par Jean Juvénal des Ursins* (Paris, 1653), p. 662).

[101] Cited, for instance, by J. Harthan, *Books of Hours and their Owners* (London, 1977), pp. 34–5.

[102] *Le Ménagier de Paris*, ed. G. M. Brereton and J. M. Ferrier (Oxford, 1981), p.11 (I, ii, 15).

[103] Sauval, *Histoire*, p. 360.

Many English men and women did want books of the use of Sarum and could commission what they wanted, provided that texts to serve as models were available. The combination of French manufacture and Sarum Use is a sure indication of an English patron. Talbot and his wife, Margaret Beauchamp, ordered very similar distinctively shaped books of hours.[104] Other patrons whose Hours survive with coats of arms and owner portraits are Thomas, Lord Hoo,[105] Sir William Porter,[106] and Sir William Oldhall.[107] In other cases an original coat of arms has been obscured by a later owner[108] or, despite lavish decoration and a miniature of the owner at prayer, there are no identifying armorial clues.[109] Some owners wished to commemorate their lords rather than themselves. In B. L., Harleian ms. 1251, the date of the Duke of Bedford's death and his badge have been added to the calendar, and the coats of arms in the miniature for the office of the dead altered to represent his funeral.[110] The wounding and subsequent death of the earl of Salisbury in 1428 were recorded in the calendar of an Hours now in the Victoria and Albert Museum, London, possibly made for a member of the Hussey family who inserted anniversaries dating from 1430 to 1442.[111] Unless marks of ownership are clearly part of a book's original design, it is impossible, as with the Hussey Hours, to be certain of the original owner. John and Eleanour Umfray owned their Hours of Sarum Use in 1453, but may not have bought the manuscript new.[112]

The number of books of hours without original marks of ownership suggests a thriving open market which could easily realise speculative investments in standard texts. Popular secular books are also likely to have been manufactured as speculative ventures. A French-made *Quatre Fils d'Aymon* has been in the royal collection since the first surviving inventory of the sixteenth century, and could have been acquired by an Englishman soon after being produced about 1440.[113] A French translation of Boccaccio's *De Casibus* belonged, at one point, to the second wife of Earl Rivers, and may also have been made with the English market in

---

[104] Cambridge, Fitzwilliam Museum, mss. 40–1950 and 41–1950. See F. Wormald and P. Giles, *A Descriptive Catalogue of the Additional Illuminated Manuscripts in the Fitzwilliam Museum acquired between 1895 and 1975* (Cambridge, 1982), II, pp. 444–53.

[105] L. L. Williams, 'A Rouen Book of Hours of the Sarum Use c. 1444 belonging to Thomas, Lord Hoo, Chancellor of Normandy and France', *Proceedings of the Royal Irish Academy*, lxxv, section C (1975), 189–212.

[106] New York, Pierpont Morgan Library, ms. M. 105; Plummer, *Last Flowering*, pp.15–16, no. 22, with illustrations.

[107] B. L., Harleian ms. 2900; J. Backhouse, *Books of Hours* (London, 1985), p. 73 and pl. 66. For the provenance, see C. E. Wright, *Fontes Harleiani* (London, 1972).

[108] B. L., Harleian ms. 1251, fo. 86, for example.

[109] Bodleian Library, ms. Auct. D inf. ii. See J. J. G. Alexander, 'A Lost Leaf from a Bodleian Book of Hours', *The Bodleian Library Record*, viii (1971), 248–51.

[110] B. L., Harleian ms. 1251, fos 12v, 145.

[111] 'New Acquisitions at the National Museums', *The Burlington Magazine* (1903), 389–90.

[112] Backhouse, *Books of Hours*, p. 52 and pl. 51.

[113] B. L., Royal ms. 16 G II; Warner and Gilson, *Catalogue*, pp.619–22.

mind.[114] A more ambitious compilation, like Talbot's Shrewsbury Book, had to be specially written and, as a gift, plentifully emblazoned with both his and Margaret of Anjou's arms. Sir John Fastolf had a copy of Le Livre des Quatre Vertus and Christine de Pisan's Épitre d'Othéa illuminated in French style, but the date of 1450 means that the miniatures must have been painted in England by a French artist who found sufficient promise of employment to follow the English in their retreat across the Channel.[115] The Fastolf Master, named from this book, seems to have prospered in England working on, for instance, the book of hours B. L., Harleian ms. 2915 and the psalter, Bodleian Library, Hatton ms. 45.[116] In general, however, English illuminators were oriented stylistically towards the Netherlands, a major source of artists and finished works.[117]

While the English were in France, they naturally turned to local scribes and artists. The books adapted for the Duke of Bedford, Henry VI, and the Neville family can all be assigned to Paris from the painting styles of the additions, whereas manuscripts made in their entirety for the English seem to have come predominantly from Normandy, and from Rouen in particular, as would be expected from the pattern of settlement and the course of the fighting. This can be established both by date and by what would have been available to an English patron at the time (as for the Shrewsbury Book of 1445) or by the presence of the painting styles of the Sarum Use books in manuscripts of Norman Uses or those made for Norman patrons. The Fastolf Master, for instance, decorated a book of hours for a member of the Guerin, or Garin, family (probably for Jean, one of the judges of Joan of Arc)[118] and another for the Use of Coutances.[119]

Rouen had a flourishing book trade, centred on the cathedral, and the English provided a new and important market for its products.[120] Some of the trade probably fell into English hands for, in March 1420, William Bradwardine, seigneur of St Vaast and La Poterie, hired Jacquet le Craon to exercise his 'metier d'ecrire et d'enluminer' for one year at a salary of 20 livres, Bradwardine undertaking to lodge, feed and clothe him, and provide his materials.[121] While a great noble may have needed a court painter to supply the trappings of life or to indulge his aes-

---

[114] B. L., Royal ms. 18 D VII; Warner and Gilson, Catalogue, p. 313; Exhibition Catalogue, Giovanni Boccaccio, (B. L., 1975), no. 35 and illustration.

[115] Alexander, 'Lost Leaf'.

[116] Backhouse, Books of Hours, pp. 30–1 and pl. 26.

[117] R. Marks and N. Morgan, The Golden Age of English Manuscript Painting 1200–1500 (London, 1981), pp. 29–31.

[118] New York, Pierpont Morgan Library, ms. M. 27; Plummer, Last Flowering, p.15, no. 21, and illustration.

[119] Paris, Bibliothèque de l'Arsenal, ms. 560; J. D. Farquhar, Creation and Imitation. The Work of a Fifteenth-Century Manuscript Illuminator (Nova University Studies in the Humanities I, Fort Lauderdale, 1976), pp. 85–8.

[120] R. Watson, The Playfair Hours (London, 1984), pp.19–34.

[121] C. de Beaurepaire, Nouveaux Mélanges historiques et archéologiques (Rouen, 1904), pp. 360–6, cited by Watson, Playfair Hours, pp. 23–4.

thetic sensibilities, Bradwardine was not in that class, and was presumably acting as an entrepreneur, perhaps taking advantage of the new English market from a stock of model Sarum Use texts.

The opportunities offered by the English were most apparent and most exploited in Normandy. Just as Parisian institutions jealously tried to defend their rights against Anglo-Norman rivals, so the painters of Paris may have looked enviously at their fellows in Rouen, where English patronage was concentrated. In the most part it was patronage for the middle range of the market; yet it helped to turn Rouen from a provincial capital into a major centre of book production, a position maintained into the age of printing. In Paris, the Duke of Bedford's two great manuscript commissions demanded an innovative creativity from illuminators otherwise largely dependent on more standardised productions. The exemption of the Duke of Bedford from the strictures of the 'Bourgeois' would surely have been accepted by the painters of Paris, even if they agreed with his assessment of the effects of English rule in general. Through the duke's patronage, the workshop named after him was able to preserve something of the standards of the first decades of the century, and to carry the traditions of the Limbourgs and the Boucicaut Master into the generation of Fouquet and the French resurgence.

'Morisques' and 'Momeryes': Aspects of Court Entertainment at the Court of Savoy in the Fifteenth Century

ALISON ROSIE

At first sight, late fifteenth-century Savoy seems an unlikely locale for a thriving court life. Beset by factionalism within its borders and faced with the ambitions of its rapacious neighbours (namely the empire-building Louis XI, the Burgundians, and the Milanese), Savoy, in the period of Yolande de Savoie's regency, has been viewed primarily as a state in dramatic decline. The spectacular achievements of the first duke, Amedée VIII, at the beginning of the century contrast sharply with the bungling and mismanagement of his son, Louis. The political dramas of the 1460s and 1470s have thus distracted historians' attention from the singular court which had developed in this Alpine region. And despite the personal traumas of her regency, including her kidnap and imprisonment by Charles the Bold in 1477, Yolande succeeded in imprinting her own particular style on a court already noted for its patronage of the arts. Her enthusiasm for music and dance meant that 'mommeries' and 'morisques', then in great vogue, had a particular role to play at her court.

A century after Yolande's death, when dance manuals were the order of the day, Thoinet Arbeau compiled his influential compendium of the court dances of the time, the *Orchesography*. 'Dancing,' he wrote, 'is practised to make manifest whether lovers are in good health and sound in all their limbs, after which it is permitted to them to kiss their mistresses whereby they may perceive if either has an unpleasant breath or exhales a disagreeable odour as that of bad meat.' But he pointed to more serious implications: 'in addition to diverse other merits attendant on dancing, it has become essential for the good governing of society'![1] A century earlier the dance might not have met Arbeau's lofty expectations, but it was certainly recognised as an integral and essential component of all manner of court festivity. That sector of society most alive to this fact, whose members furnish us with precious indications on it, were the chroniclers.

---

[1] Thoinet Arbeau, *Orchesography*, trans. C. W. Beaumont (London, 1925), p.18.

Jean Servion compiled his *Chroniques de Savoie* in the years 1464–5, during a period of imprisonment with his master, Philippe sans Terre. A passage in the chronicle described the famous tournament of 1348 at which the then Count of Savoy, Amedée VI, first donned the green apparel which earned him the sobriquet 'Le Comte Vert'. The celebrations at the end of the day's joust are depicted in glowing, if familiar, terms: 'chescung souppa et apres menestriers, trompettez, sacquebottes, et clerons prindrent a sonner, et mommeries furent atornés de toutes fassons.' On the second evening 'recommencerent dances, morisques et momeriez, durans iusques apres mynuyt'. ['After each had dined, minstrels and players of trumpets, sackbuts and bugles struck up, and all sorts of 'mommeries' were performed'] . . . ['. . . the dances, 'morisques' and 'momeries' began again, lasting until after midnight'].[2] In the effort to convey the scene to his readers, Servion, not an eye-witness, merely translates the popular court dances and entertainments of his own day back to the 1340s. Some ten years later, Perinet Dupin, secretary to the Duchess Yolande, already the author of a chivalric romance, 'Philippe de Madien', and of a life of Amedée VIII, began to assemble material for a chronicle. This work, if ever completed, has not survived, but we can get a fair idea of its scope from the questionnaire which Dupin drew up of the fifty-six points on which he required some clarification. Question 35, for instance, concerns the ceremonies surrounding the election of Amedée VIII as Pope Felix V in 1440:

> Item est necessire que Dupin saiche . . . le mistiere qui fut tenu à icellui coronner . . . le tryomphe que on mena à ceste feste cy faire, les dons qui furent donnéz et à qui on les donna; l'assiepte qui fut faicte en table des haulx princes et signeurs, la forme des entremes, mourisques et exbatemans . . . .

> [It is necessary for Dupin to find out . . . the ceremony of the enthronement . . . the proceedings of the 'triumph' of the 'fête', the gifts that were given, and to whom, the courses served up at the table of the great princes and lords, the forms of the entremets, morisques and other entertainments].[3]

These excerpts reflect a predilection for 'morisques' and 'mommeries' that was a European, and not merely a Savoyard, phenomenon. At his Provençal court, the twilight days of René d'Anjou were enlivened by performances of 'morisques' which have been singled out as a further sign of the man's penchant for the exotic. But at the court of Savoy of the 1460s and 1470s they far surpassed in popularity all other theatrical or ceremonial display. Between 1465 and 1478 at least thirty incidences of their performance, involving the *ad hoc* purchase of materials and accessories, and requiring the talents of a variety of craftsmen, may be traced in

---

[2] Jehan Servion, *Gestez et croniques de la maison de Savoie*, ed. F. E. Bollati (Turin, 1879), p. 82.
[3] D. Chaubet, 'Une Enquête historique en Savoie au XVe siècle', *Journal des Savants* (1984), 93–125.

the accounts of the treasurers-general and in other household accounts. By contrast, only half a dozen performances of mystery or morality plays are documented, and tournaments, so popular a theatrical event at the courts of Burgundy or Anjou, rarely made an appearance at all. During this period, indeed, there were no special purchase of clothing destined to be worn at a tournament. But before considering the reasons for their popularity, something of the nature of these entertainments needs to be established.

The terminology involved is not straightforward. The words 'morisque' and 'mommerie' were often used interchangeably. An example drawn from the treasurer's accounts for the year 1471 is a case in point. The amusements presented at Chambéry as part of the festivities for Quinquagesima Sunday manifested many of the hallmarks which, as we shall see, characterised a typical 'morisque'; yet the same passage uses both terms.

> Ay livré le 23 jour de fevrier 1471 à Jehan Romans taillandier 35 aulnes de drap de leyra pour fere de robes pour jouyer une momerie à la facon de Paris . . . et fut jouyer ladite moresque ledit 23 jour dudit moys de fevrier qui fut la feste de caresmentrand . . .

> [Delivered the 23rd day of February, 1471, to Jehan Romans the tailor, 35 aulnes of 'drap de leyra' (woollen cloth) to make costumes for a 'momerie' in the fashion of Paris . . . and the said 'moresque' was performed on the said 23rd day of the month of February, which was Shrove Tuesday . . .][4]

One answer is that the 'morisque' was often performed as part of a 'mommerie' as well as on its own; however the two are distinct, and perceptibly so.

The 'morisque' was the theatrical dance *par excellence* of the fifteenth century. Its origins were Spanish, 'morisco' being the slightly derogatory name given to those Moors who had converted to Christianity. In Spain, as in Italy, the 'morisque' retained an element of religious conflict watered down into a symbolic form. At the marriage of Alfonso de Ferrara to Lucrezia Borgia, Roman warriors are reported to have brandished weapons while they danced and Moors executed torch dances. Often the performers were disguised, had their faces blackened, or wore dark masks and woolly wigs to resemble Moors. René d'Anjou, who had his own real Moorish retainers, was spared this expense. The dance itself contrasted dramatically with the other popular court dance of the later Middle Ages, the 'basse danse'. Where the latter was measured and stately with gliding steps – 'basse' here meaning earthbound – the 'morisque' was lively, energetic to the point of being grotesque. A surviving German illustration of a 'morisque' aptly demonstrates some of the contortions involved.[5] Arbeau, who had seen it performed in his own day, described it as a dance executed to the rhythm of the stamping of the feet or

---

4 Archivio di Stato di Torino (A.S.T.), Inv. 16, no.116, fo.130v.
5 E. A. Bowles, *Musikleben im 15 Jahrhundert* (Leipzig, 1977), p. 63, illustr. 45.

heels and to the accompaniment of a pipe and tabour, though, he added, too rigorous stamping was not advisable, being conducive to gout!

The 'mommerie', on the other hand, was an early form of pantomime, and the
dance which the mummers performed was the 'morisque'. 'Mommerie' derives
from the word 'momer' meaning 'to mask'. An important element of the 'mommerie' was the disguising of the performers as a series of stock characters from the
world of myth, chivalric romance literature or the bible (for example angels or
saints). It was a very colourful frolic which, as a rule, centred around some particular theme or idea, though this need not necessarily have been the case. The English word 'mum' derives from the same root, and some historians of the dance have
indeed concluded that silence was the feature distinguishing it from its successor,
the Italian 'masquerade'. Though sharing some of the characteristics of the 'mommerie', the masquerade involved male and masked dancers mingling and convers-
ing with the spectators before leading them off to the dance. The 'mommerie'
however maintained a physical and therefore psychological distance between the
audience and the rather burlesque scenes represented before them.

Essentially then, the intention of both the 'morisque' and 'mommerie' was to
divert, entertain and amuse, rather than edify. Thus they were performed on high
days and holidays, at Christmas, on Saints days, during the Lenten period, at wed-
dings and at banquets, or *ad hoc* on non-spectacular occasions.

The sources available for a study of the 'mommeries' and 'morisques' at the
court of Yolande de Savoie leave much to be desired. The almost complete lack of
literary accounts, such as exist for Burgundy, necessitates a reliance on the evidence which may be gleaned from the household accounts. The sole contemporary eye-witness description surviving from the fifteenth century concerns an event
of some thirty to forty years earlier, as reported in the *Mémoires* of Lefèvre de
Saint-Rémy. A member of the entourage of Philip the Good of Burgundy, he was
among the guests at the wedding in 1434 of Louis, then Prince of Piedmont and
soon to take over from his father as Duke of Savoy. The lavish festivities, spread
over five days, were obviously intented to impress the assembled guests (including
René d'Anjou, the Prince of Orange and the Count of Freiburg) with the magni-
ficence of the court of Savoy. On each successive evening the audience was entertained to the spectacle of a different fantastic world, wildmen ('sauvages') bore a
huge rose-filled garden of wax into the hall, in the midst of which a live, and un-
comfortable, billy goat was tied; a man disguised as an eagle burst out of a pastry
case and a host of white doves flew out from under his wings; forty masked
dancers, clad dramatically in black and gold, whirled up and down the length of
the hall. Saint-Rémy, at least, was favourably impressed:

> . . . et fut la feste, sans tournoy et jouste, aussi belle qu'on povoit veoir; et
> pour la beauté d'icelle, je le mis par escript.
>
> [. . . and the celebration, with neither a tournament nor a joust, was as

fine as you could ever see; and for the beauty of it, I have set it down in writing.][6]

In comparison with the relative clarity of Saint-Rémy's description, the household registers offer a somewhat incoherent picture of events. In order, then, to make some sense of the information, it will be helpful to concentrate initially on several of the aspects involved, namely the performers, the organisers and, first of all, the scale of performances.

At the court of Savoy, the complexity of a 'mommerie' or 'morisque' was graded according to the importance of the occasion for which it was performed. At the most basic it was, for example, a 'morisque' danced by Jaquet, 'varlet de sale', before Yolande and a restricted number of her courtiers in November 1469, or the 'mommerie' staged by Yolande's young daughters, Marie and Louise, at Moncalieri for St Catherine's day in 1473. On both occasions the expenses involved were minimal – two ducats for the former and six florins for the latter for the purchase of material.[7] More complex and costly events included the 'mommeries' performed at the marriages of members of a limited court circle. When Jeanne de Mouxy, a favourite lady-in-waiting, married Ysobbe d'Avanchier at the end of December 1473, over seventy florins were spent on the costumes, including twelve florins to the embroiderers and artists who embellished them. The cloth used was itself not the reason for the expense – 'fusteyne', a cotton/wool mix, was not a luxury material. On this occasion the cost was increased by the twenty-eight pounds of 'or quiclant' and 'argent batu', the gold and silver thread used to garnish the costumes.[8]

Fellow courtiers, numbering eighteen in all, performed two 'morisques' at Alleran Provana's marriage in 1475, some decked out in silver and gold-spangled material to look like leopards. The cost amounted to well over 100 florins in all, in addition to the price of 150 small pennons and twelve large banners displaying the ducal arms, used to decorate the dishes at the banquet. The care and expense involved here can no doubt be ascribed to the presence at the feast of ambassadors from Burgundy and Milan and 'beaucop de dames de Thurin que madite dame fait venir pour veoir ladite feste' ['a large number of ladies from Turin whom my lady had brought here to witness the said feast'][9]

Full-blown theatrical displays were reserved for the visits of ambassadors and other dignitaries. 'Kings and Princes', wrote Arbeau, 'give dances and masquerades

6 Lefèvre de Saint-Rémy, *Mémoires*, in *Chroniques d'Enguerrand de Monstrelet*, ed. J. A. Buchon (Paris, 1826), VIII, p. 461; *Chronique de Jean le Fèvre, seigneur de Saint-Rémy*, ed. F. Morand (2 vols, SHF, Paris, 1876–81), II, p. 297.
7 A.S.T., Inv. 39, no.11, fos 226, 344v: '. . pour payer toyle et aultres menues bagues pour fere une maumerie devant madite dame. . '.
8 A.S.T., Inv. 16, no.122, fos 185 et seq., account of Lancelot de Lans for purchases for a momerie totalling 73 florins and 6 gros. See also Inv. 16, no.123, fos 232 et seq.
9 A.S.T., Inv. 16, no.122, fos 182v et seq, 192, 193.

for amusement and in order to afford a joyful welcome to foreign nobles.' Savoy's geographical position, straddling the Alps and guarding the passes into Italy, gave her a considerable strategic importance. A country of meagre economic resources, she was nevertheless often to play a pivotal role in the intrigues of the fifteenth century. The stream of diplomatic visitors and courtesy callers was therefore fairly continuous, and the necessity of providing a dignified and fitting reception was an onerous yet time-honoured obligation. In 1478 the then duke, Philibert, felt obliged to send six silver gilt cups valued at 249 florins to a Milanese ambassador purely because 'ci devant il avoit fait de dons a mondit Sr que montoient a tant ou plus que ce que ly a esté donné'. ['before this he had made presents to my lord whose value was equal or greater than that which was given to him'].[10] The lesson was clear; a prince must not be outdone in generosity by a mere emissary.

Some thirty years earlier, Amedée VIII had written to his son, Louis, reprimanding him for his unnecessary expenses and advising him to make sacrifices. Louis retorted that such cutbacks were impossible. The 'great concourse of nobles and others toing and froing which war and embassies lead to Turin', he wrote, were forcing him to be more magnificent in order to keep up appearances.[11] Yolande's position was equally grave. The house of Savoy was linked politically and through marriage to a number of families from countries throughout Europe – France, Burgundy and Milan being the foremost; embassies were the order of the day, keeping up the constant flow of information between one court and another. In a curious document called the 'Registre des choses faictes par tres haulte et tres excellente dame et princesse madame Yolant de France, duchess de Savoie . . . ', Jacques Lambert, councillor and 'maistre des requetes' to duke Philibert, provided a detailed vindication of the expenses Yolande had been called upon to make during the period of her regency. Lambert stated that the 25,000 florins spent on provisioning the household whilst in residence in the Vaudois in no sense constituted an extravagance, 'car ainsy le failloit faire pour le honeur de madite dame de mondit seigneur et de la maison de Savoye a cause de la presence de mondit seigneur de Bourgoigne' ['for this had to be done for the honour of my lady, my lord and the house of Savoy on account of the presence of my lord of Burgundy.'][12] This demonstrates very neatly how the problems of strained budgets could be set aside on occasions when family honour and reputation were at stake.

The arrival at Chambéry of the Count of Geneva and his wife in 1476, coin-

---

[10] A.S.T., Inv. 16, no.128, fo. 67v.

[11] E. H. Gaullieur, 'Correspondance du Pape Felix V et de son fils, Louis duc de Savoie, au sujet de la ligue de Milan', *Archiv für Schweizerische Geschichte*, xviii (1851), 345. In 1434 Amedée VIII took the unusual step of resigning his title in favour of his son, Louis. He went into a religious retreat founded by him at Ripaille. During this period Amedée was elected pope by the Council of Basle in 1439. He nevertheless continued to try to advise his son in a stream of letters.

[12] Léon de Menabrea, *Chroniques de Yolande de France, duchesse de Savoie* (Chambéry, 1859), p. 62.

ciding as it did with the visit of ambassadors from France, Milan, and Montferrat, was the grounds for a lavish banquet that December. Approximately 215 florins were spent 'tant en morisques, momeries, entremes, viandes couvertes et aultres choses'. The 'mommerie(s)' involved a large cast: Goliath, a 'cappitaine' and four maidens (sharing thirty-seven ostrich feathers and thirty-five pounds of 'or cli-cant' between them), four Moors, and nine 'petis homes darmes'. In addition, 1,800 'follies dargent' were bought for a variety of purposes, including the masks of the 'morisque' dancers ('visaiges des morisqueulx').[13] Between 6 and 13 February 1475, the court at Turin played host to Frederick, Prince of Tarento, son of King Ferrante of Naples, and the future husband of Yolande's daughter, Anne. As was customary, only the first three days of the visit were defrayed by the Duke of Savoy. Seventy five of the prince's 500 strong retinue were lodged at the bishop's palace, the others in hostelries throughout the city. Their upkeep amounted to 1,400 florins. The entertainments at the banquet held in his honour on 7 February cost well over 400 florins alone and, as will be described more fully below, the ac-counts indicate that they were particularly splendid.[14] All around the banqueting hall hung banners displaying the arms of Savoy, of King Ferrante, Milan, and Burgundy, a forceful reminder of Savoy's powerful new allies, for only the month previously she had signed an important treaty allying herself with her two neigh-bours. Frederick was the son of an important prince, a potential suitor and ally; the welcome he received was therefore tailored not only to reflect and respect his status, but also to impress and remind him of the dignity of the house of Savoy.

It has been said that the 'morisques' were not, strictly speaking, 'court dances', that they did not belong to those 'qu'un courtisan put danser sans manquer aux bienseances' ['which a courtier can dance without some loss of propriety'].[15] Cer-tainly, it was beneath the dignity of a Philip the Good or a Charles the Bold to partake in such festivities, except as a spectator. Thus mainly professional dancers performed the 'morisques' and 'mommeries' at the court of Burgundy. Savoy was not affected by such a rigorous etiquette, despite the efforts of Amedée VIII who, married to Mary of Burgundy, had sought to introduce many of the aspects of the court style he had witnessed and admired on his visits to Burgundy. Among these importations was Amedée's interest in ceremonial and more specifically, the office of Chamberlain. The full development of his ideas was enshrined in the *Statuta Sabaudia*, and particularly the sumptuary laws contained therein. But these were promulgated in 1430, only four years before Amedée made over the rule of the duchy to Louis. Despite his well-documented love of festivities, Louis was not made in his father's mould, and failed dismally to learn the lesson of how to use ceremonial effectively to underline his authority. At any rate, by the time of Yolande's regency, and doubtless as the result of her influence, the atmosphere of

13 A.S.T., Inv. 16, no.124, fos 90 et seq.
14 A.S.T., Inv. 16, no.122, fos 172 et seq.
15 P. Reyner, *Les Masques anglais* (Paris, 1909), p. 455.

the court was far more relaxed. Thus the duchess herself was often to be found among the performers, though admittedly this was restricted to certain selective occasions. It was a mark of her special favour and affection that she should have joined eleven of her ladies-in-waiting and twelve of the gentlemen of her household to dance a 'morisque' at the wedding of Catherine de Genève in 1471.[16] Catherine appeared regularly on the list of the duchess' companions from 1465 onwards, and was the frequent beneficiary of gifts. Yolande, however, did not partake in any of the entertainments performed for visiting dignitaries; perhaps this would have been considered too great a lapse of decorum.

A keen dancer, Yolande was also an avid spectator. Small-scale 'mommeries' requiring next to no expense or preparation were often performed before her in the privacy of her own quarters, and her particular delight must have been to watch her own children perform for her. At the wedding feast of Catherine de Genève, the young duke Philibert, then all of six years old, danced a 'morisque' with his brother Charles, aged three, and their two sisters.[17] The four children often combined with that other youthful sector of the court community, the pages. For instance, Philibert, Charles, and their brother, Jacques-Louis, were joined by three of the ducal pages in a 'mommerie' presented for the visit of the Milanese ambassadors in 1478.[18] This was, however, fairly uncommon as children were rarely to be found among the performers when important guests were present, when, perhaps, the quality of the presentation was held to be of particular importance.

Other children who participated were the novices of the Collège des Innocents. Founded in 1468 by Yolande, the Collège was comprised of six to eight boys ranging from the age of six to fifteen, who generally departed when their voices broke. Their appearances among the performers were relatively infrequent: in a 'morisque' presented for Yolande at Chambéry in 1470, and in another at Moncalieri in 1475.[19] On the second occasion they were joined by Anthoine Guinat, the 'abbé des chantres', and Golbet, both members of the famed ducal chapel. It was fairly unusual for the members of the chapel to partake in these more secular entertainments, as they were considered to be considerably above the household 'menestraux' in the court hierarchy, and were remunerated accordingly. Their artistry was normally restricted to the performances of masses on ceremonial occasions, important visits, or high points of the religious calendar. The final and most significant group seen to be performing the 'mommeries' and 'morisques' were drawn from a fairly restricted number of the household officers and ladies in wait-

---

16 A.S.T., Inv. 16, no.123, fos 222 et seq.
17 Ibid.
18 A.S.T., Inv. 16, no.126, fo.130v.
19 A.S.T., Inv. 39, no.11, fo. 230v; Inv. 16, no.122, fos 183v et seq: 'A mess[i]re Anthoyne Gaynat, abbé des chantres, sept fo. pour acheter deux pieces de fustaine blanc qui costent 4 fo, de quoy il as (sic) fait des abbiz des novices à ly et à daultre pour jouer une morisque . . . comme ausy pour acheter dor cliquant pour garnir lesdites abbis'.

ing. These did not hold the highest or most responsible positions at court, nor, generally, did they belong to the most influential Savoyard or Piedmontese clans; if they did, they were normally junior relatives. Moreover, they were predominantly young. There may have been a practical reason for this last characteristic: the antics of the 'mommeries' and the acrobatics of the 'morisque' must have demanded a certain energy, if not agility, from their performers. The disparate nature of the Savoyard territories, too, and the demands of an active participation in external affairs, must have combined to remove many of the most influential members of the court for considerable spells. Some, like the de Montmayeur, were even busy fomenting trouble against Yolande with her recalcitrant brothers-in-law.

Thus, it is most noticeable that the male performers belonged to the 'middle management' and were heavily involved in the day-to-day running of the household. Let us take, for example, a 'morisque' presented at Rivoli in 1478 for the ambassador of Milan. Thirteen gentlemen were involved. Glaude de Marcossey, *Maître d'Hotel*, and Claude de Seyssel, Mareschal de Savoie, might be said to represent the upper echelons, the others were predominantly 'escuiers' like François d'Allinge, seigneur de Servete, whose wife was one of the duchess's closest attendants, or Hugonin (Gonyn) de Montfalcon, 'escuier d'escuierie', Anthoine de la Forest, 'escuier tranchant', and Philippe de Visques, 'escuier d'honneur'.[20] In 1471, de Montfalcon (at this date merely described as 'escuier du duc') and de la Forest performed a 'mommerie' with Loys de Mataffellon, 'escuier du duc', Gaultier de Chignin and Joffroy de Rivarol, both 'escuiers d'escuierie'.[21] The latter was responsible for snatching the young duke to safety when Yolande was taken captive by the duke of Burgundy. This pool of retainers remained very loyal to Yolande throughout this period, and there is little fundermental change among them for at least the last ten years of her regency. This held true for her female attendants, too; there are few fluctuations, and the same names occurred again and again – for example Catherine de Genève, Catherine de Lornay, Jaqueme de Challes and Anthoynette de Villars. There was a strong element of stability within the core of Yolande's household, and to that extent it was a fairly exclusive group.

Yolande was not so fortunate as to have an Olivier de la Marche at court to create and direct her extravaganzas, yet one man emerged consistently from the accounts from 1469 onwards in connection with their organisation. Lancelot de Lans first appeared in 1467 as one of the pages to Amedée IX. By 1470, he was described as 'escuyer et maistre de cuisine'. A Jacques de Lans, 'maistre queu', who may well have been his father, served in the household of the duke, Louis, in the 1450s. Lancelot's aptitude for things theatrical must have manifested itself early. In 1470 he took charge of the preparations for the staging of the 'Moralité de Ste Suzanne', performed before the duchess and the court at Chambéry by the bur-

20 A.S.T., Inv. 16, no.126, fo.130v.
21 A.S.T., Inv. 16, no.116, fo.130v.

gesses of Montmelian. In 1472 he was granted four florins for his direction of 'mommeries' the previous Christmas 'quant levesque de Valence estoit ici' ['when the bishop of Valence was here'].[22] There is no direct evidence that he choreographed the 'morisques' himself, but the likelihood is that he did. In similar fashion to the dance instructors who were currently establishing themselves as essential members of the Italian courts, Lancelot might be seen leading his pupils into the dance. It was a rare 'morisque' from which his name was absent, and on all occasions on which these festivities appear in the accounts, Lancelot was in charge of their payment. Thus Lancelot was a key figure in the performances – as in 1475, when he danced a 'morisque' with Marquet le Fol – and was the co-ordinator of the behind-the-scenes activities, his account for the 'mommeries' for the visit of the Marquise de Montferrat including payment to 'vi compaignons . . . qui mont aydé à toutes choses fere' ['six assistants who have helped me do everything']. He was frequently well rewarded for his endeavours – 100 florins in August 1474, for example, and a further 100 the next February after the hectic Christmas period and the flurry of preparations for the visit of the prince of Tarento.[23] Strangely, there is no sign in all this of another court player, Perinet de Normes. Formerly an archer to duke Louis, de Normes first appeared at Yolande's court as 'larchier qui fait les farses', the archer turned comedian. Thereafter, until his death in 1477, he appeared as 'joyeur des farses' (1469 and 1473) as 'farceur' (1472) and 'mestre de farses' (1469 and 1474). He performed 'farses' at Chambéry in March 1471 and a 'moralité' at Geneva in 1469; yet his talents never seem to have been exploited for the 'mommeries' and 'morisques'.[24]

However, the successful staging of these event was not merely the result of one man's activities, but of the fruitful co-operation between de Lans and other junior members of the household, the master-cook, the artist and the musician. As the 'mommeries; and 'morisques' performed at banquets formed part and parcel of the 'entremes', entertainments enacted between courses, the collusion of the organiser and the master-cook was inevitable. In his task, then, de Lans was aided and abetted by Mermet Brigant, 'mestre de cusine' and later one of the three ducal 'maistres cueux' until his death in 1476.[25] This was some position to live up to, as in the time of Amedée VII the post had been filled by one 'maitre Chiquart', whose culinary skills were preserved in a treatise written on the orders of the duke. His *Du fait de Cuisine*, though drawing much of its inspiration (and recipes) from

22   A.S.T., Inv. 16, no.113, fo.116 (8 Apr. 1467); Inv. 16, no.116, fo. 318 (1470); Inv. 16, no. 98, fo. 349v (Jaquet de Lans appears on a list of recipients of 'etrennes' for Jan. 1451); Inv. 39, no.11, fo. 228.
23   A.S.T., Inv. 16, no.122. fos 181 et seq., 186.
24   A.S.T., Inv. 16, no.11, fo. 291v; Inv. 39, no.11, fos 59v, 228, 307v, 345v; Inv. 16, no.122, fo.144; Inv. 39, no.11, fos 250, 66.
25   A.S.T., Inv. 16, no.123. fo. 281v; Inv. 16, no.114, fo.102v; Inv. 16, no.129, fo. 295v, where his son, Deifilio, is referred to as a 'lardonier' in the ducal service. A Pierre Brigand is also noted in the same year as 'ducalis coquus'.

Taillevant, chief cook to Charles V of France, was a tacit recognition that the banquet was 'the most satisfactory means by which to impress visiting neighbours and potentates, and to gratify a taste for conspicuous opulence'. In the treatise, Chiquart described in some detail the organisation of an 'entremes' for a sumptuous banquet. It is difficult not to believe that de Lans and Brigant drew some of their ideas from this manual, though it must be admitted that the themes contained therein were commonplaces of medieval chivalric literature. Chiquart described a 'fountain of love' 'from which rosewater and mulled wine would gush through a spout'.[26] In 1471, at a banquet held at Chambéry for the 'dames de ceste ville', a fountain in the castle courtyard 'gestoit vin blanc et rouge', and in 1475 a gilded fountain ran with wine for the visit of the prince of Tarento.[27] Chiquart also described an elaborate crenellated 'castle of love' with four towers protected by archers, with a group of musicians nestling inside who 'should also have good voices and be singing melodiously in such a way that they really seem to be sea sirens for the clarity of their singing'.[28] This same motif cropped up in 1471 in a 'morisque' 'faicte a chastel d'amours et a xvi personnes . . . a festier le frere du duc de Millan' ['performed at a castle of love by sixteen persons, to welcome the duke of Milan's brother], while the banquet held for Frederick of Tarento also centred around a 'chasteau damours'.[29] Chiquart's castle was of meat paste, his archers of cloth; similarily Brigant was responsible for manufacturing the gardens of red and white wax roses used to transport the dishes to the guests' tables in 1475. Brigant himself actually made an honourable appearance in a 'morisque', with five of the ladies-in-waiting, dressed in silk 'en guise de dame'.

The dukes of Savoy had an eclectic taste in the arts. The courts of Amedée VIII, Louis and his wife, Anne of Cyprus, were noted for the encouragement and patronage given to artists, and the fifteenth century saw the production there of a number of high quality illuminated manuscripts. Jehan Bapteur, Peronet Lamy, Colombe and Jacopo Jaquerio all benefited from the fusion of influences – Burgundian, Germanic, Flemish, Provençal, and Tuscan – meeting in this area. Bapteur, 'pictor ducis' in the 1430s and 1440s, and responsible for the masterpiece, The Apocalypse, and the Heures de Savoie, was the artistic force behind 'mommeries' performed before Charles, duke of Bourbon, in 1442.[30] His successor in the 1460s and 1470s was maître Nicolas Robert, a Piedmontese, who turned his hand mainly to the demands of the court festivities; his other work, for example that in the chapel of the château d'Ivrée, was not nearly as masterful as that of Bapteur. Robert was working for the court between 1465 and 1477. His repertoire ranged from covering plates for banquets with 'feuilles d'etain' to more complicated art-

---

[26] Chiquart's 'On Cookery': a Fifteenth-Century Savoyard Culinary Treatise, ed. T. Scully (American University Studies Series, vol. 22, New York, 1986), pp.xi, 33.
[27] A.S.T., Inv. 39, no.11, fo. 251; Inv. 16, no.123, fos 256–7.
[28] 'On Cookery', p. 36.
[29] A.S.T., Inv. 16, no.119, fos 153v et seq.
[30] A.S.T., Inv. 16, no. 88, fos 214–16.

work. In 1475, for example, he painted the banners of the ducal arms at the 'banquet triumphans' given for the Marquis de Monferrat and modelled the figures of St Morice, two sirens and thirty-two men-at-arms for the same event; in the same year he moulded large giants' and dwarfs' heads for a 'morisque'; and later, for a banquet at Carignan, he painted the mummers' costumes with *fleurs-de-lis* and the initials A and Y interlaced, stressing the connection of the house of Savoy to the French royal dynasty.[31] If Robert's position within the court hierarchy was not elevated, his role in the presentation of its entertainments should not be underestimated, as the visual aspect of the 'mommeries' was vitally important.

The final group involved in the presentation of 'morisques' and 'mommeries' were the court musicians, a group on which the accounts are disappointingly reticent. There is no record of payment made to a musician which can be positively tied to his performing at a particular 'morisque' or mommerie'. The typical accompaniment for the 'morisque' was a pipe/fife and tabour, but a more complex 'orchestra' was required for performances in a banqueting hall where a larger volume of sound was necessary – a blend of the so-called 'haultz instruments', sackbuts and trumpets. A special stage or raised platform ('haut siege') was constructed for the musicians at the festivities which accompanied the visit of the Count and Countess of Geneva on 15 December 1476. A list of the recipients of the annual 'étrennes' (new year gifts) for the following month named six musicians – 'clerin, Alexandre le trompete, Guilleaume l'aveugle, au tabourin et maistre du Rebec, au maistre de larpe'. It was normal practice on such an occasion for the minstrels accompanying the visitor to join forces with the court musicians, though in this instance they do not appear in the accounts. However, an acount for September 1474 records payment made to six 'trompetes' and 'menestriers' in the retinue of the bishop of Turin, and three 'trompetes de Verceil' who were boarded at Turin at the duke's expense, 'les queulx ont este ycy à la court à jouer de leurs instruments des la feste de noye jusqu à carementrant des bordes' ['. . . who were here at court playing their instruments from the feast of Christmas to the first Sunday in Lent'], a period coinciding with the visit of the Marquise de Montferrat. Half a dozen seems to have been about the normal complement of household musicians at Savoy, though as a group they were less stable than the chapel, some of whose members remained for many years. In 1474 only five were mentioned among those receiving 'gaiges' – a 'maitre des orgues', a 'trompete' and three 'menestriers'. Three years later there were three 'trompetes' and four 'menestriers'.[32] The musical reputation of Savoy had always rested on her chapel choir, whose excellence had attracted the talents of Guillaume Dufay in an earlier period, and it seems evident that Yolande's interests lay more with this choir than with the ministrels whose

[31] A.S.T., Inv. 16, no.116. fo.167; Inv. 16, no.122, fos 189v, 183 et seq.
[32] A.S.T., Inv. 16, no.124, fos 90v et seq (Dec. 1476); Inv. 16, no.126, fo. 91v (Jan. 1477); Inv. 16, no.122, fo. 200v (Sept. 1474); Inv. 16, no.126, fo.125 (1477)

relatively low status in the court hierarchy conveyed the appreciation of their skills.

Given the popularity of Sir John Mandeville's travels in the Middle ages, recounting his visits to strange lands, it is not surprising that the most outstanding feature common to both 'morisques' and 'mommeries' was the element of the exotic or bizarre. This was first conveyed to the onlookers through the costumes. These were either cut in a distinctive style, and hence are described as tailored 'à la facon de momerie' or 'a la mode de la morisque', or were in the fashion of a foreign land, for example Germany, in the 'abilliement dalamant' worn for a 'mommerie' in 1475, or the 'chapperons d'allemagne' of a year earlier. In February 1471, Jehan Romans, the tailor, fashioned fourteen 'chapironx au mode de Paris' for fourteen ladies to 'jouyer une momerie à la facon de Paris'.[33] The court had long since abandoned the practice of sending to Paris for dress patterns, as had been the case for most of the fourteenth and early years of the fifteenth century, so these costumes must have struck the audiences as distinctive and significantly different from the norm, and thus marked out the revellers immediately. One typical feature of the costumes lay in the unusually long sleeves, as in, for example, the fifteen 'aulnes datours pour fere les manges treynant jusqz a terre' bought for 'mommeries' in 1474, or again the 'troys auquetons descoupés avesque grans manches pendans' ['15 aulnes of fine cloth to make the sleeves which hang right down to the ground' . . . ' the three tunics cut with long sleeves hanging down'][34]

All manner of accessories were added to the costumes to heighten their comic or outlandish appearance. Most commonly applied, and the one with the most spectacular effect, was 'or clicant', a type of fine copper wire used to embroider material like gold thread. In the *Glossaire*, Laborde notes that the 'or cliquant' 'n'était porté que par les laquais, les batteleurs et les masqués'.[35] Some costumes may be positively identified as destined for a 'morisque' purely on the basis of the presence of this 'or cliquant', as it never seems to have been used on non-spectacular occasions. Take, for instance, a 'morisque' performed before the assembled ambassadors of Anjou, Burgundy and Milan in December 1474. The costumes themselves were unremarkable in design and not very costly. The material was of poorish quality – the eighteen aulnes only cost 7 florins and 6 gros, whereas that same month eleven aulnes of 'drap pers de Beaune', bought to make garments for the ducal pages, cost as much as 49 florins and 8 gros. But the low value of the material is easily explained – it served only as a back cloth for the decoration, namely one pound of 'or cliquant' and a half pound of 'filz dorain'.[36] In 1476, no less than thirty-five pounds of 'or cliquant' adorned the wax figures of 'le capitaine et

---

[33] A.S.T., Inv. 16, no.116, fo.130.
[34] A.S.T., Inv. 16, no.122. fos 180v, 181v.
[35] L. de Laborde, *Glossaire français du Moyen Age à l'usage de l'archéologie et des amateurs d'art* (Paris, 1872).
[36] A.S.T., Inv. 16, no.122, fos 182 et seq, 122.

les quatre pucelles', while 25,000 'pailletes', or spangles, garnished the costumes of ten 'morisque' dancers at this same banquet for the count and countess of Geneva.[37] Ostrich feathers and tiny bells were also *de rigueur*. These same 'morisque' dancers sported an ostrich feather each, and 230 bells worn as anklets. Fourteen sets of these 'jambieres de sonnettes' were purchased for a 'morisque' performed at Aleran Provana's wedding in January 1475.[38] Vibrant colours of material were also used. Clearly nothing was to be omitted in the effort to obtain maximum impact, noise and visual excitement. To modern tastes the 'spectacle dance' may have seemed merely garish, but to medieval eyes it was a feast of colour and entertainment.

The mummers were often masked or disguised, sometimes as Moors or Turks; hence the 'morisque' was called 'la sarrazine'. At a banquet at Chambéry in 1476, four Moors featured in a 'mommerie' narrating the story of Goliath, all clothed in black in a striking constrast to the crimson taffeta of the 'capitaine du triumphe'. They wore ostrich feathers and masks of silver: 'Item pour xviii^c follies dargent fin pour argenter les chouses dessus dites, enclus estandars et bandieres et les visaiges des morisqueulx' ['Item, for 1,800 leaves of fine silver to plate the above items including the standards and the masks of the morisque dancers']. The 'entremes' and 'morisques' at Moncalieri in 1475 included a 'momerie des géans et des nains' [giants and dwarfs] each of the four performers wearing a large mask ('grans testes').[39]

'Sauvages', or wildmen, were a borrowing from folklore. They had particular associations with the Carnival period, their appearance heralding the arrival of Spring. They were quickly appropriated and absorbed into chivalric art, literature and heraldry throughout Europe. A Burgundian tapestry in the church of Notre-Dame de Nantilly depicts an early wildman masquerade, but as early as 1347 the wardrobe accounts for festivities at the English court record 'tetes de wodewose', that is, wildmen's masks. The most notorious, and an early French example, of the wildman masquerade is the 'Bal des Ardents' of 1393, when Charles VI narrowly escaped being burnt alive when the animal skins he and his companions were wearing were set alight. This event was graphically illustrated, and thus widely circulated, in many chronicles. The wildman makes an early appearance at the court of Savoy in 1434 as part of the 'entremes' at the wedding of Louis de Savoie. Later, in the above-mentioned 'mommerie des géans', Lancelot de Lans danced a 'morisque' with Marquet le Fol dressed as a savage in an 'abilliment de sovage chargé dor clicant'. A sack of cow's tails was used to 'couvrir labit dung souvage', as well as for making the hair of three ogres and sirens in 1475.[40]

'Mommeries' took place in a fantastic world peopled by all manner of real and

---

[37] A.S.T., Inv. 16, no.124, fos 90v et seq.
[38] A.S.T., Inv. 16, no.122, fo.183v.
[39] A.S.T., Inv. 16, no.124, fo. 91; no.122, fo.183
[40] *Ibid.*, and no.122, fos 172 et seq.

imaginary deviant groups: sirens, dwarfs, giants, wildmen, dragons, unicorns, god-desses and fools. Much has been written on the role of the fool in medieval society – the fool as 'locale of disorder' and the 'enemy of all organised systems'.[41] The world turned upside down inhabited by the fool is aptly symbolised in the fool's costume in which the 'coqueluchon' forms the principal component. Deriving from and indeed parodying the episcopal mitre, the 'coqueluchon' was a hood from which two asses ears protruded. Returning to Saint-Rémy's account of the 1434 wedding festivities, we find on the final evening eighteen knights and squires, apparelled in yellow (the colour symbolic of folly, commonly worn by fools as well as prostitutes, Jews and traitors), dancing a morisque, bells a-jangling, 'et avoient les chapperons grans oreilles comme folz' ['their hoods having great ears, like fools have'].[42] An echo of this is found at the banquet of the 'Toyson d'Or', the Golden Fleece, held at Geneva on St. Valentine's Day 1469. A gilded sheep formed the edible centrepiece, wearing the 'collier de Bourgogne': (the exact significance of this is unclear – there may have been present at the feast a member of the order who had come to Geneva to take a part in the jousts held there that same month). Five 'morisque' dancers each sported a 'coculuche': the accounts record payment for the 'ocquetons de cinq compagnions et les cacquelles de leur teste . . .'.[43] The 'compagnions' here may have been professional dancers as, unusually, they remain unidentified in this instance. We have already seen the court fool, Marquet, perform on several occasions; but the fool need not necessar-ily be acted by one! In 1474 it was Johanin de Rivolte who 'fait le fol' at the ban-quet for the Marquise de Montferrat. However, his costume was the same parti-coloured red and white worn by the other three performers,[44] which would seem to suggest that his 'folly' was made explicit through his movements rather than through his costume. The presence of fools, wildmen, giants and sirens did make for a very comic effect, as a certain amount of buffoonery seems to have in-formed these entertainments. At the same time, the certainties of the spectators' world was never seriously threatened, and they were reassured of their own sophis-tication.

Trying to tease a more rounded picture of the events proves rather more diffi-cult. Some of the themes are more easily indentifiable than others. Take, for example, the banquet for the Marquise de Montferrat in 1474, in which St. Morice rescued two sirens from their towers. St. Morice was particularly venerated in Savoy, and indeed the banquet was held on his feast day, 15 September. The ring of St. Morice was passed down through generations of counts and dukes of Savoy as a revered heirloom and, in 1434, Amedée VIII dedicated his newly founded religious order to this saint. Other 'mommeries' were more obviously in-

---

[41] For example, M. Lever, Le Sceptre et la Marotte (Paris, 1983).
[42] Lefèvre, Mémoires, ed. Buchon, p. 460; Chronique, ed. Morand, II, p. 296–7.
[43] A.S.T., Inv. 16, no.114, fos 128 et seq.
[44] A.S.T., Inv. 16, no.122, fo.189.

spired by the world of chivalric romance literature. The main characters in the 'morisque' of the 'Chasteau d'amours' were the 'dieu damours et les quatre déesses', the god of Love and the four goddesses; Amedée VIII is known to have possessed a tapestry of the same subject. It was considered a most apposite theme for a wedding: Saint-Rémy informs us of the God of Love who shot pink and white roses from his bow into the laps of the ladies at the marriage of Louis de Savoie.

The most complex in terms of organisation and presentation were, without doubt, the 'mommeries' performed before the Prince of Tarento in 1475.[45] A fairly coherent picture of events may be extrapolated from the information provided in the accounts. Preparations began on 25 January with the leasing of a house close to the castle in Turin to facilitate the production and storage of the necessary artifacts. Lancelot de Lans was, as usual, in charge of proceedings, assisted by a number of kitchen staff including the three senior 'cousiniers', Mermet Brigant, Benoit Mangeon and Le Bossu, the 'enfans de cousine', le Pelloux and Tabellet, the carpenters, Pierre Ros and Jehanin Cosa, and the tailor, 'maitre Glaude'. Nicolas Robert took control of the artwork, though some minor tasks were undertaken by Maîtres Michiel and Bernard, both from nearby Pinerolo.

Dominating the action was a white and yellow 'chasteau damours' with four towers, in each of which sat a maiden (variously described as 'pucelles' or 'dames' in the accounts). These maidens were to be carried into the 'grant salle' throwing pieces of gold at the assembled guests. Each tower was guarded by a wild animal, a lion, a bear, a boar, or a unicorn, the gate of the 'chasteau' by a wildman (a stuffed dummy). Two other 'sauvages' then attacked a mechanical dragon, manipulated by four men, as it emerged from the nearby wood (actually seven trees made from laurel branches brought especially from Rivoli for the purpose). In the meanwhile three regal ladies wearing 'couronnes demperieure et deux de royne' were seated in the 'jardin damours' which they shared with a single tree and a green serpent. The 'chasteau' was held in position by the means of chains held by eight 'chantres' or choristers – presumably from the ducal chapel whose members had been seen participating on previous occasions. The role of the three ogres in the drama is unclear. They sat astride three of the 'besties sauvages' and may have been taken part in a 'morisque' with de Lans, Marquet le Fol and Monsieur de Chivron, as they each carried torches, a common enough element in the 'morisque'. Five women, in addition to Mermet Brigant 'en guise de dame', performed in the 'mommerie', though we are not told explicitly that they danced a 'morisque'.

On the costumes worn, however, the accounts are quite specific. The nine sirens (dummies made of 'mollure') who held up the dishes or 'mes' ('neuf grans plas faits comme ung panier argentés dedans et dorés') [('nine great dishes in the shape of a basket, plated with silver and gold inside')] and the four maidens were all clothed in 'chemises' of silk 'croveché' (a fine gauze-like material), the collars em-

---

[45] The following information is contained in A.S.T., Inv. 16, no.122, fos 172 et seq, 194v et seq.

briodered with 'fil dor'. Each wore a feather of 'or clicant' attached to her fore-head. The 'morisque' dancers' outfits had sixty sets of 'sonneaux fins', or tiny bells sewn on to them. Lancelot and his two companions wore 'cornetes', a type of conical hat, made of white taffeta with the device of Yolande and the duke picked out in gold. 'Guiches doubles', long straps which fell from the shoulders to the ground, accoutrements commonly sported for the 'morisque', were attached to their 'hauquetons' (short padded tunics), and the final touch consisted of 'petits franges dor' used as beards. Marquet and the three ogres were the only ones to wear masks, the ogres' hair being made of twenty-one pounds of silver thread. We may only guess at the source for the idea for this 'mommerie'. A clue may lie in the centrepiece of the banquet, a 'toyson d'or' bearing the gold and azure collar of the chivalric order of Savoy, the 'Ordre du Collier'. It would be stretching things a bit too far to suggest that Yolande used the banquet to celebrate the anniversary of Amedée VIII's revision of the statutes in January 1434, as there is little indication that she had any interest in the order (we have no record of the creation of new members of the order during this period). The presence of the collar therefore tends to add to the impression that this was a 'no holds barred' attempt to convince the prince of the prestige of this ancient dynasty.

Notwithstanding their assured flamboyance or their mechanical sophistication, the court entertainments were not strikingly innovative or original, and from the information we possess on similar activities of some thirty or forty years earlier, they had evolved surprisingly little. Given the proximity of Savoy to the Italian courts and Yolande's own tendency to flirt more and more with Italy and Italian ideas, one might have expected a stronger influence on the court from that quarter. The majority of the 'morisques' and 'mommeries' were indeed performed in a number of ducal establishments in Piedmont, most notably in its capital Turin, but also at Moncalieri, Yvorée and Rivoli. Yolande began to spend increasingly longer periods south of the Alps, a trend particularly unpopular with the Savoyard nobility which saw its political hegemony being eroded by the Piedmontese. Beleaguered on all sides in the north, Yolande retreated to the south to find the financial and personal support for her policies, support which she was hard-pressed to find in Savoy where the aristocracy was only too eager to be bought off by the French or the Burgundians. In Piedmont, she could pursue her interest in the classics; she purchased copies of the early printed editions of Cicero, Ovid, and Lorenzo Valla. Dante and Boccaccio in 'lombardic' were already in her library, inherited from Amedée VIII. The humanists, Andrea Rolando of Vercelli and Niccolo da Tarsi, were employed to educate the young duke and his brother. Francesco Filelfo was commissioned to write the 'Instructione del ben vivere utilissima' for the duke, though he was paid the rather paltry sum of 10 florins for his pains. But beyond these indications there is no sign that the new renaissance-style entertainments (to be viewed at the neighbouring court of Milan, for instance) were being emulated or admired at the court of Savoy. The Alps, it is true, were not a barrier to the spread of cultural ideas, and Savoy itself had in many spheres seen fruitful cross-fertilisation of ideas. Yet, in the realm of court entertainments, she remained firmly rooted in a heritage which for long had linked her to Burgundy. The cultural and political hegemony of Burgundy continued to fetter Savoy even in this matter.

But at the same time as reflecting the decline in court life of this particularly difficult period, the entertainments very much reflect the personality of Yolande and her need for amusement as a solace from her troubles. They are 'divertissements' pure and simple, shorn of the layers of meaning that were often part and parcel of their Burgundian counterparts. They represented a court turning in on itself, constricting its spectacular occasions to the exclusive confines of the 'grant salle' rather than the more expansive occasions allowed, for instance, by the tournament. Under threat, Yolande took refuge with her select group of courtiers in the performance of 'morisques' and 'mommeries'. The deaths of Charles the Bold, of Yolande herself, along with the dislocations and French invasions of the succeeding twenty years were required to set Savoy on a new track and inject some renewed vigour and dynamism into her court culture. Shaking off the shackles of the north, the court of Savoy now accepted its Italianisation wholeheartedly.

English and French Artistic Propaganda during the period of the Hundred Years War: Some Evidence from Royal Charters.[1]

ELIZABETH DANBURY

In January 1340, Edward III formally adopted the style and title of King of France, and set about prosecuting his claim to the French throne. The various efforts of English artists and craftsmen to underline the rights of English kings to the throne of France, and the corresponding efforts of their French counterparts to undermine them, form the main subject of this paper. Much of the evidence is taken from the decoration of charters. These, the most formal products of the royal chanceries, are the more important as a source because the larger-scale vehicles for such propaganda – the tents, the flags and pennons, the surcoats and horse-trappers and large parchment broadsheets – only survive as individual rarities, or as depicted in heraldic and other illuminated manuscripts.

In England, the practice of omitting the initial letter of the kings's name in royal charters and the most formal letters patent, and of inserting a decorated or illuminated letter in the resulting space, appears to have begun in about 1250. The earliest examples of royal instruments having such inserted decorated letters relate to East Anglia and appear from 1255 onwards.[2] From the 1340s, space was created for additional decoration by omitting certain other letters from the top line of the text of formal royal instruments and by not completing the elongated ascenders of the letters of the words setting out the king's style and title. The decoration and illumination of such documents was normally done at the expense of the grantees,[3] and until the end of Richard II's reign it is not possible to identify any uniformity of subject or style, or to isolate any individual, workshop, group of workshops or geographical centre, in which the majority of royal instruments may have been decorated. After 1399, there seems to have been a complete change in

---

[1]   I am grateful to Mr J. Campbell for his helpful comments on this paper.
[2]   Norfolk Record Office, King's Lynn Muniments, Aa3, Aa4a, Aa4b; H. Grieve and F. Roberts, *Ornament and Decoration in Essex Records* (Essex County Council, 1950), p.1.
[3]   H. C. Maxwell-Lyte, *Historical Notes on the use of the Great Seal of England* (London, 1926), pp. 266–7.

practice. Most, though by no means all, documents were decorated in pen and ink, and in a uniform style.[4] This suggests that there was a central workshop (most probably in London) to which royal grants could be taken by the grantees to be embellished. It has even been argued that some of this decoration may have been undertaken within the royal writing office; the title 'Master of the Decorated Documents' has been applied to the artist or artists who embellished certain royal grants and legal records during the reigns of Edward IV and Richard III.[5] The large majority of grants were never decorated, probably because decoration or illumination was an expensive optional extra to add to the already costly necessity of obtaining charters and letters patent. When decoration was added, this was apparently normally done very soon after the document was written.[6] The subjects chosen for illustration were often of symbolic or heraldic importance to the grantee: decoration could be employed to underline the civic pride of towns, the lands and liberties obtained or corporate bodies such as towns, religious houses and universitites, or the aspirations and achievements of individuals.

In France, too, the practice of decorating royal grants seems to have started in the thirteenth century, though only a few isolated decorated grants have been

---

[4] A charter of Henry V to the city of Canterbury, 10 Oct. 1414 (Canterbury Cathedral, City and Diocesan Record Office, AA27); letters patent to the City of Hull, 10 Dec. 1414 (Kingston upon Hull City Record Office, BRC 11); and a charter to the city of Gloucester (Gloucestershire Record Office, GBR 1 1/16) have almost identical decoration, based on an enlarged pen and ink letter H. In each case, one of Henry V's mottoes, 'In deo salutare meum', is written on the left-hand stroke and bow of the H. In the Canterbury and Hull documents, the H is surmounted by a crown of *fleurs de lis* with Henry IV's motto 'soverain' inscribed on the rim.

[5] *Richard III*, ed. P. Tudor-Craig, (National Portrait Gallery, 1973), pp. 33, 48–9, pls 20–3.

[6] This is difficult to prove or disprove on other than stylistic grounds. Very few accounts of payments for the decoration of documents survive. One exception is found in the Bursar's Accounts for Winchester College of 1442–3. These include a reference to the payment of 5s. 4d. 'clerico Kirkeby pro illuminacione litterarum patencium domini Regis et scribenti diversas bullas et capias . . ' The letters patent referred to in the accounts are those of Henry VI to Winchester College of 9 Feb. 1443, permitting it to acquire lands to the yearly value of 100 marks (Winchester College Muniments, Charters 21). I am indebted to Mr. John Harvey for this reference.

The existence of certain decorated or illuminated documents which had been cancelled or invalidated soon after their issue also indicated that, if documents were embellished, this was done soon after they were written. P.R.O., E156/29/41 is letters patent, dated 8 Sept. 1385, granting to Michael de la Pole, who had been created Earl of Suffolk on 6 Aug. 1385, the reversion of the lands of William de Ufford, late Earl of Suffolk, to the yearly value of £500. Michael de la Pole was impeached in Oct. 1386, and it was ordered that lands and revenues previously granted to him by Richard II should be taken back into the king's hands (*Rot. Parl.*, III, p. 219). The original grant itself is elaborately decorated in pen and ink with Michael de la Pole's name and arms. To have decorated the document after Oct. 1386 would have been an obvious waste of time and money.

found from before the reign of Charles V (1364–1380).[7] One of the earliest decorated French royal grants is of 1283, a confirmation by Philippe III (1270–1285) of a ruling made by the lord of Rosnay concerning the cutting of wood in the forest of Chevrie, near Mantes.[8] The first two letters of the king's name, 'Philippus', are ornamented with elaborate pen and ink flourishes and with grotesques. As in England, it seems that only a minute proportion of French royal documents were ever decorated, but the practice of embellishing the initial letter or first two letters of the king's name did become more common in the fourteenth century, partly because the script employed in the most formal documents lent itself to such elaboration.[9] Before the reign of Charles V the style of ornamentation of royal documents was, on the whole, abstract in character. For example, a grant of 1318 of Philippe V (1316–1322) to the Sainte-Chapelle in Paris,[10] and the formal *procès-verbal* of the oath taken by John II (1350–1364) on his accession[11] are, like the grant of Philippe III mentioned above, decorated in pen and ink with grotesques and flourishes. The earliest royal document with a representation of the king is one of July 1364, forbidding the alienation of the Hôtel St. Pol from the French Crown.[12] The use of such royal or donor portraits had a shorter life in France than in England; it seems to have been restricted to the reign of Charles V and to the twenty-five years immediately following.[13]

Until the end of the fourteenth century English practice differed markedly from French, both in regard to the style of decoration favoured and to the materials used for the embellishment of documents.[14] Even after that date there were some obvious distinctions. The main differences centred on the artistic treatment

---

[7]   C. R. Sherman, *The Portraits of Charles V of France (1338–1380)* (New York, 1969), pp. 37–42; M. E. Dupont, '1337, 1389, 1402 – Trois Chartes à Vignettes', *Notices et documents publiés pour la Société de l'Histoire de France à l'occasion du Cinquantième Anniversaire de sa fondation* (Paris, 1884), pp.187–218; *Musée des Archives Nationales, Documents originaux de l'histoire de France exposés dans l'Hotel Soubise* (Paris, 1872), pp.130–272.

[8]   A. N., K 35, no. 8; *Musée des Archives Nationales, Documents originaux*, pp.156–7; Dupont, 'Trois Chartes', pp.188–9.

[9]   G. Tessier, *Diplomatique royale française* (Paris, 1962), p. 238.

[10] A. N., J 155, no. 23; *Musée des Archives Nationales, Documents originaux*, pp.180–1; Dupont, 'Trois Chartes', p.189.

[11] A. N., K 47, no. 6; *Musée des Archives Nationales, Documents originaux*, pp. 208–9; Dupont, 'Trois Chartes', p.189.

[12] A. N., J 154, no. 5 (Musée AE 383). See pl.1.

[13] Dupont, 'Trois Chartes', pp.193–4; *Musée des Archives Nationales, Documents originaux*, pp. 247–72.

[14] There is no specific study of the palaeography, diplomatic and embellishment of decorated documents in either England or France. Many of the decorated charters in the Archives Nationales are listed, with a brief commentary, in *Musée des Archives Nationales, Documents originaux*, pp.130–272. C. T. Clay, 'An Illuminated Charter of Free Warren, dated 1291', *The Antiquaries Journal*, xi (1931), 129–32, and Maxwell-Lyte, *Historical Notes on the use of the Great Seal of England*, pp. 266–70 provide the starting point for investigation of English practice.

Plate 1. Charles V in Majesty: letters patent forbidding the alienation of the Hôtel St Pol from the French crown, July, 1364 (A.N., J 154, no. 5 [Musée, AE 383])

of the initial and other letters to be decorated, and on English preference for illumination rather than pen and ink decoration. Before 1399, the most elaborate
and expensive charter decoration in England took the form of illumination, rather
than pen and ink embellishment, which was the favoured, though not the invari-
able practice in France. Many English charters were illuminated in the same style
(and probably by the same artists) as contemporary illuminated manuscripts. The
initial letters of the documents were therefore treated in the same way as in manuscript illuminations: they acted as frames which enclosed or supported repre-
sentational or abstract designs. In France, both before and after the end of the
fourteenth century, the style of charter decoration was by no means always identical to that of contemporary manuscript illumination; instead, it gives the impression of having been developed for the specific purpose of the ornamentation of
documents. The decorated French charters, though illustrating a variety of subjects, often have a similarity of style and iconography which unites them and suggests that the organisation of any decoration was probably, from the first, far more
centralised than in England, and that the ornament may have been added in or
near the royal chancery in Paris. The distinctiveness and uniformity of approach
to charter decoration in France is best illustrated by the treatment of the initial
and other letters to be decorated. Instead of acting as frames or supports for the ornamentation, the actual strokes forming the letter were made into an integral part
of it. For example, in the contract of marriage between Jean, Duke of Berry, and
Jeanne de Boulogne, dated 5 June 1389,[15] the left and right hand strokes of the initial letter A are the contracted couple: Jeanne de Boulogne on the left and the
Duke of Berry on the right. A bar across the centre of the A is formed by the pair's
joined hands. This integration of the actual form of the letter into the decoration
only became part of English practice after the end of the fourteenth century; similarly an increasing number of English documents were decorated in pen and ink,
rather than illuminated, after that date.

The main purpose of the present paper is to show how, both in England and in
France, charter-decoration was sometimes part of what may loosely be called the
propaganda of the Hundred Years War. In the iconography of their symbolism and
of the scenes which they depict, some of these decorations appear to make express
claims and counter claims. Some English documents of this kind were sent to
France and some French documents were sent to England. Most, however, could
hardly have been expected to reach or affect the enemy. Indeed, by their nature,
they were intended for home consumption; and even at home it is a question of
how many people saw them. Yet, as important survivors from a world of decorated
objects of various kinds, most of which are lost, they provide significant clues to
the ways in which war may have been fought in pictures.

The first way in which English artists attempted to assert their kings' rights to

---

[15] A. N., J 1105, no. 8 (Musée AE II 411); transcript, commentary and illustration in Dupont, 'Trois Chartes', pp.192, 198–202, 208–16.

the French throne was to portray them in the royal robes of the kings of France. One representation of a king of France in majesty appears in the first folio of the only surviving copy of the great inventory of the jewels and regalia of Charles V, drawn up in 1379–80.[16] The copy dates from the late fifteenth century, but the portrait itself is probably derived from an exemplar of the reign of Charles VI (1380–1422) as it features one of his badges, the broom plant, and his motto *Ja mès*. The king is shown robed, crowned, holding a long sceptre in his right hand and, in his left, a shorter sceptre surmounted by a hand in the attitude of benediction (the *main de justice*, a vital symbol of French royal authority, which appears on French royal seals from the time of Louis X (1314–16)). In late 1373 the city of Bristol was created a county in its own right. Three crucial documents were the charter of 8 August, the letters patent of 30 October confirming the boundaries, and those of 20 December inspecting and notifying, with parliamentary approval, the other two grants.[17] All three documents were elaborately illuminated by a very fine artist, or group of artists, possibly some of those who worked on the manuscripts associated with the Bohun family. All three illuminations portray King Edward III in the initial E, with his arms (quarterly, France ancient and England), the arms of Bristol to the left of the initial.[18] The portrayal of the king in the letters patent of 30 October shows him standing, crowned with a crown of *fleurs de lis*, holding a sceptre in his left hand, and wearing, over a scarlet gown, the royal robes of France.[19] These blue robes with gold *fleurs de lis*, lined with ermine, may even have been intended specifically to represent the seamless coronation robes of the French kings. In any case the image of Edward III in the Bristol letters patent was intended to portray him as king of France in full majesty; the robes are identical to those attributed to kings of France when thus depicted.

Seals were also used to bear the same message and to express the claim of English kings to rule in France. The importance attributed by English kings to their claim to the throne of France is most obviously reflected in the use of the title *Rex Francie* in royal documents and on royal seals. The title *Rex Francie* was made to precede the title *Rex Anglie* on the legend of the third seal of presence of Edward III, which was used between February and June 1340. The same order was maintained on at least one of the great seals used by all but two of his successors up to and until Henry VII.[20] It is strange that Henry V was one of the exceptions (Richard III being the other). However, under Henry VI not only did *Rex Francie* precede *Rex Anglie*, but the seals for French affairs showed the king crowned and

---

[16] B. N., ms. fr. 2705, fo.1; *Les Fastes du Gothique: le siècle de Charles V* (Paris, 1981), pp. 337–8.

[17] All three documents are transcribed and translated in N. Dermott Harding, 'Bristol Charters, 1155–1373', *Bristol Record Society*, I (1930), pp.118–41, 168–73.

[18] City of Bristol Record Office, 01208, 01209, 01210.

[19] City of Bristol Record Office, 01209. See pl. 2.

[20] A. B. and A. Wyon, *The Great Seals of England* (London, 1887), pp. 31–67.

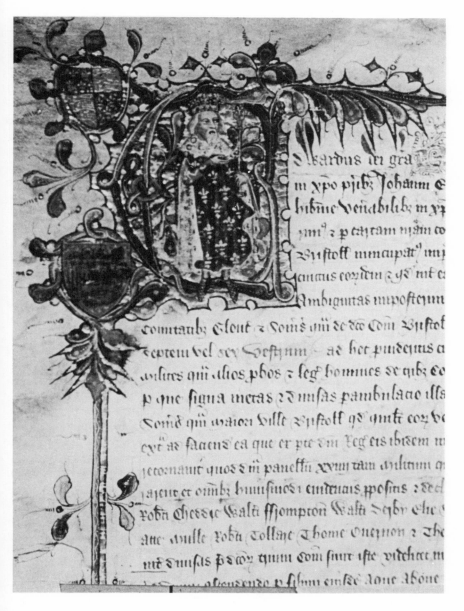

Plate 2. Edward III in majesty, wearing the royal robes of France: letters patent confirming the boundaries of the newly created county of Bristol, 30 Oct., 1373 (City of Bristol Record Office, 01209)

holding both the sceptre and the *main de justice*.[21] The last known occasion on which a great seal was used on which the title *Rex Francie* precedes all others is that on the confirmation of the treaty of Étaples, 11 November 1492.

Perhaps the most obvious visual way in which English artists demonstrated their kings' claims to the throne of France was in their arrogation of the *fleur de lis*. The *fleur de lis* appears to have been first used on the obverse of French royal seals, on banners and on royal robes, during the reign of Louis VII (1137–1180),[22] and it has been suggested that Abbot Suger of Saint-Denis (d.1151) may have promoted its use as a Capetian emblem. The *fleur de lis* possessed both ecclesiastical and political significance, and could be used to link the later Capetians with, on the one hand, Christ and the Virgin Mary, and, on the other hand, with earlier imperial and royal houses on whose regalia it had appeared.[23] Edward III's quartering (in 1340) of the *fleurs de lis* of France with the lions of England was therefore a particularly strong visual statement of his claim. This quartering (incidentally the first known use of quartering by an Englishman in England)[24] was such as to give greater prominence to the French rather than to the English arms; the former are in the first and fourth quarters which later practice would have reserved for the paternal arms. The *fleurs de lis* continued to be quartered with the lions until George III finally abandoned the formal claim to France in 1801.

The royal quartered arms in full, acting as a lasting reminder of English claims to France, were employed to decorate a variety of documents, not all emanating from the royal chancery, and served to emphasise the recipients' links with their sovereigns. Letters patent from Richard II to the city of Canterbury of 8 February 1380 are lavishly illuminated on three borders, and feature, within the initial let-

[21] *Ibid.*, pp. 53–5. B. Bedos-Rezak, 'Idéologie royale, ambitions princières et rivalités politiques d'après le témoignage des sceaux (France, 1380–1461)', *La 'France Anglaise' au Moyen Age (Actes du 111ᵉ Congrès National des Sociétés Savantes (Poitiers, 1986)*, (Paris 1988), i, 483–511, was published after the completion of this paper.

[22] B. Bedos-Rezak, 'Suger and the Symbolism of Royal Power: the Seal of Louis VII', *Abbot Suger and Saint-Denis*, ed. P. L. Gerson (New York, 1986), p.100.

[23] Carolingian kings and Ottonian emperors had employed *fleurs de lis* on their regalia, and early Capetian kings from Robert II (996–1031) had incorporated a *fleur de lis* onto the end of their sceptres. The earliest surviving physical evidence of *semée of fleurs de lis* as the arms of the royal family of France is on a seal of Louis (later Louis VIII), son of Philip II Augustus (1180–1223). The seal is appended to a document of 1211. It seems likely that Philip Augustus himself used the arms *azure semée of fleurs de lis or*. Thereafter gold *fleurs de lis* on a blue background remained the arms of the kings of France (M. Pastoureau, 'La fleur de lis: emblème royal, symbol Marial où thème graphique', *L'Hermine et le Sinople; Études d'Héraldique Médiévale*, ed. M. Pastoureau (Paris, 1982), pp.158–78.

[24] A. C. Fox-Davies, *A Complete Guide to Heraldry* (London, 1969), pp. 206–7. The quartered arms of Queen Eleanor of Castile (d.1290), first wife of Edward I, survive as fragments of the Eleanor Cross at Cheapside (*Age of Chivalry: Art in Plantagenet England 1200–1400* ed. J. J. G. Alexander and P. Binski (London, 1987), pp. 361–6).

ter R, the royal arms (Quarterly, France ancient and England) supported by ostrich feathers.[25]

Throughout the period of the Hundred Years War and later, the *fleur de lis* was used not only in the decoration of royal and other charters as an integral part of the royal arms, but also as decoration in its own right, at first only on the initial letter of the king's name, but under Henry VIII and the later Tudors and Stuarts, as a royal badge, often crowned, as part of the decoration in the top margin of the document. The documents in which *fleurs de lis* appear as decoration are not necessarily of great political moment. For example, in letters patent of Henry VI to Michaelhouse, Cambridge, dated 1 February 1425,[26] giving permission to the college to dig a ditch at the end of its garden, the initial letter H of the name 'Henricus' is decorated in pen and ink with five *fleurs de lis*.

Some of the decorations under consideration were very skillfully executed, as appears from those illustrated in plates 3 and 4. The documents concerned are not of the first importance, though relating to a foundation which was, for they are duplicate copies of the public instrument of 1440 declaring that the parish church of Eton had been created the collegiate church of the Blessed Mary of Eton, and appropriated to the Provost and Fellows.[27] Both have closely similar decoration, which is at once grand and subtle, and presents a touching image of the piety of Henry VI, king of England and, (as the artist carefully brings home) of France, too. Both feature the arms of Henry VI (quarterly, England and France modern) in the initial letter U of 'Universis', and both use the lions of England and the *fleurs de lis* as decoration while retaining their heraldic significance. The first copy features, in the left-hand shaft of the letter U, three lions, and in the right-hand shaft three *fleurs de lis*, represented unheraldically, one below the other in vertical line.[28] The space within the letter is filled by an angel, wings outspread, holding a shield of the royal arms in the correct heraldic form. Above the letter U is a closed (imperial) crown, composed of alternate oak leaves and trefoils (possibly *fleurs de lis*) and surmounted by a cross. The king's style and title, 'Henricus d(e)i gra(tia) Rex anglie et ffranc(ie) + d(ominus) hib(ernie)', is written in the rim of the crown. The whole letter is further decorated with strapwork and elaborate pen flourishes.

The second, more elaborate and more finely executed copy features, in the left-hand upright of the letter U, a lion sejant, bearing a banner of the arms of Henry VI, and in the right-hand upright, the *fleurs de lis* and lions again unheraldically, one below the other in vertical line.[29] The space within the letter U enclosed the Virgin Mary as Queen of Heaven, crowned by God the Father and supported by

[25] Canterbury Cathedral, City and Diocesan Record Office, AA12.

[26] Trinity College, Cambridge, Michaelhouse muniments, no. 92.

[27] Eton College, ECR 39/5A and 5B; H. C. Maxwell-Lyte, *A History of Eton College (1440–1898)* (London, 1899), pp. 7–8.

[28] Eton College, ECR 39/5A. See pl. 3.

[29] Eton College, ECR 39/5B. See pl. 4

Plate 3.   Royal arms of Henry VI: public instrument appropriating the parish church of Eton to the Provost and Fellows of Eton College, Dec., 1440 (Eton College, ECR 39/5A)

Plate 4.   Henry VI's arms and the Virgin in majesty: duplicate of the public instrument of Dec., 1440 [pl. 3] (Eton College, ECR 39/5B)

six angels. Above the letter U an angel, wings outspread, holds an open (royal) crown composed of alternative trefoil leaves and small globes, with the words 'Henricus d(e)i gra(tia)' on its rim. The purpose of the elaborate embellishment of these, as of other decorated documents at Eton, was to underline the heavenly and earthly patronage of the new foundation. The details of the decoration appear to have been meticulously worked out by someone who knew the college very well : the crowned Virgin with God the Father and the six angels is identical to the design of Eton's first seal.[30] The stress laid on Henry VI's arms and titles underlines the regality of the king and the importance of his new foundation. The *fleurs de lis* were employed both as a decorative motif and to emphasise the power and prestige of the founder, and his sovereignty over France, even at a date (1440) when these were fast waning.

A few English documents may have been illustrated at royal expense with the possible effect upon the French recipient specifically in mind. The English counterpart of an Anglo-French agreement relating to the appointment of a joint commission to investigate and arbitrate upon the dispute concerning Belleville, dated at Westminster on 20 January 1366, was delivered into the *Trésor des Chartes* on 29 May of that year.[31] Edward III's arms are displayed in the space within the initial letter E of Edward, while in the left-hand curved upright of the E itself a single *fleur de lis* is shown, supported between two lions. Furthermore, the initial letter A of 'A tous' is filled with Breton ermines. The inclusion of these elements seems likely to have been deliberately provocative rather than accidental.[32]

How offensive the English use of *fleurs de lis* must have been to the French can be seen in the emphasis placed on them in documents, manuscripts and objects produced for Charles V. Charles was highly conscious of the capacity of the visual arts and of literature to defend and strengthen the authority of the Crown.[33] He commissioned French translations of classical texts concerning the conduct of government, new histories and political treatises, and studies of holy legends and myths surrounding the special powers and attributes of French kings, all of which emphasised the divine sanction of the kings of France and their authority on

---

[30] Maxwell-Lyte, A *History of Eton College*, pp.17, 73–4. Two shields of the royal arms are incorporated within the first seal of Eton College: the first shield bears the arms of France alone, the second those of England.

[31] A. N., J 642, no. 9bis; P. T. V. M. Chaplais, *English Diplomatic Practice* (London 1975, 1982), Part II (Plates), pp.14–15, pl. 31.

[32] *Ibid.*, p.14. The political undertones of the embellishment of this document are deepened by the possibility that the artist who worked on it may have been French rather than English. Stylistically, the decoration is French (the letters are part of the decoration, not merely a frame for it) and shows a marked similarity to that found in other French documents: the A of 'A tous' is almost identical to the A of 'Ad' in A. N., Musée AE II 395 II. It has no parallels in English charter decoration of the second half of the fourteenth century.

[33] Sherman, *The Portraits of Charles V*, pp. 8–16; B. Guenée, 'Les Grandes Chroniques de France', *Les Lieux de Mémoire*, II: *La Nation*, ed. P. Nora (Paris, 1986), pp.189–214.

earth.[34] Among the attributes specifically associated with the kings of France was the *fleur de lis*. It was not only employed as a major decorative motif,[35] but functioned as a symbol of the links between the monarchy and God and as a special attribute of French kingship. In this latter role, *fleurs de lis* were used to decorate two of the three versions (all originals) of an *ordonnance* of August 1374 which fixed the age of majority of French kings at fourteen years.[36] The two versions are not identical, but in both the initial letter K of 'Karolus' is illuminated, *semée of fleurs de lis* or on an azure field, and surmounted by a gold crown composed of *fleurs de lis*. In one of the two exemplars, reference is made in the decoration to the king's eldest son: the second part of the initial letter K is formed of two interlocked fish, representing dolphins. 'Dauphin' (lat. 'delphinus') was a new title in the royal house of France: Charles V's son, the future Charles VI (born on 3 December 1368) was the first eldest son of the reigning monarch to bear the title and hold the Dauphiné of the Viennois, which had been ceded to the crown by Humbert II, the last non-royal Dauphin of the Viennois.[37] Regulations governing the majority of the kings of France had obvious relevance to the eldest son of the monarch: the choice of decoration is therefore not surprising. The use of a crown composed of *fleurs de lis* to top the initial letter K reinforces the emphasis on the emblematic importance of the *fleur de lis* to the French royal house.

By an edict of February 1376, Charles V reduced the number of *fleurs de lis* in the French royal arms to three, in honour of the Holy Trinity. The intentions behind the edict may have included the desire to distance the French royal arms from the English, and hence to make the English claims to the French throne appear more remote. The idea may, however, have had its origin earlier in the reign. In July 1364, in the letters patent forbidding the alienation of the Hôtel St. Pol, the shield of arms to the left of the king already bore three *fleurs de lis*.[38] These are shown clearly in this document (and in others) as linking the king of France and the King of Heaven. Above and to left of the king, two angels support, each with one hand, a crown of *fleurs de lis* and, with the other hand, a single *fleur de lis*. Above them is God, right hand raised in blessing over angels, crown, *fleur de lis* and Charles V himself.

---

[34] Sherman, *The Portraits of Charles V*, pp.13–14.

[35] Examples of the employment of the *fleur de lis* as a decorative motif on regalia, precious objects and jewelry in the second half of the fourteenth century are illustrated in *Les Fastes du Gothique*, pp. 231, 238, 244, 250, 252–3. Some recently discovered pieces of early fifteenth-century armour and insignia are discussed in M. Fleury, *Point d'archéologie sans histoire* (Oxford, 1988), pp.14–16, figs 10–11.

[36] A. N., J 401, nos 6A, 6B, 6C (Musée AE 395 I, II, III.); Dupont, 'Trois Chartes', p.191; *Musée des Archives Nationales, Documents originaux*, pp. 226–9. See pl. 5.

[37] A. N., J 279, no. 4; Dupont, 'Trois chartes', p.189; *Musée des Archives Nationales, Documents originaux*, pp. 201–2.

[38] A. N., J 154, no. 5 (Musée AE II 383); Sherman, *The Portraits of Charles V*, pp. 75–6; *Les Fastes du Gothique*, pp. 360–1; *Musée des Archives Nationales, Documents originaux*, pp. 217–19; Dupont, 'Trois Chartes', p.189. See pl. 1.

Plate 5. Initial K[arolus], illuminated in blue with gold *fleurs de lis*, surmounted by a gold crown composed of *fleurs de lis*: letters patent fixing the majority of French kings at fourteen years, Aug., 1374 (A.N., J 401, no. 6A [Musée, AE 395 I])

Plate 6. Charles V in prayer before the Virgin and Child: act of the Dean and Chapter of Rouen cathedral, instituting solemn masses for the good estate of Charles V, 20 July, 1366 (A.N., J 463, no. 53 [Musée, AE II 385])

In the initial letter U of 'Universis' of an act of the dean and chapter of Rouen, dated 20 July 1366, instituting solemn masses for the good estate of Charles V during his life and for his soul thereafter, the king is shown in prayer before the Virgin and Child.[39] The Virgin is seated in front of a curtain beneath a canopy powdered with *fleurs de lis*. Above, two lions, employed as heraldic supporters, each holds a shield, one of France, the other of France quartering the Dauphiné. The *fleurs de lis* in the shields, and those behind the Virgin Mary, create and emphasise the bonds linking France and its king to Heaven and its Queen. Other documents emphasised the particular favour of heaven towards the French king, and expressed this by incorporating visual references of special local significance. In a grant of 1380, Charles V endowed the cathedral chapter of Reims with Vauclerc.[40] It was in Reims cathedral that French kings were consecrated. It was held that the oil used for the sacring had been brought by a dove from heaven, on Christmas Day 496, for the baptism of Clovis by St. Remigius. This baptism is represented in the space between the strokes of the initial letter K of Charles V's grant. Clovis is shown kneeling before St. Remigius, who appears to be crowning, rather than baptising him. The dove with the holy oil in a vial (the *Sainte Ampoule*) hovers above and to the left of Clovis and St. Remigius. Charles V himself is shown standing, crowned, before a background of *fleurs de lis* in the left-hand stroke of the K of 'Karolus'. His crown is supported by two angels, and further evidence of heavenly approval for him and his actions is provided by the representation of the Virgin and Child in the top right-hand stroke of the K, and of God the Father, within a semicircle, right hand raised in blessing towards Charles V.

The significance of the pictorial association of earthly rulers with the powers of heaven obviously extended beyond war propaganda. Nevertheless, it was essential to the justification of any cause that God and His saints should be represented as being firmly on the side of one protagonist. Saints were called upon in battle cries, and heraldic arms attributed to them were born on shields, surcoats and banners. Edward III designated a warrior saint, George, as patron of the Order of the Garter. His arms, a red cross on a white ground, became an almost indispensable part of the heraldry of any English war-band, as the practice developed of depicting the arms next to the staff of the standard (the long tapering flag used by lords to act as a mustering point for their troops in battle).[41]

Even the least warlike of monarchs could be associated in art with the fighting saint. The cross of St. George was attributed to Henry VI as one of his badges.[42] A grant of William Alnwick, bishop of Lincoln, dated September 1443, conferring

---

[39] A. N., J 463, no. 53 (Musée AE II 385); L. Delisle, *Recherches sur la librairie de Charles V* (Paris, 1907), pp. 57, 61; *Musée des Archives Nationales, Documents originaux*, p. 219; Dupont, 'Trois Chartes', p.189. See pl. 6.

[40] Reims, Archives Municipales, G 1549, (*olim* Fonds du Chapitre métropolitain, Vauclerc, liasse I, no. 4), cited by Sherman, *The Portraits of Charles V*, pp. 39–40.

[41] Fox-Davies, *A Complete Guide to Heraldry*, pp. 360–3.

[42] College of Arms, London, Vincent ms. 152, fo. 53.

Plate 7. The Virgin, the royal arms of Henry VI, and the banner of St George: grant of William Alnwick, bishop of Lincoln, exempting the Provost, College, and parishioners of Eton from the jurisdiction of the archdeacon of Buckingham, Sept., 1443 (Eton College, ECR 39/27)

upon the Provost, College, and parishoners of Eton exemption from the jurisdiction of the archdeacon of Buckingham and assigning to the Provost archidiaconal authority within the college, survives in duplicate.[43] Both exemplars show, within the initial letter U of 'Universis', the Virgin (to whom the college is dedicated) supported by four angels. Both make pictorial reference to St. George. In the less elaborate version, the saint's banner is held by an antelope (Henry VI's heraldic supporter),[44] while the right hand upright of the initial letter U of the more elaborate document shows St. George himself slaying the dragon, the king's arms being represented in the left hand upright. Below and to the left of the initial, King Henry VI kneels in prayer to the Virgin, with the words 'Salve Regina Mater Misericord(ie)' issuing from his mouth.[45]

Both the French and the English monarchs claimed the throne of France as the true heirs of the French royal house. In consequence, much visual emphasis was placed on genealogy and on real and legendary predecessors whose renown and

[43] Eton College, ECR 39/27 and 28; Maxwell-Lyte, A History of Eton College, p.19.
[44] Eton College, ECR 39/27. See pl. 7.
[45] Eton College, ECR 39/28. See pl. 8.

Plate 8. The Virgin, the royal arms, St George, and Henry VI kneeling in supplication: duplicate of the grant of Sept., 1443 [pl. 7] (Eton College, ECR 39/28)

sanctity added lustre to their successors' claims. An ornate genealogy showing Henry VI uniting the royal lines of France and England appears in the volume of romances and poems presented by John Talbot, Earl of Shrewsbury, to Margaret of Anjou on the occasion of her marriage to Henry VI in 1445.[46] Attempts were made by English kings to associate themselves with saints who previously had been firmly connected to the French royal house. Small statues of St. Denis as well as of St. George fill the niches of Henry V's tomb at Westminster Abbey. A psalter owned by Henry VI, which may originally have belonged to Louis of France (d. 1415), the eldest son of Charles VI, was altered so that seven of its miniatures feature a figure wearing the royal arms of England. In one of these, this figure, presumably Henry VI, is shown being presented to the Virgin by St. Louis.[47]

When the Hundred Years War began, the English royal house already had saints to whom it was especially devoted; namely Edward the Confessor and Edmund the Martyr, after whom Henry III had named his two sons. The emphasis on these two royal saints and on the lustre lent by their lives to the projects of later kings remained constant during the period of the war.

Both Richard II and Henry VI had a particular devotion to St. Edward the Confessor. Richard II impaled his own arms with those attributed to St. Edward and, as a special mark of favour, granted to three men, on whom he had conferred dukedoms, permission to impale the arms also. One of the newly-created dukes, Thomas de Holland, Duke of Surrey, founded the Carthusian priory of Mountgrace in 1398. In the initial letter of the foundation charter he is portrayed, wearing a surcoat of the impaled arms, being presented to the Virgin Mary by St. Nicholas.[48] The arms of both St. Edward and St. Edmund feature prominently in the three instruments spectacularly illuminated by William Abel for Henry VI's foundations at Eton and Cambridge.[49] Even the rapid development of the cult of St. George after 1348 did not displace St. Edward and St. Edmund from their central positions as special patrons of the royal house and symbols of its greatness. Rather, the warrior saint and the two kingly saints were linked together to underline heavenly support for Edward III and his successors.[50] The arms attributed to

[46] London, B. L., Royal ms. 15 E VI; J. J. G. Alexander, 'Painting and Manuscript Illumination for Royal Patrons in the Later Middle Ages', *English Court Culture in the Later Middle Ages*, ed. V. J. Scattergood and J. W. Sherborne, (London, 1983), p.151.

[47] B. L., Cotton ms. Domitian A XVII; Alexander, *ibid.*, p.151; D. H. Turner, *Illuminated Manuscripts exhibited in the Grenville Library* (British Museum, London, 1967), p. 44.

[48] Ingilby of Ripley Castle no. 25 (privately held).

[49] Eton College, ECR 39/8, ECR 39/57; King's College, Cambridge, muniments A20. J. J. G. Alexander includes the two latter documents in his study of William Abel: 'William Abell 'Lymnour' and 15th-century English illumination', *Kunsthistorische Forschungen Otto Pächt zu ehren*, ed. A. Rosenauer and G. Weber, (Salzburg, 1972), pp.166–72.

[50] The association of saints Edward and Edmund with St George is discussed in A. B. Wyon, 'The Great Seals of Henry IV, Henry V, and Henry VI', *Journal of the British Archaeological Association*, xxxix (1888), 139–67; also Wyon, *The Great Seals of England*, pp. 43–6.

St. Edward and St. Edmund appear in shields on the first seal of the Order of the Garter, one on each side of the representation of St. George.[51] The Wilton Diptych shows Richard II being presented by St. Edmund, St. Edward and St. John the Baptist to the Virgin and Child. The Virgin is surrounded by angels wearing badges showing Richard II's personal device of a white hart. One angel, standing between Richard II and the infant Christ, holds a banner with the red cross of St. George.

Iconographic programmes linking the powers of heaven and the greatness of the patron's family to his current ambitions and projects may also be found in English charter illumination. On 19 July 1362 Edward, the Black Prince, was granted by his father the newly created principality of Aquitaine and Gascony.[52] The initial letter E of 'Edwardus' is surmounted by a four-arched architectural structure. Angels playing musical instruments appear in the arches and on top of the structure itself, as well as on the illuminated borders of the document. The initial letter features, above the bar of the E, a representation of the Holy Trinity, to whose cult the Black Prince had a particular devotion, and below the bar, two angels supporting a shield of his arms, quarterly France ancient and England, with a label of three points argent. On the right hand side of the document is another shield with the Black Prince's device of three ostrich feathers (sable, three ostrich feathers with scrolls argent). The inclusion of both these shields is significant. The three ostrich feathers are defined in the Black Prince's will as his arms for peace, while his quartered arms are described as those for war.[53] The combination of the Holy Trinity, the triumphant angels, one holding a scroll with the motto of the Garter, and the Black Prince's own arms, showing him prepared to govern his new principality both in peace and in war, confirm the coincidence of earthly policy with heavenly approval.

The same care to link the interests of crown, family and heaven may be found in the work of French artists and propagandists. The cult of the Emperor Charlemagne was carefully fostered at the court of France in the second half of the fourteenth century. The coincidence of the name of both Charles V and his eldest son with that of the Emperor gave additional force to the attempts of the Valois kings to associate themselves with Charlemagne. The sceptre made for Charles V in Paris between 1365 and 1380 is surmounted by a statuette of the Emperor Charlemagne seated in majesty, and other objects reputedly belonging to him, or with a

[51] D. and S. Lysons, *Magna Britannia, I. Bedfordshire, Berkshire and Buckinghamshire* (London, 1806), fig.1; and Juliet Vale, *Edward III and Chivalry: chivalric society and its context 1270–1350* (Woodbridge, 1982), frontispiece.

[52] P. R. O., E 30/1105. The document is discussed in R. Barber, *Edward, Prince of Wales and Aquitaine* (London, 1978), pp.177–8, and pl. 4.

[53] J. Nichols, *A Collection of all the Wills now known to be extant of the Kings and Queens of England, Princes and Princesses of Wales, and every branch of the Blood Royal from the reign of William the Conqueror, to that of Henry the Seventh exclusive* (London, 1780), p. 68.

representation of him, circulated in the court.[54] The cult of St. Louis (1226–1270) was also exceedingly important, as his greatness and holiness must reflect favourably on his legitimate successors. Illustrations of his life and death may be found both in the histories and in the prayerbooks commissioned by and for his successors and their families. The saint was seen by Charles V as the model of Christian kingship.[55] When, in January 1372, Charles V gave to his brother Jean, Duke of Berry, a portion of the True Cross which had been brought to France by St. Louis and lodged in the Sainte Chapelle, this bore witness to the glory of God, and to the honour and piety of the ruling family of France, and linked both Charles V and his brother with their saintly ancestor. In the document certifying that the gift had been made, Charles is shown standing and crowned in the left hand stroke of the initial letter K of 'Karolus' offering in his right hand a cross to his brother, who is kneeling to receive it.[56] The Duke's figure takes up the lower right-hand stroke of the K while the upper right-hand stroke is occupied by an angel playing the viol. The eyes of the angel and of the Duke are turned towards the king, who dominates the scene.

Visual symbols produced strong reactions. On the morning immediately preceding the battle of Poitiers, Sir John Chandos rode out to reconnoitre the French positions, and Marshal Jean de Clermont those of the English.[57] The two men met. Each noticed that the other bore the same device as himself, not on the shield, but on the left arm, 'une bleue dame ouvrée de broudure ou ray d'un soleil'. An argument broke out, in which each claimed the device as his own, and challenged the other to prove his right to bear it. Physical action had to be deferred, as their meeting took place on a day of truce between the two armies. As a parting verbal shot, Jean de Clermont claimed that the English could never invent anything new of their own, but plagiarised the inventions of others: 'Chandos, Chandos, ce sont bien des posnées de vos Englès qui ne scevent aviser riens de nouvel; mès quanqu'il voient, leur est biel'.

This incident testifies to the power of symbols and emblems to create or foster friction and antagonism. It also gives voice to the French assertion that the English, having no imagination, were forced to appropriate ideas and emblems not their own, an opinion which may well have been held in view of English attempts to arrogate the title, authority and attributes of the French kings. The nature of the device born by both men is also significant. Although it is possible, since Froissart describes the two knights as 'jone et amoureus', that the lady represented was a noblewoman whose favour both carried, it is far more probable that she was

---

[54] Les Fastes du Gothique, p. 249.

[55] Sherman, The Portraits of Charles V, p.13; J. de Pange, Le Roi très chrétien (Paris, 1949), p. 413.

[56] A. N., J 185, no. 6 (Musée AE II 393); Musée des Archives Nationales, Documents originaux, p. 225; Dupont, 'Trois Chartes', p.190. See pl. 9.

[57] Oeuvres de Froissart, ed. Kervyn de Lettenhove and A. Scheler (Brussels, 1867–1877), V, pp. 416–19.

Plate 9.   Charles V presenting his brother John, Duke of Berry, with a portion of a relic of the True Cross: instrument confirming the donation, Jan., 1372 (A.N., J 185, no. 6 [Musée, AE II 393])

the Virgin Mary.[58] According to Froissart, the lady was dressed in blue (the colour most commonly associated with the Virgin in heraldry) and stood within a mandorla of gold. If both Sir John Chandos and Jean de Clermont carried the Virgin's image, then this suggests the fierce competition between the French and the English to provide visual evidence of heavenly support for their earthly causes and for the kings on whose behalf they fought. Each side emphasised, in every available medium, the faith, rights, just claims and beneficent rule of its true christian king.

An important example of this, and of the main theme of this paper, is the decoration of the surviving exemplar of the treaty of Troyes, 21 May 1420.[59] This decoration was accomplished by an artist aware of the iconographic significance of his work. Hopes for the intended dual monarchy were expressed in the initial letter of the document. The letter H (for 'Henricus') was decorated in pen and ink, not illuminated. Within the left-hand stroke of the H are three *fleurs de lis*, one above the other, while the bow of the H contains three lions, also one above the other, illustrating the fusion of France and England by and within Henry V. The letter is surmounted by a crown, composed of alternate oak leaves (which may represent England) and *fleurs de lis*. Within the rim of the crown are inscribed the words *fides pax justicia*, indicating the threefold aspirations for the new monarchy, and emphasising by the use of the words *fides* and *justicia* that the blessing of God and man attends the longed-for peace.[60] A great deal is expressed in the embellishment of this initial letter. The high ability of the artists who illustrated royal and other documents in France and England during the fourteenth and fifteenth centuries was shown not only in their artistic skill, but in their capacity, within a small space, to illuminate a cause.

---

[58] R. Dennys, *The Heraldic Imagination* (London, 1975), pp.104–5.

[59] A. N., J 646, no.15 (Musée AE III 254); Archives Nationales (Musée de l'Histoire de France) *La France du VIIe au XXe siècle: à travers soixante et onze documents* (Paris, 1980), p. 32.

[60] The words on the inscription were carefully chosen. 'Justicia' was the name by which Henry V was known at the Council of Constance, 1414–18 (Oxford, Bodleian Lib., ms. Ashmole 845, fo. 224r); while 'fides' was associated in French royal historiography both with France and the *fleur de lis*. William of Nangis (d.1300) argued that 'fides' (faith), 'sapientia' (learning) and 'militia' (chivalry) had been joined together to form the *fleur de lis*, borne on the arms and banners of the kings of France, 'fides' being the central element. (J. W. Baldwin, 'Masters at Paris from 1179 to 1215: a social perspective', *Renaissance and Renewal in the Twelfth Century*, ed. R. L. Benson and G. Constable (Oxford, 1982), pp.162–3. I owe this reference to Dr Margaret Gibson).

Mixing Business with Leisure:
Some French Royal Notaries and Secretaries and their Histories of France, c.1459–1509[1]

KATHLEEN DALY

In November 1482, an important royal ordinance confirmed the privileges and status of the college of notaries and secretaries of the kings of France. In addition to the information which it supplies on the tasks of these royal officials and the important positions which they occupied in various branches of the royal administration, the ordinance stresses the close association of the notaries and secretaries with the history and the mystique of the French crown. It traces the origins of the office to the origins of the French kingdom, and the duty of recording 'toutes les choses solempnelles et autenticques, qui perpetuellement par le temps avenir, seroient faites . . . par les roys de France' is compared to that of the Four Evangelists who recorded the deeds of Christ, and the protonotaries of the Holy See who recorded those of the early church.[2]

A small group of notaries and secretaries extended their duty of recording the deeds of the kings of France beyond the routine tasks described by the ordinance, and compiled works on French history. This paper will consider the works of four fifteenth-century notaries and secretaries, Noël de Fribois, Nicole Gilles, Jacques Le Picart and Louis Le Blanc, who combined a career in royal service with historical writing. These men and their texts have been recognised as important evidence of the general, and more specifically historical, culture of this group of royal officials. However, no comparative study of the authors and their texts has been made, although they provide evidence of the attitudes of two successive generations of royal officials, whose careers spanned almost a century, to the history of

---

[1] My thanks are due to the trustees of the Susette Taylor Travelling Fellowship and the Susette Taylor Fund, Lady Margaret Hall, Oxford and to the British Academy for financial assistance during research for this paper.
[2] *Ordonnances des rois de France de la troisième race*, (Paris 1835, reprinted 1968), XIX, pp. 62–4. The four evangelists were considered to be patrons of the confraternity or college of notaries and secretaries. (P. Robin, *La compagnie des secrétaires du roi [1351–1791]* (Paris, 1933), pp.19–21.

the crown and dynasty which they served. This paper is intended to provide an introduction to the topic, by considering how and why these men composed their historical works, and to what extent their texts reflect the professional and cultural milieu in which they were produced.[3]

Although all the texts required the authors to investigate events which took place in the distant past, they varied in scope and length. Three authors compiled texts which began with the legendary Trojan origins of the French. Noël de Fribois, notary and secretary to Charles VII from at least 1425 until 1444, notary to the Council of the Gallican Church at Bourges in 1438, and royal counsellor from 1452 at the latest until 1459, composed an 'Abrégé des Chroniques de France', ending in 1383, also known from its opening words as 'C'est chose profitable'.[4] Nicole Gilles, notary and secretary in the royal chancellery from 1476 at the latest, and *clerc et contrôleur* in the royal *Trésor* from 1484 to his death in 1503, composed the *Annalles . . . des Gaulles . . .*.[5] Jacques Le Picart, notary and secre-

[3]   R.-H. Bautier, Introduction, in A. Lapeyre & R. Scheurer, *Les Notaires et Secrétaires du roi sous les règnes de Louis XI, Charles VIII et Louis XII* (Paris, 1978), I, pp.xxxvi–viii, and notices 295, 379, 408; B. Guenée, *Histoire et culture historique dans l'Occident médiéval* (Paris, 1980), pp. 322–3; N. Pons, 'Chancellerie et culture. Les chancelleries parisiennes sous les règnes de Charles VI et Charles VII', *Rapports présentés à la Commission Internationale de Diplomatique, XVIe Congrès International des Sciences Historiques* (Stuttgart, August 1985), forthcoming; the author kindly permitted me to consult her typescript. Both H. Michaud, *La Grande Chancellerie et les écritures royales au 16ème siècle* (Paris, 1967), p.182, and R.-H. Bautier, *op. cit.*, p.xxxvii, note that this ordinance made the notaries and secretaries responsible for composing the official chronicle of the reign: there is no explicit reference to this task, however, in the ordinance.
[4]   K. Daly, 'Histoire et politique à la fin de la Guerre de Cent Ans: "l'Abrégé des Chroniques" de Noël de Fribois', *La "France Anglaise" au Moyen Age (Actes du 111e Congrès National des Sociétés Savantes (Poitiers, 1986),* (Paris 1988), i, 91–101, For manuscripts, textual families and the 'Mirouer Historial Abregié de France' (1451), probably also by Fribois, see K. Daly, 'The "Miroir Historial Abrégé de France" and "C'est Chose Profitable": a Study of Two Fifteenth-Century French Historical Texts and their Context' (D. Phil. thesis, 2 vols, Oxford, 1983); and A. Labat, 'L'Abrégé des Chroniques de France de Noël de Fribois' (unpublished thesis, École des Chartes, 1953), which the author kindly allowed me to consult. Citations are taken from Vatican Library, Reg. ms. lat. 829.
[5]   B.N., Nouv. acq. fr. 1417 is an autograph manuscript containing a preliminary version of the *Annalles . . . des Gaulles . . .*. The beginning and end of the text are missing: fos 1–242v correspond to (Book) I, xxvii^v–II, xlv^v in the edition. I have consulted 'Les tres elegantes et copieuses Annalles des tres preux . . . et excellens moderateurs des belliqueuses Gaulles . . .' (Paris, 1538); the first known printed edition was published in 1525 (but see n. 49 below). The manuscript ends with an account of the battle of Roosebeke (1382). An editor's note in the printed edition indicates that Gilles's text ended with the reign of Louis XI; continuations were added to modernise the text.
   The text in the printed edition is much fuller than that in the manuscript. For these problems, see J. Riche, 'L'Historien Nicole Gilles, 14? –1503', (unpublished thesis, École des Chartes, 1930), pp.141–262; Lapeyre & Scheurer, *Notaires* I, notice 295.

tary from at least 1475 and clerk in the *Chambre des Comptes* from 1487 until 1505, adopted the same time span for his 'Chronique Abrégée' compiled in 1489.[6]

In contrast, Louis Le Blanc, who served as *greffier* in the *Chambre des Comptes* from 1467 until 1509, composed works which blended history and hagiography:[7] an account of the devotion of successive kings of France to St Denis, and the role of the saint as intercessor for the kingdom, composed for Charles VIII in 1495;[8] a short history exalting the deeds of kings of France, and the house of Orléans, for Louis XII in 1498;[9] and 'La sainte vie et les haultz faictz de Monseigneur saint Louis' between 1495 and 1509.[10]

It is probable that Louis Le Blanc also composed a short historical treatise, beginning 'Pour vraye congnoissance avoir', refuting English pretensions to the crown of France. The text was composed in November 1471; the author gave his name as Louis, shared Louis Le Blanc's personal devotion to Saint Louis, and displayed a knowledge of the royal archives, and particularly those of the *Chambre des Comptes*, which might be expected of the *greffier*. The treatise has therefore been included in the present paper as an example of the historical work of Le Blanc.[11]

Let us look first at the authors and their texts as the products of the professional milieu. Do the professional activities of these men explain their interest in history?

---

[6]   Lapeyre & Scheurer, *Notaires* I, notice 408; Troyes, Bibliothèque Municipale ms. 812, dated 1489, with his signature and a note on the first flyleaf that the text has been 'extraicte d'une cronique de France', probably the *Grandes Chroniques de France* (for example fos 1–20v, vols. I, pp.10–344 *passim*, II, pp. 30–9, 78–82). As Le Picart consulted other texts as well, and his personal comments and annotations bear comparison with those of Nicole Gilles, his abridged chronicle is considered here as an independent historical text.

[7]   Lapeyre & Scheurer, *Notaires* I, notice 379. M. François, 'Les Rois de France et les traditions de l'abbaye de Saint-Denis à la fin du xve siècle', *Mélanges Felix Grat*, (Paris, 1946) I, pp. 367–82.

[8]   François, 'Rois de France', pp. 368–72, 374, identified two versions of this text: B.N., ms. fr. 5868 (belonging to Charles VIII), and mss. fr. 5706 and 5870 (the latter manuscript was prepared for Louis XII). References will be given to ms. fr. 5870.

[9]   Citations from B.N., ms. fr. 5869, the date being given in the text, fo.xxvi; François, 'Rois de France', pp. 376–7.

Oxford, Bodleian Library, ms. Douce 92 (1509–10) contains chapters from this text, and from the chronicle of the kings of France and Saint-Denis mentioned above, n. 8, with a continuation to 1509. The manuscript was originally identified by R. Scheller, 'Ensigns of Authority: French Royal Symbolism: the Age of Louis XII', *Simiolus*, xiii (1983), 91, 115, fig. 21.

[10]   B.N., ms. fr. 5721; François, 'Rois de France', pp. 377–80.

[11]   B.N., mss. fr.15490, 25159, identified by P. S. Lewis, 'War Propaganda and Historiography in Fifteenth-Century France and England', *Transactions of the Royal Historical Society*, 5th series, xv (1965), 1–21 (11, n.1, 20, n.1). Citations are taken from ms. fr.15490, which contains references to documents and other details, such as the author's name, not found in ms. fr. 25159. For authorship and date, see fos 4v, 14v. For evidence of the author's devotion to St Louis in each text, see François, 'Rois de France', pp. 377–8; and compare

In general terms there is ample evidence of a tradition of historical knowledge among royal clerks. In the reign of Philip Augustus, lists of popes, emperors and kings of France were copied into registers of royal letters kept in the royal chancellery. In the fourteenth century, these were copied into the Memorials of the Chambre des Comptes. [12] In each case, they provided a guide for officials who needed to place the documents with which they were dealing in an historical context. In the early fifteenth century, a more elaborate chronicle, the Origo Regum Francie, was circulating among officials in the Chambre des Comptes. This was abridged from the universal chronicle of Géraud de Frachet, giving a short account of the reigns of the kings of France, but also included two references to documents in the Chambre. It enjoyed a certain vogue in the milieu until the early sixteenth century.[13]

Further indications of the need for chronicles are provided by the manuels of Jean Le Bègue, greffier in the Chambre des Comptes from 1407 to 1456, and that of his pupil and clerk, Pierre Amer, clerc in the Chambre from 1449 (d. 1484). These are principally of interest as a testimony to the authors' knowledge of the archives of the institutions in which they worked, but both supplemented these with ex-

ms. fr. 5721, fo.106, and ms. fr.15490, fo. 4v. 'Pour vraye congnoissance avoir', fos 4v, 9v, observes the same numbering for the kings of France named Louis as that noted by François for Le Blanc's other works.

The author also intended to compose another 'traicté' on Philip VI and his successors to the time of Louis XI (fo.13). None of Le Blanc's identified works fulfil this promise.

12 Recueil des Actes de Philippe Auguste, ed. H. F. Delaborde (Paris, 1916), I, pp. xxxiii–iv (register E). For the implications of the list see E. A. R. Brown, 'La Notion de légitimité et la prophétie à la cour de Philippe-Auguste', La France de Philippe-Auguste – le temps des mutations (C.N.R.S., Paris, 1982), pp. 77–111. The list appears in B.N., ms. lat.12814, fo. 8. C.-V. Langlois identified this manuscript as the Memorial 'Noster' in his introduction in J. Petit, Gavrilovitch, Maury and Téodoru, Essai de restitution des plus anciens mémoriaux de la Chambre des Comptes de Paris (Université de Paris, Bibliothèque de la Faculté des Lettres, vii, 1899), pp.ii, x–xii. See also A. M. de Boislisle, La Chambre des Comptes de Paris. Pièces justificatives pour servir à l'histoire des premiers Présidents (Nogent-le-Rotrou, 1873), pp. vii–xii, and Brown, op.cit., p. 83, n. 30. The earliest Memorials were copied by clerks in the Chambre for their own benefit, but quickly acquired an official character.

13 Boislisle, Chambre des Comptes, p. xiv, drew attention to this chronicle in the Advaluationes. Ten manuscripts of the Origo Regum Francie can be identified. The original version, represented by B.N., ms. lat. 6185, ended in 1383. In the earliest manuscript (ms. lat. 9848) later additions were made, to the time of Louis XI. See also ms. lat. 5932A, with additional notes on the regency of Henry V, and the duke of Bedford. Ms. lat. 5933 follows 5932A; ms. fr. 4924 follows 9848; ms. fr. 4429 and B. L. Harleian ms. 4362 continue to the reign of Louis XII; B.N., mss. lat. 5940, 2834, 9849 continue to the reign of Francis I. The author or compiler consulted the Memorials of the Chambre for the coronation expenses of Louis IX (actually Louis VIII) and the baptism of Charles VI (ms. lat. 6185, fos 26, 31).

B. Guenée, Histoire et culture historique, p. 323 and n. 73, identified the major source for this work as Frachet's chronicle; but the existence of B.N., ms. lat. 9848 indicates that the author could not have been Pierre Amer, as Guenée suggested. This manuscript belonged originally to Adam des Champs, notary at the Châtelet, and clerk in the Chambre des Comptes from 1427; it is possible that he may have been responsible for adding the Origo Regum tracts from chronicles.[14] Pierre Amer provided valuable information about the circulation of chronicles within this milieu, for he noted how, in 1451, he was shown an anonymous abridged chronicle by Master Jean Lescuier, *auditeur* in the *Chambre*, from which he copied extracts into his manual.[15]

What began as professional necessity may well have stimulated curiosity about history among these officials, and encouraged them to undertake further investigations. This is certainly the impression given by Nicole Gilles in the prologue to his *Annalles . . . des Gaulles . . .* He stated that his history evolved from the research which he undertook in his leisure hours, because he could not easily establish the order in which the kings of France had ruled. The fruit of his experience was carefully presented, complete with dates and lengths of reigns.[16] Jacques Le Picart's annotations in his 'Chronique Abrégée' reveal similar concerns. Where he found conflicting accounts, he corrected his text or at least noted alternatives. But in Le Picart's case, his history had a practical function, more intimately connected with his professional work. His marginal notanda drew attention to passages in the text which might be of practical use: for example, in February 1494 (n.s.) he marked passages referring to the kingdom of the two Sicilies with the comment that these could aid the king (Charles VIII) in pursuing his claims to these lands.[17]

With the possible exception of Fribois, whose career is insufficiently documented, these notaries and secretaries had ample opportunities to familiarise themselves with the archives of the institutions in which they worked. Louis Le Blanc seems to have made a personal collection of copies of documents, probably using the archives of the *Chambre*, and in 1482 he was also commissioned to compile an inventory of documents in the *Trésor des Chartes*. Jacques Le Picart compiled an inventory of documents in the *Chambre de France*, part of the *Chambre des Comptes*, in 1495.[18]

Francie to an *Advaluatio*, and may even have been its compiler; but I have not to date been able to corroborate this hypothesis.

[14] B.N., ms. lat.12815 (Jean Le Bègue); ms. fr.10988 (Pierre Amer); Boislisle, *Chambre des Comptes*, pp. xiv–xv, and, on the archives, pp. viii–xii, with H. Jassemin, *La Chambre des Comptes de Paris au xve siècle* (Paris, 1933), p. 300–08.
These manuals have been the subject of an unpublished paper by P. Contamine and F. Autrand, 'Fonctionnaires au travail. Les manuels de Jean Le Bègue, greffier et de Pierre Amer, correcteur à la Chambre des Comptes du roi, à Paris, au xve siècle', Groupe de recherche: Les Pouvoirs, xiie–xvie s. Lettre III (École Normale Supérieure, Paris, 1985) pp.17–28.
See also Daly, 'The "Miroir Historial" ', I, pp.182–3 on Amer's manual.
[15] B.N., ms. fr.10988, fo. 31.
[16] *Annalles . . . des Gaulles . . .*, I, i^r–v.
[17] Le Picart, Troyes, ms. 812, fos 134v–35.
[18] This is the implication of a comment by Étienne Le Blanc, 'Genealogie de Bourbon', B.N., ms. fr. 5719, fo. 7, who used a copy of a letter made by Louis, his father, for this text. For the 1482 inventory, see Dessalles, 'Le Trésor des Chartes: sa création, ses gardes et leurs travaux', *Mémoires présentés par divers savants à l'Académie des Inscriptions et Belles-Lettres*, I

This familiarity with documents seems to have been reflected to varying degrees in the texts.[19] It is especially prominent in 'Pour vraye congnoissance avoir', which is very heavily documented in proportion to its length, with many direct references to documents; on occasion, the author attempts to resolve chronological problems by comparing the evidence of different documents, and even uses epigraphical evidence.[20] The other texts attributed to Louis Le Blanc contain very few documents; however, he must have consulted one of the Memorials, or even the original manuscript of the *Enseignements de St Louis*, which he incorporated into his history of France written for Louis of Orléans.[21]

In view of the expertise of the authors, it seems unlikely that the discrepancy in their use of documents can be explained by reference to the 'grant desordre' of the royal archives, bemoaned by successive kings of France:[22] it must, in the final analysis, have depended on individual choice. As they were composing narrative history, Fribois, Gilles, Le Blanc and Le Picart required access, above all, to histories and chronicles of France. They were still able to draw on their professional expertise: chronicles could be cited as evidence to prove legal claims, be given the status of archival documents, and sometimes described in similar terms.[23]

The range of narrative sources also varies from one author to another. All the texts reflect the influence of the *Grandes Chroniques de France*, a fundamental

---

(1844), 439–42, and Delaborde, *Recueil*, pp. clxxiii–iv. For Le Picart, see Rouen, Bibliothèque Municipale, Collection Leber, tome XII, fos 90–96. The earliest document was dated 1160 (fo. 90v). None of these seems to have been used in his text.

[19] For examples which suggest that Gilles consulted documents, see I, cxxii[r], cxxiv[v], and n. 36 below. For Fribois, see Daly, 'The "Miroir Historial" ', I, p.115. Le Picart does not cite documents directly.

[20] The author gives references to the Memorials 'Noster', 'Croix', 'St-Just', 'Rouge' or 'Rubeus': 'A', 'B', 'C', and the fifth Book of Charters of the *Chambre des Comptes*; the *Journal du Trésor* and documents in the *Trésor des Chartes*; and epitaphs from the convent of the Jacobins and Cordeliers. On the Memorials, see Boislisle, *Chambre des Comptes*, pp. vii–xi; C.-V. Langlois in *Essai de Restitution*, pp. v–xix.

For an example of the author's method, see 'Pour vraye congnoissance avoir' (B.N., ms. fr.15490, fos 4v–5v), where he draws on various documents and chronicles to resolve the confusion in his sources on the date at which Louis IX began his reign.

In general, on the growth of the use of documents in historiography, see Guenée, *Histoire et culture historique*, p.100.

[21] B.N., mss. fr. 5869. fo.lii[v]; fr. 5721, fos 83–93v; François, 'Rois de France', p. 381, n.1.

[22] Delaborde, *Recueil*, pp. clxxiii–clxxxvi; Dessalles, 'Trésor', pp. 444–53.

[23] B. Guenée, *Histoire et culture historique*, p.100; and ' "Authentique et approuvé": recherches sur les principes de la critique historique au Moyen Age', *Actes du Colloque international sur la lexicographie du latin médiéval* (C.N.R.S., Paris, 1979), pp. 261–88; reprinted in B. Guenée, *Politique et histoire au Moyen age: recueil des études sur l'histoire politique et historiographie médiévales* (Paris, 1981), retaining original pagination of reprinted articles.

For the contemporary use of chronicles and documents as diplomatic evidence, see P. Contamine, 'The Contents of a French Diplomatic Bag in the Fifteenth Century: Louis XI, Regalian Rights and Breton Bishoprics', *Nottingham Medieval Studies*, xxv (1981), 52–72.

source for the history of the French crown, while Noël de Fribois and Nicole Gilles were more ambitious in their choice of historical material.[24]

What can we learn about the authors' attitude to the history of France from these historical works? The association of the notaries and secretaries with the prestige and interests of the French crown in the 1482 ordinance is also reflected in their texts.[25] They stress the special relationship between the kings of France and God, manifested in French history. Fribois, Gilles and Le Blanc celebrate the 'grace et prerogative, benediction . . . et autres tres grans dons espirituelz', bestowed on the kings and the kingdom of France, channelled through abstract symbols of royalty, such as the sceptre, royal arms and crown of France. The history of the kingdom, with its succession of saintly kings, shows why God has exalted 'sa maison en terre en la maison de France'. France has a unique vocation as defender of the Christian faith, 'singulier protecteur et deffenseur' of the church militant, home of a devout and valiant nobility, and a centre of Christian learning. Its kings are conquerors, crusaders and saints, patrons of churches, and extirpators of schisms in the church.[26]

This glorification of French history forms a striking contrast to the authors' attitude to enemies of the crown, and especially the English. These are depicted as an heretical and perfidious nation, and provokers of unjust wars against the French. Thus Le Blanc praises St Louis for maintaining one of the chief glories of France, when he prevents the scholars of the University of Paris from migrating to England at the invitation of Henry III:

> quelle esclipse eust esté de lescu de la tres chrestien et tres loyal maison
> de France se ladite université feust allé[e] en Angleterre, qui est lan-

---

[24] For the *Grandes Chroniques*, and their importance in French historiography, see G. M. Spiegel, *The Chronicle Tradition of Saint-Denis: a Survey* (Brookline: Leyden, 1978); for Fribois' sources, see Daly, 'The "Miroir Historial" ', I, pp.107–09; for Gilles, see Riche, 'Nichole Gilles', pp. 290–312, 331–4. The inventory made after the death of Gilles' wife in 1499 gives a partial impression of the range of his books (R. Doucet, *Les Bibliothèques parisiennes au seizième siècle* (Paris, 1956), pp. 83–9).

[25] 'Apres ce qu'il eust pleu à Dieu prendre et accepter les très glorieux Roys . . . la couronne et le royaume de France en si espéciale et particulière élection, que par les Saints Anges du ciel il envoya au glorieux Clovis, premier roy de France chrestien, la sainte onction . . . et les armes et enseignes que perpétuellement ils porteroient, et qu'il les a esleus en telle dignité que sur tous autres ils ont héréditairement le nom de tres Chrestien', *Ordonnances*, XIX, pp. 62–3. For these attributes, see C. Beaune, *Naissance de la Nation France* (Paris, 1985), chs 2, 7, 8.

[26] Citations from Fribois, Reg. ms. lat. 829, fo. 2v; Le Blanc, ms. fr. 5869, fo. iv^v; Gilles, *Annalles . . . des Gaulles . . .*, I, i^r.
For examples of these themes in Fribois' work, see Daly 'Histoire et politique', 93–5.
Le Blanc, mss. fr. 5870, 5869 are devoted to these issues. Note also the comment in the 'Vie de St Louis' (ms. fr. 5721, fo. xv) where Louis' acquisitions of relics are compared to Philip Augustus' territorial conquests.
Fribois (Reg. ms. lat. 829, fo. 2), and Gilles (*Annalles . . . des Gaulles . . .*, I, i^r) note that

cienne maison ennemye de la tres chrestienne et royal maison de France,
car ledict escu . . . eust esté esclipsé de son costé dextre qui signifie cler-
gie, id est sapience. . . . Ledit monsr. Sainct Loys n'eust pas fait les dignes
oeuvres quil fist en son temps s'il eust perdu le dextre coste departie de
son escu envoyé du ciel.

[How the arms of the very Christian and very loyal house of France
would have been eclipsed, had the University moved to England, which
is the hereditary enemy of the . . . house of France; for the right side of
the said coat of arms signifies the clergy, that is, wisdom. . . . Saint Louis
would not have done the worthy things which he did in his time, had he
lost the dexter side of his coat of arms sent from heaven.][27]

The authors' hostility is focused above all on the claims of Edward III and his
successors to the crown of France, and the need to justify the accession of Philip
VI de Valois and his descendants, including the kings of their own time. They
could draw on arguments which had been developed by royal apologists in the
course of the Hundred Years War.

The treatise against the English by Jean de Montreuil (d. 1418), who was also a
royal notary and secretary, inspired Noël de Fribois to include a justification, in
both Latin and French, of the exclusion of Edward III in his account of the reign
of Philip VI. Fribois, like Montreuil, made use of the Salic Law, interpreted to ex-
clude the descendants of women from the royal succession, and placed it in an historical context: it was promulgated by the first king of France, Pharamund, and
ratified by the first Christian king, Clovis, and by Charlemagne and Louis the
Pious. Fribois' treatment of the Salic Law and the Valois succession also included
new arguments, drawn from Baldus de Ubaldis, and reflected the elaboration of
traditional arguments which took place in the entourage of Charles VII in response to the English presence in France. In the 'Abrégé des Chroniques de
France', the historical narrative itself provided an implicit justification of Valois
legitimacy, while the more recent threat posed by the treaty of Troyes (1420),
which disinherited Charles in favour of Henry V and his heirs, was demolished by
a series of arguments probably derived from the *Oratio Historialis*, presented to
Charles VII in 1449 by Robert Blondel.[28]

the kings of France have healed twenty-three schisms in the church ; Le Blanc attributes
twenty-four to them (ms. fr. 5869, fo. iv). On this theme, see Beaune, *Naissance*, pp. 213–
14.
    These themes are less explicit in Le Picart, but see his comment (Troyes, ms. 812,
fo.105v), that the Church 'tousjours a esté remis sus . . . par les Franceys'.
[27] Fribois, Reg. ms. lat. 829, fos 31r–v, 53v–56v; 'Pour vraye congnoissance avoir' ms.
fr.15490, fo. 4r–v; Le Picart, Troyes, ms. 812, fos 115 (on King John), 120, 129r–v (on dis-
loyalty of the English); Le Blanc, ms. fr. 5721, fo.10r–v (citation).
[28] Reg. ms. lat. 829, fos 5v–6, 9v, 19v–20, 48–58v, 84v–86; Daly, 'The "Miroir Historial" ',
I, pp. 260–73; Jean de Montreuil, 'Traité contre les Anglais [étape III]', *Opera II: L'Oeuvre
historique et polémique*, ed. N. Grévy, E. Ornato, G. Ouy, (Turin, 1975), pp. 270, 272, 274–
5, 284–5, 288–9; Daly, 'The "Miroir Historial" ', I, pp.113–14, 262–73; N. Pons, 'Propa-

Nicole Gilles and Jacques Le Picart also commented on the Salic Law in their historical narratives, taking arguments from Fribois's 'Abrégé des Chroniques de France'. Gilles gave a justification of Philip VI's claim to the throne: and his use of extracts from the *Droiz de la couronne de France*, a translation of Blondel's treatise, gave much of his historical narrative an anti-English, polemical flavour.[29]

In his chronicle of the kings of France and St Denis, Le Blanc echoed the arguments for Valois legitimacy, when he noted that Philip VI's almsgiving 'monstre bien qu'il estoit des hoirs du glorieux roy monsr Saint Loys' ['shows well that he was one of the heirs of the glorious king, my lord saint Louis'].[30]

But fuller treatment was given to the issue in 'Pour vraye congnoissance avoir'. This was in effect an historical treatise devoted to proving that the English could not justly claim the crown and kingdom of France. The painstakingly constructed genealogy of St Louis and his descendants, to Philip VI, served as a prelude to, and historical justification of, the author's arguments against Edward III's claims inspired, again, by Jean de Montreuil.[31]

Although the sentiments expressed by these authors were not exclusive to the royal notaries and secretaries, there are important indications that this milieu fostered them, and that these authors were representative of attitudes held more generally by their colleagues. Jean de Montreuil's treatise against the English certainly circulated in the milieu: during the reign of Louis XI an abridgement of the Latin text was included in a chancellery formulary, with a genealogy of the kings of France and a list of royal prerogatives. Jean Budé, notary and secretary of Louis XI, owned a copy of 'Pource que plusieurs', a treatise refuting English claims in France, which was composed in 1464. The experience of notaries and secretaries in compiling memoranda and preparing diplomatic dossiers made these men particularly well equipped to contribute, in their turn, to a justification of the legitimacy of the ruling dynasty.[32]

---

gande et sentiment national pendant le règne de Charles VI: l'exemple de Jean de Montreuil', *Francia*, viii (1980), 127–45; Beaune, *Naissance*, pp. 267–90; Robert Blondel, *Oeuvres*, ed. A. Heron (Société de l'Histoire de Normandie, Rouen, 1891), I, pp. 273–5.

[29] Le Picart, Troyes, ms. 812, fo. 8: compare the 'Abrégé des Chroniques de France', Reg. ms. lat. 829, fos 5v–6v, 9v (this manuscript was used by Le Picart). Compare also Gilles, *Annalles . . . des Gaulles*, Nouv. acq. fr.1417, fos 170v–171 (II, iʳ), and the 'Abrégé des Chroniques de France', Reg. ms. lat. 829, fos 48–49; Gilles, Nouv. acq. fr.1417, fos 103v–104 (I, ciiʳ⁻ᵛ); and Blondel, *Oeuvres*, I, pp. 369–70.

[30] B.N., ms. fr. 5870, fo. xxxi.

[31] See B.N., ms. fr.15490: Prologue, fo. 4–4v; genealogy, fos 4v–13; justification, fos 13–14v.

[32] B.N., ms. fr.14371, fos 287v–88; Montreuil, 'Traité', pp. 224–6 (lines 90–148).

J. Budé, Vatican Library, Reg. ms. lat.1933 (1486).

E. Langlois, 'Notices des manuscrits français et provençaux de Rome antérieurs au xvie siècle', *Notices et extraits*, xxxiii.2 (1899), 243. Budé is not the author, as Langlois believed, since the treatise was composed in 1464.

See also the comments of Pons, 'Chancellerie et culture' on the patriotism of notaries and secretaries in the first half of the fifteenth century.

The Valois succession was not the only occasion on which the continuity and legitimacy of French kingship was brought into question. There had been two previous changes of dynasty, from the Merovingians to the Carolingians and then to the Capetians. Although their relationship seemed to pose few problems for Noël de Fribois, Nicole Gilles and Jacques Le Picart were more concerned to determine why the dynasties had changed. The deposition of the last Merovingian, Childeric III, by Pipin 'qui n'estoit heritier de la couronne de France mais vassal et serviteur' ['who was not heir to the crown of France, only a vassal and servant'] baffled Nicole Gilles, who concluded that Pipin must have acted at divine instigation because 'il ne povoit veoir la ruyne de la tres noble monarchie de France dont il estoit l'ung des princes et pilliers laquelle il veoit aneantir par la negligence' ['he could not watch the downfall of the most noble monarchy of France, of which he was one of the princes and pillars, which he saw being brought about by the negligence . . .'] of the last Merovingian. The accession of Louis III and Carloman, brothers of Charles the Simple, caused difficulties for Jacques Le Picart. He concluded that they must have reigned during the minority of their brother Charles the Simple, and they must have been regents, not kings,

> puisqu'il y avoit heritier legitime et s'ils ont regné ce a esté par force et contre raison ainsi que par la loy et ordonnance des roys et royaume de France peult estre congneu, et n'est point depuis trouvé que bastard ne s'est nommée (roy) en France ne qu'il ait regné, n'y aussi fille.
>
> [because there was a legitimate heir and if they ruled, it was by might and unlawfully, as the law and ordinance of the king and kingdom of France reveal; since when no bastard has reigned as king of France: neither has a woman.][33]

The end of the Carolingian dynasty and the accession of Hugh Capet in 987 caused Le Picart even greater problems. He found it difficult to excuse the rejection of Charles of Lotharingia by the French: 'en ce temps ne furent pas Francoys loyaulx . . . car ledit Charles estoit leur seigneur et roy. Ilz oublierent leur loyalté' ['at that time the French were disloyal . . . for the said Charles was their lord and king; and they forgot their loyalty (to him)'].[34]

The problem of loyalty to the crown, particularly among the nobility, was commented on by Fribois and Gilles. Fribois embellished his account of the punishment of Bernard, king of Italy, by Louis the Pious, with an admonition to the princes of his own day: 'Cy doivent prandre exemple les seigneurs du sang des roys et par especial ceulx de la tres noble maison de France qui ont pour chief roy singulierement honnoré de ce tres noble mot tres chrestien' ['The lords of the blood of kings, and in particular those of the very noble house of France who have as their head a king specially honoured with the very noble title of "Most Christian",

---

33 *Annalles . . . des Gaulles . . .*, I, xlii[r] (only); Le Picart, Troyes, ms. 812, fo. 63.
34 Le Picart, Troyes, ms. 812, fo. 72v.

must take this as a moral']. Fribois may well have had in mind the threats posed by noble leagues to royal power, and most recently, the hostility between Charles VII and his son Louis, then in exile in the court of Burgundy. But Gilles felt it to be equally applicable at the end of the century, for he discouraged potentially rebellious subjects with the warning 'Car on a tres souvent veu que à tous ceulx qui ont fait aucunes machinations et entreprinses contre les roys et la couronne de France qu'il leur est mescheu et mal prins de leur besongnes'. ['For it has often been shown that ill has befallen all who have plotted against or attacked the kings and crown of France.']³⁵

The supremacy of the king of France over his greater vassals was further emphasised by reference in the 'Abrégé des Chroniques de France' and the Annalles . . . . des Gaulles . . . to the origins of some of the great fiefs. For Noël de Fribois, the origin of the county of Flanders was illegitimate. Nicole Gilles emphasised that both Flanders and Normandy were integral parts of France: the 'foy hommage et souveraineté' of Flanders could not be alienated from the crown, while all the authors stressed the subjection of Brittany.³⁶

The power of the French king was further celebrated by references to his imperial status. These invoked the traditional claim that the king and kingdom of France were exempt from the empire, but were also used by Fribois to emphasise royal power over all the inhabitants of the kingdom, and by Le Picart to stress French exemption from unjust tributes. Gilles' allusions seemed designed to exalt

---

³⁵ Fribois, Reg. ms. lat. 829, fo. 21; Gilles, Nouv. acq. fr.1417, fo. 56 (as a marginal note); Annalles . . . des Gaulles . . . I, lix^{r-v}.

³⁶ Fribois, Reg. ms. lat. 829, fo. 22r–v; his attitude to Normandy is more favourable, perhaps reflecting his Norman origins, or the conciliatory policy of the king. See Daly, 'Histoire et politique', 97. Contrast Gilles, Annalles . . . des Gaulles . . ., I, lxix^{r-v}, 'appert que tous les successeurs du Rou [Rollo] ont possedé le pays à mauvais titre'. This passage is not in the manuscript.

Gilles, I, lxv^v emphasises that Charlemagne has reserved 'la foy hommage et souveraineté en sa court souveraine' (not in Nouv, acq. fr.1417, fo. 64v); he also notes treaties between the king of France and the Flemings, for example I, cxxx^{r-v} (not in Nouv. acq. fr.1417, fo.156v), and their treachery to 'leur roy souverain et naturel seigneur' II, vi^r. The implications of the term 'naturel' are discussed by J. Krynen, 'Naturel: essai sur l'argument de la nature dans la pensée politique française à la fin du moyen âge', Journal des Savants, (1982), 169–90.

See also Louis Le Blanc's references to wars with the Flemings (for example, ms. fr. 5870, fos xxx^v, xxxv^v–xxxvi, xlii, xliv–lii^v); also Le Picart, Troyes, ms. 812, fo.111v, who stresses the legitimacy of Philip Augustus' invasion of Flanders, 'par conseil'.

On Brittany, see Fribois, Reg. ms. lat. 829, fo. 24r; Gilles, I, xxxiiii^r–lxiii^v, passim; Le Picart, Troyes, ms. 812, fos 25, 55, 59r–v, 67v and marginal notes in the 'Abrégé des Chroniques de France', Reg. ms. lat. 829, fos 1, 13v. For these, see Daly, 'The "Miroir Historial" ', I, p. 36; II, plates 19a, b.

Le Blanc, ms. fr. 5721, fos 7v, 8v. See P. Jeulin, 'L'Hommage de la Bretagne en droit et dans les faits', Annales de Bretagne, xli (1934), 380–473.

the prestige of the French language and French victories, at the expense of Roman and medieval emperors.[37]

In addition both Gilles and Fribois emphasised the king's power over, and duties towards, the Gallican church. Gilles, in particular, stressed the occasions on which kings of France had legislated for the French church, citing the example of St Louis, to whom he attributed a document which was in fact a forgery, which he believed to be the forerunner of the Pragmatic Sanction issued by Charles VII in 1438. He emphasised how both the False Pragmatic of St Louis and Charles VII's Pragmatic Sanction were 'juste, saincte et canonique' and should be observed for 'le grant prouffit et utilité de l'eglise gallicane'.[38]

The authors were not indifferent to the faults of earlier French kings. In keeping with the didactic function of history, the texts emphasised good examples, to be emulated, and evil deeds, to be eschewed. They criticised kings who failed to live up to their glorious ancestry and fulfil the exalted mission to which they had been called, by following bad counsel, leading dissolute lives or imposing unjustified taxes on their people.[39] Nevertheless, the general impression given by the

[37] The authors note the exemption of the king of France from the empire and the imperial quality of the king's power: Fribois, Reg. ms. lat. 829, fos 48v, 64v; Le Picart, Troyes, ms. 812, fos 109v–110v, 138v, 141r–v, and the 'Abrégé des Chroniques de France', Reg. ms. lat. 829, annotations, fo.19v; Daly, 'The "Miroir Historial" ', I, p. 36; II, plate 19c.

G. Post, 'Two Notes on Nationalism in the Middle Ages: II, Rex Imperator', *Traditio* ix (1953), 296–320.

A. Bossuat, 'La Formule, "Le roi est empereur en son royaume", son emploi au xve siècle devant le Parlement de Paris', *Revue historique de droit français et étranger*, 4e série, xxxix (1961), 371–81.

Gilles, *Annalles . . . des Gaulles . . .*, I, i[r] on French kings: 'Si leurs faictz et gestes eussent esté mis par escript et par langage eloquent, ainsi que ont esté les faictz des Rommains et autres, on trouveroit que leur vertu, vaillance et proesse precederoit et surmonteroit les faictz desditz Rommains, qui plus ont faictz de langue que d'espée'. See also iii[r], xvi[r] on French prowess; Nouv. acq. fr.1417, fo. 68, (with interlinear additions), lxviii[v] on imperial decline.

[38] Fribois, Reg. ms. lat. 829, fos 40 (defence of the church and its liberties); 68v (royal right to levy régales); 70v–73v (elections to bishoprics). Fribois does not mention the Pragmatic Sanction, in spite of his office of notary to the Council of Bourges. See N. Valois, *Histoire de la Pragmatique Sanction de Bourges sous Charles VII* (Paris, 1906), pp.lxxviii–xc.

Gilles, Nouv. acq. fr.1417, fo.134 I, cxvii[r] (St Louis); II, xcv[r–v] (Charles VII). See Valois, *Pragmatique*, pp. clix–clxxiv for the False Pragmatic Sanction of St Louis.

[39] Le Picart's comments in his 'Chronique Abrégée', Troyes, ms. 812, fo. 51v, and annotations in the 'Abrégé des Chroniques', Reg. ms. lat. 829, fo.19v, imply a critical attitude to taxation: it is linked with tribute, subjection, and bad counsel, while he praises Louis the Pious for suppressing 'treux et subsides', 'Chronique Abrégé', Troyes, ms. 812, fo. 54. Compare Gilles, *Annalles . . . des Gaulles . . .*, I, xxiv[v], lviii[v] for similar sentiments.

Le Blanc's allegation that Louis IX's ransom was raised miraculously, without burdening his subjects, may reflect hostility even among royal servants to the burden of royal taxation, and his desire to show that his patron saint was not responsible for increasing it.

See also Beaune, *Naissance*, pp.146–9, for St Louis' association with freedom from taxation, as an implied criticism of the exactions of his successors.

texts was favourable to royal power, prestige and mystique. They provided a moral and historical justification for the ecclesiastical and secular privileges of the French crown, which the authors and their colleagues were called upon to defend in the course of their careers.[40] Their historical works therefore represented an extension of their professional activities: they were, in the words of Bernard Guenée, 'by-products of bureaucracy'. In this respect, these notaries and secretaries resembled officials in the chancelleries and entourages of other late medieval rulers.[41]

For whom were the texts composed, and for what purpose? Were they commissioned by the king to promote his image and power? The extent of royal intervention is difficult to assess. It is not always clear whether a work was commissioned by the king, or composed by the author on his own initiative and subsequently presented to the king, who approved the work and then rewarded the author. Although we have no direct evidence that any of the works discussed here were direct royal commissions, Fribois certainly benefited from royal patronage. After resigning his office as notary and secretary in 1444, he may well have devoted himself to investigating the history of France. He was rewarded for the 'Abrégé des Chroniques de France', which he presented to Charles VII in June 1459, received a further payment for work 'touchant le fait des chroniques de France' in the same year, and may even have received a pension specifically for his historical work. Charles VII may have considered that he needed a supplement to the official history of his reign, composed by Jean Chartier, chanter and monk of Saint-Denis, just as Louis XI was subsequently to appoint a royal 'istoriografe', Guillaume Danicot, who was commissioned to collect all the legends and historical facts concerning the kingdom of France, 'et icelles mectre par livres especiaulx'. There is, unfortunately, no evidence that Fribois held such an office; but it seems highly

---

[40] On royal privileges, see Beaune, Naissance, pp. 226–9. Some aspects of these texts recall the lists of privileges mentioned by Beaune; François noted the analogy between Louis Le Blanc's texts and the Memorials ('Rois de France', p. 382).

[41] In general, see Guenée, Histoire et culture historique, pp. 65–9. For historical works composed by seigneurial officials, see K. Daly, 'Some Seigneurial Archives and Chronicles in Fifteenth-Century France', Peritia, ii (1983), 59–73; J. Kerhervé, 'Aux Origines d'un sentiment national: les chroniqueurs bretons de la fin du Moyen Age', Bulletin de la Société archéologique du Finistère, cviii (1980), 165–206. Much has been written on the important contribution of Italian secretaries, particularly on the Florentine Leonardo Bruni: but for a valuable methodological approach, see G. Ianziti, 'Patronage and the Production of History: the case of Quattrocento Milan', Patronage, Art and Society in Renaissance Italy, ed. F. W. Kent and P. Simons (Oxford: Canberra, 1987), pp. 299–311. At present, less is known about the role of contemporary English officials, particularly chancellery clerks, in the promotion of culture generally, and history in particular; but see T. F. Tout, 'Literature and Learning in the English Civil Service in the Fourteenth Century', Speculum, iv (1929), 365–89; A. Gransden, Historical Writing in England ii (London, 1982), pp.160 and notes, 261–5; The Crowland Chronicle Continuations, 1459–1486, ed. N. Pronay and J. Cox (London, 1986), pp. 78–98.

likely that the 'Abrégé des Chroniques de France' was composed in response to royal command, for it is addressed directly to the king.[42]

Le Blanc also received royal patronage. His historical work was taken into account by Charles VIII in 1496 when he awarded the *greffier* 1000 *livres tournois* for his 'bons et agreables services' to the king and his father; and his 'grant soin, cure et diligence ... à congnoistre et entendre à nous les droitz et appartenans de nostre couronne pour ... nous aider à la protection et garde diceulx, et aussi les haulx faiz dignes de memoire de nos progeniteurs pour nous en advertir et les ensuiyvir' ['good and agreeable services ... great care and diligence ... in declaring and making known to us the rights and possessions of our crown, to help us in protecting these; and also the high and memorable deeds of our ancestors so that we may be aware of them and imitate them'], as well as to raise his eleven children![43] Unfortunately, we do not know which of his works were written in response to royal command. In his *Annalles . . . des Gaulles . . .*, Nicole Gilles emphasised the value to the king of the lessons of history. However, there was no direct allusion to royal patronage; and although he received a pension, there is no evidence to connect this directly with his historical writing.[44] Le Picart's text, as we have noted, seems to have been composed for his own use.

Whether or not a king commissioned them, the texts provided a means for the authors to express ideas on royal power and its exercise, to educate both the king and his subjects. In the case of 'Pour vraye congnoissance avoir', these were 'simple gens ayans nobles courages, ... qui ont vouloir de garder et defendre la noble couronne de France, affin de y encliner tousjours leurs cueurs et courages' ['simple people with noble courage, who wish to protect and defend the noble crown of France, to direct their hearts and courage always [to this end]']. The author thus intended to influence a wider public, although the small number of surviving manuscripts of the text may indicate that he failed to achieve his aim. Fribois' 'Abrégé des Chroniques de France' enjoyed a wider circulation and a more varied public; twenty-two manuscripts containing a fragment, or the complete text, have been identified to date. Gilles' text was even more successful, and was reprinted many times in the sixteenth and early seventeenth century. The influence of these texts thus merges with that of the mass of chronicles, political

---

[42] A.N., KK 51, fo. 97; B.N., ms. fr. 32511. fo. 210v; Daly, 'The "Miroir Historial" ', I, pp.167–8, 189–93; C. Samaran, *La Chronique latine inédite de Jean Chartier* (Paris, 1928), pp. 87–8; J. Lesellier, 'Un Historiographe de Louis XI demeuré inconnu: Guillaume Danicot', *Mélanges d'archéologie et d'histoire de l'École Française de Rome*, xliii (1926), 1–42; C. Samaran, 'Un Ouvrage de Guillaume Danicot, Historiographe de Louis XI', *Ibid.*, xlv (1928), 8–20.

[43] B.N., Pièces originales 361, dossier 7820, pièce 2; Lapeyre & Scheurer, *Notaires* I, notice 379.

[44] Lapeyre & Scheurer, *Notaires* I, notice 295, p.150. The edition of 1525 describes Gilles as 'historiographe et indiciaire du roi' but, as there is no corroborating evidence, it is probable, as Riche concludes ('Nicole Gilles', p. 37), that this was added by the printer, to increase the authority, and attraction to readers, of the *Annalles . . . des Gaulles . . .*

treatises and other works, many anonymous, which both reflected and helped to shape royal ideology in later medieval France.[45]

However, it seems probable that most of the texts were intended for a more restricted public: the royal court. G. Ianziti recently noted the role of Milanese chancellery officials in providing materials for, and eventually composing, history favourable to the Sforza dukes, to promote solidarity within the princes' clientele. Noël de Fribois evidently hoped that princes of the blood would heed his warnings against rebellion, a tone that was also adopted by Nicole Gilles. Historical writing enabled the authors to promote favoured causes among the politically powerful: and at a more basic level it served to remind the latter of the prestige of the crown to which they owed obedience and which could, in turn, reflect glory on them.[46]

This applied particularly to the authors' own milieu. Noël de Fribois's 'Abrégé des Chroniques de France' found favour with other notaries and secretaries. Jean Le Bègue, the *greffier* in the *Chambre des Comptes*, acquired an early version of the text before his death in 1457; as it predates the version presented to Charles VII in 1459, it is possible that Fribois circulated his work among friends and colleagues before presenting it to the king. Étienne Chevalier, notary and secretary, then *trésorier* to Charles VII and Louis XI, owned a manuscript of the completed text.[47] In the following generation, Le Picart's annotations in one of the best manuscripts of the 'Abrégé des Chroniques de France', and the use to which both he and Gilles put the text in their own historical writings, were to indicate how solidarity could be encouraged in the milieu, and useful arguments could be propagated among men who would have practical use for them.[48] Nicole Gilles himself may have envisaged that the *Annalles . . . des Gaulles . . .* would circulate among royal officials: he urged the 'juges de France' and 'les presidens, conseillers, advocatz,

---

[45] B.N., ms. fr.15490, fo. 4v. A list of manuscripts of the 'Abrégé des Chroniques de France' is given by P. S. Lewis, 'War Propaganda', p.10, n. 5. I have added the following manuscripts: Paris, Bibliothèque Ste. Geneviève, ms. 3034 (fragment) and OE.xv.s. 490; Wolfenbüttel, Herzog August Bibliothek, ms. Cod. Guelf. Helmstadt 1051; Stockholm, Kungliga Biblioteket, ms. D.1281; Baltimore , Walters Art Gallery, ms. Walters 306 (fragment). For details, see Daly, 'The "Miroir Historial" ', I, pp.19–28, 295–336; see Paris, Institut de Recherche et d'Histoire des Textes, Section Romane, for Cracow, Bibl. Jagiellonska, ms. gall. 8° 1 (fragment).

Riche, 'Nicole Gilles', p. 316–18, and P. S. Lewis,'The Making of Political Mentalities in Later Medieval France' (unpublished paper presented to the Colloque Historique Franco-Britannique: Communications et représentations collectives, Lyon, 1974), which the author allowed me to read, provided many useful ideas. See also P. S. Lewis, 'War propaganda', *passim*; and N. Grévy-Pons, 'La Propagande de guerre avant l'apparition de Jeanne d'Arc', *Journal des Savants* (1982), 191–214, especially p. 214, which indicate that royalist literature was not restricted either to the chancellery or to the immediate royal entourage.

[46] Ianziti, 'Patronage and Production', pp. 302–11.

[47] B.N., ms. fr.13569; B.L., Additional ms.13961, on fo. 2 of which Chevalier's initials (EE) appear in the illuminated initial. Claude Schaefer kindly confirmed my identification of this manuscript.

[48] Vatican Library, Reg. ms. lat. 829.

procureurs et autres officiers tant de la court de Parlement que dailleurs' to enforce the Pragmatic Sanction and restrictions on usury.[49]

The debt of Fribois to Montreuil, and of Le Picart and Gilles to Fribois indicates a certain similarity in the attitudes, ideas and cultural interests of royal notaries and secretaries between the early fifteenth and sixteenth centuries. It seems appropriate therefore to conclude with the next generation of notaries and secretaries: and Louis Le Blanc's son, Étienne, who epitomises aspects of both continuity and change in the milieu and its culture during the fifteenth and early sixteenth centuries. Successor to his father in his offices of notary and secretary and *greffier* in the *Chambre des Comptes*, and third generation in his family in royal service, Étienne symbolises the growing stability and increasingly hereditary nature of the office of royal notary and secretary, officially recognised by the ordinance of 1482, which allowed members to resign in favour of their sons or relatives. The Le Blanc family also reflects the nexus of relationships in the milieu of the college; Étienne's maternal uncle was a *conseiller* in the *Parlement* of Paris. His paternal uncle had also been a notary and secretary, and *greffier*, while he himself married the daughter of Dreux II Budé, *trésorier* and *garde des chartes* and member of a powerful family in royal service for five generations. His marriage also linked him with new cultural trends, for his wife's uncle was the humanist, Guillaume Budé, while Étienne himself translated four discourses of Cicero.

As *greffier*, Étienne completed the inventory of the *Trésor des chartes* which his father had begun. His experience in the royal archives was put to further use when he prepared collections of copies of treaties for Louis XII. He composed a discourse on the marriage of Isabella, daughter of Charles VI, to Richard II of England in 1395, in celebration both of the marriage between Mary Tudor and Louis XII in 1514 and of the king's Orléanist ancestry.[50] He also composed a genealogy of the

---

[49] *Annalles . . . des Gaulles . . .*, I, cxvii', II, c', I, cvi'. Gilles' brother-in-law, Robert Turquan, was a *Conseiller* in the *Parlement* of Paris, and it is possible that Gilles' work originally circulated in this milieu. J. Riche suggested that it was printed only after the death of Turquan in 1523. However, R. Scheurer's study of the connection between Gilles and Antoine Vérard, the Parisian printer, indicates that we cannot rule out the possibility of an earlier printed edition of the text, now lost ('Nicole Gilles et Antoine Vérard', *B.E.C.*, cxxviii (1970), 415–19).

[50] For the college of notaries and secretaries during the late fifteenth and sixteenth century, see R.-H. Bautier, H. Michaud, n. 3 above. These paragraphs on Étienne, his family and his writings are based on L. Delisle, 'Traductions d'auteurs grecs et latins offertes à François Ier et Anne de Montmorency par Étienne Leblanc et Antoine Macault', *Journal des Savants*, (1900), 476–92; L. Mirot, 'Notes sur Étienne Le Blanc et ses compilations historiques', *Bulletin de la Société de l'Histoire de Paris et de l'Ile de France*, xxxvi (1909), 38–45. For the Budé family, see Lapeyre & Scheurer, *Notaires* I, notices 116–19; II, pl. xxv. For the cultural interests of members of the Budé family other than Guillaume, see G. Ouy, 'Histoire "visible" et histoire "cachée" d'un manuscrit', *Le Moyen Age*, lxiv (1958), 115–38; M.-C. Garand, 'Les copistes de Jean Budé (1430–1502)', *Bulletin de l'Institut de Recherches et d'Histoire des Textes*, 15 (1967–68), 293–332.

dukes of Bourbon, and the 'Gestes de Blanche de Castille', both dedicated to Louise of Savoy, Francis I's mother. These works indicate the continuity not only within a professional and cultural milieu, but also within the same family: in a passage in praise of women, intended to flatter Louise, Étienne himself noted how he had been counselled on their role in history by his father, Louis,

> qui savoit tant par experience que pour avoir leu l'espace de cinquante ans en grant partie des faictes et gestes des haulz hommes qui ont esté par cy devant.

> [who knew of this as much through his own experience as from his reading, over the best part of fifty years, about the deeds of great men of the past.][51]

Étienne provides us with a well-documented case. In our present state of knowledge, we have few comparable indications of continuity in the culture of the notaries and secretaries, from one generation to the next, in a milieu or a family, for history as for humanism. Family relationships and friendships could do much to explain the transmission of ideas between individuals and milieux. It is, after all, a short step from Étienne Le Blanc to his contemporary Jean du Tillet who, though he seems to signal a new departure in national historiography linked to the *Parlement* of Paris, was the son of a notary and secretary, and held that office himself as *greffier* of the *Parlement*. We still have much to learn about the causes of change in historical mentalities; directing our attention to continuities as well may help us to understand them better.[52]

---

[51] 'Genealogie de Bourbon', B.N., ms. fr. 5719. The text was prepared in defence of Louise's claim to the duchy. The author states that he composed it in a month, after consulting documents in the *Chambre des Comptes*, the *Trésor des Chartes* and 'anciennes histoires de France'. It includes paraphrases of the most important documents, including wills, ratifications and marriages, up to Louis XII's accession in 1498. It concludes with a section which justifies the good reputation of St Louis.

'Gestes de Blanche de Castille', B.N., ms. fr. 5715, fo. 7. Although the references to St Louis in both works were clearly intended to flatter Louise, Étienne seems also to have been inspired by his father's interest in St Louis; he plagiarises his 'Vie . . . de St Louis' (B.N., ms. fr. 5721, fo. 4v; fr. 5715, fo. 2v); he also borrowed from the chronicle in honour of Louis XII (B.N., mss. fr. 5869, fo. xli[v]; fr. 5715, fo. 3v).

[52] For a stimulating discussion of these problems and of the evidence for elements of continuity within the milieu in the earlier part of the period, see Pons, 'Chancellerie et culture'. Her study underlines our dependence on the survival of a few examples of the writings of, or books owned by, notaries and secretaries. The need to investigate continuity between the cultural movements, particularly humanism, in Paris in the late fourteenth and fifteenth century, and that of the late fifteenth and early sixteenth century, was emphasised by G. Ouy in his study of Jean Le Bègue, 'Le Songe et les ambitions d'un jeune humaniste parisien vers 1395', *Miscellanea di Studi e Ricerche sul Quattrocento Francese*, ed. F. Simone (Turin, 1967), pp. 355–407, especially pp. 357–65. For Jean du Tillet, see D. R. Kelley, 'Jean du Tillet, Archivist and Antiquary', *Journal of Modern History*, xxxviii (1966), 337–54.

Rouen and the Golden Age:
the Entry of Francis I, 2 August 1517

PENNY RICHARDS

The Golden Age was one of the most popular subjects for court ceremonials in Renaissance Europe.[1] It was a wonderfully flexible and adaptable theme suitable for most royal and civic occasions. It could be used to stress wholesome simplicity or imperial grandeur; healthy toil or aristocratic ease. It was suitable for royal marriages, births and coronations, and, with great frequency, it provided a vehicle for those expressions of felicity and optimism appropriate to the ceremonial Entry of royal personages into a city. In 1517 the wealthy port city of Rouen, a *ville Parlementaire* and a centre of considerable regional importance, welcomed the young king of France, Francis I, on his first visit as king to the city. The seven tableaux, or spectacles, presented to Francis as he processed from the city gate to the cathedral used Golden Age motifs and images to praise the king. More specifically, the Entry tableaux associated the king with the marvellous boy referred to in Virgil's fourth *Eclogue* whose coming would usher in the new Golden Age. The lines in which Virgil foresees the return of Astrea (Justice) and the birth of a child had long since acquired Christian and imperial connotations,[2] and it was not unusual to associate these lines and events with kings, especially recently crowned kings.

However, the imperial implications went further than simply complimenting Francis on his accession to the throne. At this point in his reign Francis was actively and successfully engaged in expanding French territory and asserting French

[1] See, for example, Elizabeth Armstrong's discussion of the numerous applications of Golden Age mythology in court ceremonials and celebrations (*Ronsard and the Age of Gold* (Cambridge, 1968), pp.1–9; Frances Yates' magisterial study of the imperial theme in *Astrea: The Imperial Theme in the Sixteenth Century* (Harmondsworth, 1977); H. Levin, *The Myth of the Golden Age* (London, 1970), pp.112–38; and E. H. Gombrich, 'Renaissance and Golden Age', *Norm and Form: Studies in the Art of the Renaissance* (London, 1966), pp. 29–34. A. B. Giamatti, *The Earthly Paradise of the Renaissance Epic* (Princeton, 1966), confirms the importance of the Golden Age/Paradise garden for the Renaissance imagination.

[2] See H. H. Erskine Hill, *The Augustan Idea in English Literature* (London, 1983), for a discussion of the early Roman imperial applications of Virgil's *Eclogue*; Yates, *Astrea*, should also be consulted.

prestige. His victory at Marignano in 1515 had re-established French control of the duchy of Milan and reversed the humiliating defeat suffered at Novara in 1513. In support of his Italian territories Francis was cultivating papal approval, and his visit to Rouen should probably be associated with his drive to register the Concordat of 1516 between France and the Papacy.[3] The Holy Roman Emperor, Maximillian, was ageing and, like other European rulers (Henry VIII and the ultimately successful Archduke Charles of Burgundy), Francis had hopes of succeeding him. Francis must have been attracted by the power and glory of the position; but geo-political concerns were also highly important. The election of the Archduke Charles would threaten French possessions in Italy; Francis wrote frankly that

> the reason which moves me to gain the empire . . . is to prevent the said Catholic king from doing so. If he were to succeed, seeing the extent of his kingdoms and lordships, this could do me immeasurable harm; he would always be mistrustful and suspicious, and would doubtless throw me out of Italy.[4]

The Entry ceremonials at Rouen should be seen against this expansionist background and in terms of the optimism and confidence of the early years of Francis' reign when all things, from universal peace to a Valois replacing a Habsburg, seemed possible.

These political considerations and aspirations inform the Rouen Entry ceremonials which, happily, can be reconstructed from contemporary sources. These printed accounts of the Entry, hereafter referred to as *L'Entrée*, were edited in the nineteenth century by the Rouennais historian, Charles de Beaurepaire, and enable us to follow the entire progress.[5]

The 'moult grand triumphe'[6] began with a procession of the city dignitaries to

---

3   Rouen was one of the six *villes parlementaires*, and sovereign in its own area with respect to registering royal enactments; hence its support was needed to ratify the 1516 concordat between Francis I and the Papacy (J. Thomas, *Le Concordat de 1516: ses origines, son histoire au XVIe siècle* (3 vols., Paris, 1910), II, pp. 235–9. Professor R. J. Knecht (*Francis I* (Cambridge, 1982), p. 54) argues that papal support for French claims in Italy was the king's prime motive for seeking the concordat. From March 1517 he had had a series of meetings with delegates from Rouen and other cities to pave the way to ratification (R. J. Knecht, *Francis I and Absolute Monarchy* (London, 1969), p.17). This was also motivated by his need for a vote of money from the Norman estates and a desire to survey the fortifications of Normandy.

4   Knecht, *Francis I*, p. 72.

5   *L'Entrée de François Ier dans la ville de Rouen au mois d'août 1517*, ed. C. de Beaurepaire (Rouen, 1867). The edition is a compilation from two contemporary printed sources. Since neither the sources nor the compilation bears any pagination, I use my own numbering system, page 1 being the first page of Beaurepaire's edition of the entry into Rouen, hereafter referred to as *L'Entrée*. It may be noted that this edition includes a brief series of extracts from the city registers.

6   The phrase is used by the Bourgeois de Paris who notes that 'audict an mil cinq cens dix

greet the king at Sainte-Catherine-de-Grandmont, the traditional lodgings for an entering monarch. The city councillors were attended by the town's fifty *arbalesteriez* wearing gold and satin liveries decorated with the city's emblem, a lamb. The first tableau, presented at a bridge on the edge of the city, articulated the controlling themes of expansion and virtuous rule. A lamb under a gilded *fleur-de-lis* indicated the loyalty of the city to the realm of France. The lily opened as the king approached and revealed three lovely girls, richly dressed in the king's colours and in German, Italian and Milanese costumes, a tribute to the king's recent victories and an indication of the actual and projected extent of Francis's rule. The girls held attributes which identified them as three virtues: Hope, Temperance, and Perseverance. Perseverance is not usually one of the seven virtues; Hope is a theological virtue and Temperance is a cardinal virtue. This combination might suggest a carelessness over the order and nature of the virtues, but *L'Entrée* offered a careful description of the spectacle which indicated that the choice was not random. Hope, it stated, had the highest place in the tableau and was to be understood in two ways:

> que le roy represente par ceste fleur la à son esperance en dieu au moyen de quoy il a obtins ses triumphantes victoires mesmes aussi pour denoter quel est lesperance du peuple.
>
> [that the king represents through this flower his hope in God by whom he has obtained his triumphal victories and also to denote the hope of the people][7]

Temperance represented a quality necessary to all good rulers, while Perseverance gave 'la couronne de gloire à celz qui ont continué et perseveré aux autres vertues.' ['the crown of glory to those who continue and persevere with the other virtues'.][8] The king was being greeted and characterised as a mediator between God and the people. He was also being reminded, as he was to be again in the last tableau, that victories came from God, and, perhaps, he was also being cautioned that victories alone were not enough. Temperance could be seen as a warning against rash endeavours and Perseverance, a tough if uncanonical virtue, supplied the unity and continuity which made the other virtues meaningful. The Entry spectacles were to move from celebrations of the king's achievements to projections of his future glories, and Perseverance had an appropriate place in any ceremonial concerned not merely with the present but also with future and on-going achievement.

The lamb was primarily the emblem of the city but also carried a theological

---

sept, le dimanche deuxiesme aoust, le Roy fit son entrée à Rouen où il fut receu à moult grand triumphe' (*Le Journal d'un Bourgeois de Paris sous le règne de François Ier*, ed. V.-L. Bourrilly (Paris, 1910), p. 52).

[7]   *L'Entrée*, p. 7.
[8]   *Ibid.*, p. 8.

significance as the lamb of God. The lamb was presented in a triangle beneath the virtue-laden lily. *L'Entrée* gave a literal, largely secular, interpretation suggesting that it represented 'Le Roy, la Royne, et madame la regente'.[9] This interpretation indicated the power which Francis's wife and mother were perceived to possess. However, the triangle surely also symbolised the Holy Trinity, and the entire spectacle could be read both as a presentation of the sovereignty of the crown (the lily) over the town (the lamb), and as a religious presentation of the king's duty to God. It can now be seen that the trio of virtues, dressed in foreign costume, who represented French possessions and aspirations, stood firmly on a Christian and French foundation: the Holy Trinity and the lily of France.

After this introductory spectacle the king, having been presented with the ritual canopy, entered the city. The second spectacle took place at the cross roads of the Peacock and, as the first to be presented inside the city, marked the real beginning of the city's allegorical pageant. As *L'Entrée* pointed out, this tableau illustrated a scene from Ovid's *Metamorphoses*. The lines quoted in *L'Entrée* dealt with the attempt by the giants to overthrow Jupiter and the Olympians by piling up mountains and scaling them until struck down by a thunder-bolt from Jupiter. In this scene, richly dressed Olympians, Neptune, Mars, Aeolus, Vulcan, and Mercury rose and bowed to Jupiter after he had loosed his thunder-bolt. *L'Entrée* explained that

> Lintelligence dud'theatre est de facile apprehension, Par les geans on y peut entendre les turcz et infideles, ou, qui vouldra, les adversaires du Roy, et cetera.
>
> [The meaning of the spectacle is easy to comprehend. The giants may be understood as the Turks and infidels or, if one prefers, the adversaries of the king][10]

Certainly there was great concern in Europe at the advance of the Turks. In March 1517 Francis I had agreed with the Emperor Maximillian and the Archduke Charles to join in a crusade against them. Nevertheless, at this point in time it was the Christian kings who were more likely than the 'infideles' Turks to be 'les adversaires du Roy'. As with the interpretation of the triangle, *L'Entrée* offered a rather pedestrian reading of the Ovidian spectacle. The general thought that the king/Jupiter could effortlessly quell his enemies was surely there, but an examination of the context from which the scene was taken in the *Metamorphoses* indicated the ways in which the pageant masters blended political discourse with Golden Age themes.

The first book of the *Metamorphoses* describes the creation of the world and the four ages of man from the Golden Age ruled by Saturn to the Silver Age ruled by his usurper, Jupiter; then the iniquitous and war-like Bronze Age; and, finally, the

9 *Ibid.*, p. 8.
10 *Ibid.*, pp.10–11.

wretched Iron Age when Astrea, Goddess of Justice, flees a world given over to greed and warfare. In the *Metamorphoses* Astrea's flight is immediately followed by the scene shown in the second tableau of the giants' attempt on heaven. The lines then describe how earth creates a race of men out of the blood of the crushed giants. This race is so evil that Jupiter, in despair, floods the earth and creates a new breed of men. In Ovidian terms, the giants' assault represents the disorders of a violent and corrupt world which precedes the creation of a newer and better order.[11] Ovid was frequently 'moralised' in the Middle Ages and the Renaissance. For instance, Don Cameron Allen draws attention to the Lyon humanist scholar, Petrus Lavinius, who pointed out in his 1510 commentary in the *Metamorphoses* that the assault of the giants corresponded to the story of the Tower of Babel.[12] In either pagan or Christian terms, the incident represented the extravagant follies of a world fallen from grace.

In Ovidian terms Jupiter is an equivocal figure. He maintains the order of heaven against the anarchy of earth but, as the deity who banishes Saturn and the Golden Age, he is himself a manifestation of the decline in virtue and growth of violence and greed on earth. It would be rash to firmly identify Francis with Jupiter. This spectacle illustrated the regal power to destroy and control, but it also represented a decline from the Golden Age. Subsequent tableaux moved from brute force to a new era of peace and harmony – a second Golden Age.

The third spectacle was a bronze *all' antica* equestrian statue of the king, described in *L'Entrée* as 'ordonée pour aucunement ensuyvir et emuler le triumphe des romains'. ['having been designed to follow and emulate the roman triumph'.][13] The text went on to explain that the Romans honoured their consuls, emperors and men of outstanding virtue with marble or copper equestrian statues. The growing transalpine fashion for such equestrian statues and their 'power as a symbol of greatness'[14] has been well traced by H. W. Janson. More specifically, the equestrian statue was closely associated with regality and imperial grandeur. Margaret McGowan has speculated that this Rouen statue was the direct inspiration for the bronze horse presented to Henry II during his ceremonial entry into the city in 1550.[15] Francis Yates drew attention to the connection between equestrian statues of monarchs and the imperial idea.[16] The statue at Rouen was, there-

---

[11] All quotations from Ovid, other than those contained in quotations from *L'Entrée* itself, are line references from *Ovid in Six Volumes: Metamorphoses*, I, 90–345 (Loeb edn.).

[12] D. C. Allen, *Mysteriously Meant: the Recovery of Pagan Symbolism and Allegorical Interpretation in the Renaissance* (Baltimore: London, 1970), p.176.

[13] *L'Entrée*, p.12.

[14] H. W. Janson, 'The Equestrian Monument from Cangrande della Scala to Peter the Great', *Aspects of the Renaissance*, ed. A. R. Lewis (Austin: London, 1967), p. 74.

[15] Margaret M. McGowan, 'Forms and Themes in Henry II's Entry into Rouen', *Renaissance Drama*, new series, i (1968), 245.

[16] Yates, *Astrea*, pp. 22, 138.

fore, to be seen as a graceful tribute to the king's recent military victories and an intimation of present and future imperial possibilities.

In terms of the overall pattern of the Rouen ceremonial, the placing of the bronze statue was significant. It followed the somewhat ambiguous celebration of Olympian might, and continued the theme of power as it offered an heroic image of the king. Given the existence of 'les turcz et infideles' and 'les adversaires du Roy', martial enterprise was an established fact of the world, and victories were worth celebration. The bronze colour of the statue might refer to the Roman tradition; it might also indicate that the pageants had begun their movement back through time. They had moved from the Iron Age of the giants to the slightly less wicked and certainly more heroic Bronze Age. The following spectacles were to move further back to the Silver and Golden Ages. The pageants moved from representation of the world as it was to images of the world as it might be.

The fourth tableau showed a scaffold with the shield of France held by two richly dressed little girls. They were flanked by two boys disguised as Moors. The latter, perhaps, represented 'les turcz et infideles' whose projected conversion to the support of the Christian realm of France was now envisaged. On the scaffold a model world, coated with silver to represent the Silver Age, stood on one side and on the other there was a tower representing Athens, complete with a fully armed Pallas Athene. Hanging over the world was a glittering star and, as the king approached, the star opened and a child bearing three star rays emerged from it while the world below turned golden. The child walked down a ray of the opened star to the scaffold, where he was greeted by the three Graces dressed in the king's colours.[17]

L'Entrée identified the child as Perseus and noted that, as in the legend, the marvellous boy was taken by the three Graces to Athena who gave him her crystal shield, identified as Prudence, and then a place in heaven. The child was also to be associated with Francis; L'Entrée went on to explain that the three star rays held by the child denoted 'les graces et perfections de lame'. ['the graces and perfections of the soul'.][18] The child, together with the rays and the graces, 'signifie que le roy a toutes graces en luy, tant du corps que de lame' ['signifies that the king

---

[17] Here, and throughout, one notes the repetition of the number three. For an interesting and delightful discussion of the significance of numerology in Renaissance thought, see C. A. Patrides, Premises and Motifs in Renaissance Thought and Literature (Princeton, 1982). Among the many tributes to the number three which it contains is that quoted from Agrippa: '. . . a holy number, a number of perfection, a most powerful number' (p. 75). Similarly, G. Ferguson (Signs and Symbols in Christian Art (London, 1954; repr. 1974), p.154) notes that 'three was called by Pythagoras the number of completion, expressive of a beginning, a middle, and an end. In Christian symbolism, three became the divine number suggesting the Trinity, and also the three days that Christ spent in the tomb.'

The veneration accorded to the number seven is also well known and fully documented by Patrides, and it is of no surprise that, in the seven spectacles provided for the entry, the seven virtues were displayed.

[18] L'Entrée, p.13.

had all the graces in him as much of the body as of the soul'], thus combining to make Francis the 'chief doeuvre de nature'.[19] *L'Entrée* explained that the changing colour of the world indicated the return of the Golden Age and that 'le dieu Saturne regnat en iceluy pour denoter que le Roy ramene les siecles dor' ['the god, Saturn, reigned there to denote that the king is bringing back the ages of gold'].[20] Time had now been rolled back from the violence of the Iron Age to the peace and calm of the Golden Age. Francis, thus associated with Perseus,[21] was now shown not as a warrior but as a mystic and sacred ruler. Verses attached to the scaffold described this transformation:

> Clarté nouvelle est descendue
> Du ciel sur la terre et sur londe
> Quand le roy Francoys vint au monde

[A new luminosity came down from heaven onto the earth and sea when King Francis came into the world][22]

L'Entrée noted without comment that a line from Virgil's *Eclogues* was displayed over the scaffold: 'Iam nova progenies celo demittitur alto'[23] ['And now a new life comes down from the high heaven']. This line from Virgil's strange and brilliant fourth *Eclogue* predicts the birth of a marvellous boy in whose lifetime Astrea will return to earth and a new Golden Age will unfold. As Frances Yates remarked, the preceding line, 'Iam redit et virgo, redeunt Saturnia regna',[24] ['Now the virgin returns: so does the rule of Saturn'] is one which has 'never been forgotten in the West'.[25] Howard Erskine Hill, writing about English ceremonials, describes the line as 'so significant that it might almost have been deemed an obligatory part of every sixteenth and seventeenth-century royal Entry'.[26] The line may be taken as implied when the silver world turned to gold and, probably, we should see Athena, a virgin goddess, as a parallel for Astrea, just as Perseus is another version of Virgil's child as well as the young king. The line which was chosen to adorn the scaffold "Iam nova progenies" is certainly more appropriate in the case of a male ruler accompanied by his wife.

Christian interpretations of the fourth *Eclogue*, which saw the work as divinely inspired and prophetic of the coming of Christ, allow one also to associate Francis with Christ and the second coming. However, if the Christian associations endow the spectacle with spiritual qualities, they also point it more firmly in imperial

---

[19] *Ibid.*, p.14.
[20] *Ibid.*, p.13.
[21] *Ibid.*, p.14.
[22] *Ibid.*, p.15.
[23] *Ibid.*, p.14, citing Virgil, *Eclogues*, IV. 7. The line references are those adopted in the 'Penguin' translation by G. Lee (Harmondsworth, 1984).
[24] Virgil, *Eclogues*, IV, 6.
[25] Yates, *Astrea*, p. 33.
[26] Erskine Hill, *Augustan Idea*, p.126.

directions. As Francis Yates most notably pointed out, this *Eclogue* and these lines had long been related to the idea of Empire in a concept which stretched back beyond the foundations of the Holy Roman Empire to the Augustan era, the *pax romana*, and the Christian imperial mission to Rome.[27] A traditional reading of history saw the Roman Empire and the *pax romana* as essential, indeed divinely appointed, for the propagation of the Christian message. In this context, the pagan fourth *Eclogue* combines prophecy with imperialism. In *De Monarchia*, an influential and widely circulated work written at the beginning of the fourteenth century in support of Henry VII's claim to be Holy Roman Emperor, Dante directly associates the *Eclogue* with the idea of Empire. He cites the line 'Iam redit et virgo' as he argues that the Golden Age can only be renewed under a universal monarch who will have the strength to revive and enforce justice, and through this attain 'perfect order'.[28]

It is relevant to note that the fourth *Eclogue* foretells for the divine child a period of Homeric heroic warfare in his youth when the world, although renewed, will retain 'priscae vestigia fraudis' ['traces of old deceit'].[29] Only when the child has attained full maturity will war, trade and agriculture cease to trouble the earth as the world achieves perfection:

> hinc, ubi iam firmata virum te fecerit aetas, cedet et ipse mari vector, nec nautica pinus mutabit merces; omnis feret omnia tellus.
>
> [Then, when the strength of time has made you a man/ The merchant will leave the sea, and seafaring ships/ Will trade no more, and all land will produce all things][30]

In the full Virgilian context, the heroic endeavours which were celebrated by the defeat of the giants and by the bronze equestrian statue now take on a new significance. These military activities were the work of Francis' young manhood whilst the world was still impure. Such activities had been presented as necessary for the present, but the changing of the world from silver to golden indicated that warfare was an inferior activity which, happily, would have no place in Francis' realm in the future.

The fifth spectacle, presented by the monks of Saint-Ouen, constituted a warning against war as knights defended and assaulted a tower amidst fiery and destructive explosions. As Anne-Marie Lecoq has pointed out, the tower 'symbolisait la Guerre' and we may take it that the events represented warfare which was now

---

[27] In particular, see Yates, *Astrea*, p. 33, and Yates, 'Charles Quint et l'idée d'empire', *Les Fêtes de la Renaissance*, ed. J. Jacquot (3 vols., C.N.R.S., Paris, 1960), II, pp. 66–7; also Erskine Hill, *Augustan Idea*, and D. P. A. Comparetti, *Vergil in the Middle Ages*, trans. E. F. M. Benecke (London, 1908; repr. 1966), pp. 96–104.

[28] Dante, *Monarchy and Three Political Letters*, trans. D. Nicholl and C. Hardie (London, 1954), p.15.

[29] Virgil, *Eclogues*, IV, 31.

[30] *Ibid.*, IV, 37–9.

presented as destructive rather than heroic.[31] The participation of clergy in this spectacle endowed it with an admonitory quality.

The warning against warfare was amplified in the sixth tableau which took place at the Robec bridge. The whole stage represented the world born on the shoulders of Hercules and Atlas. As the king approached, Hercules and Atlas bowed to him and opened the sky to reveal a salamander, Francis's personal badge, basking in 'feu naturel'.[32] The salamander descended to the stage and in rapid succession defeated a bull and a bear and then 'retournoit triumphant au lieu du quel estoit partie' ['he returned triumphant to the place he had come from'].[33] L'Entrée did not explain the significance of the bull and bear but that was surely because, as Anne-Marie Lecoq writes, everyone had understood that they were looking at the bull of Uri and the bear of Bern, two Swiss cantons.[34] The references here are to the Swiss armies which, until Marignano, had been considered invincible. L'Entrée offered an interpretation of this spectacle which went beyond Marignano: 'le mystere diceluy theatre estoit oeuvre de grand force et prudence'. ['The meaning of this spectacle was concerned with the working of great strength and prudence.'][35] Prudence, it will be recalled, was associated with the shield which Athena gave to Perseus in the fourth spectacle. The combination of force and prudence could be understood as a unification of military strength and alert readiness.[36] The salamander had defeated not merely specific enemies but even war itself. This was indicated by a verse attached to the scaffold:

> La salamandre en vertue singuliere, Lors estaignait lhorrible feu de mars, Quant du grant ours emporta la baniere, Et du thoreau rompit cornes et dardz.
>
> [The salamander, singular in virtue, then extinguished the terrible fire of Mars when he carried away the banner of the great bear and broke the horns of the bull.][37]

In the fire motif the Rouen tableau ingeniously utilised the king's personal badge and motto. A Latin version of the motto was displayed on the scaffold, rendered as 'Nutrisco Extinguo'. Anne-Marie Lecoq, in her analysis of the various and extended meanings of the badge and motto, concludes that the motto not only signifies 'je me nourris au bon feu' but also the antithesis 'j'éteins le mauvais

---

[31] Anne-Marie Lecoq, 'La Salamandre royale dans les entrées de Francois Ier', Les Fêtes de la Renaissance, ed. J. Jacquot and E. Konigson (C.N.R.S., Paris, 1975), III, p. 96.

[32] L'Entrée, p.16.

[33] Ibid., p.17.

[34] Lecoq, 'Salamandre', p. 98.

[35] L'Entrée, p.16.

[36] I am indebted to Dr Christopher Allmand for drawing my attention to the significance of 'Prudence' in the military context.

[37] L'Entrée, p.17.

feu' ['I take strength from the good fire . . . I extinguish the evil fire'][38] The power of fire to dominate was expounded by the Renaissance Magus, Agrippa of Nette-sheim, in his *Three Books of Occult Philosophy* in which fire is described as

> Active, Powerful, Invisibly present in all things at once; it will not be af-fronted or opposed, but as it were in a way of revenge, it will reduce on a sudden things into obedience to itself, incomprehensible, impalpable, not lessened, most rich in all dispensations of itself.[39]

The power of fire to 'reduce on a sudden things into obedience to itself' had al-ready been illustrated in the fiery fifth spectacle. The sixth spectacle balanced the destructive 'feu de mars' with the virtuous and victorious fires of heaven associ-ated with the salamander/Francis. As Lecoq writes, the salamander (Francis) was being glorified here as 'une guerrière pacifique qui combat pour la Paix'.[40] As the soldier of Peace, the King extinguished the 'horrible feu de mars' and nourished himself on the fires of heaven. These images, associating Francis with the defeat of war and showing his return to the heavens, indicated that the king had moved through the stages of growth shown in the earlier spectacles and as outlined in Virgil's fourth *Eclogue*. Earlier, Francis' military competence was celebrated in the depiction of Jupiter's defeat of the giants and by the bronze equestrian statue. Now that he had attained maturity ('ubi iam firmata virum te fecerit aetas')[41] the time of war was over. The last taints of the old iniquity had been purged and the time of peace, prudence and plenty might now unfold. The king was now fully qualified to take up a position as a universal monarch, an Emperor under whose rule univer-sal peace would be enjoyed.

The last tableau was at the Gate of the Booksellers, close to the Cathedral Church of Notre-Dame, where the celebrations were to conclude with a high Mass. This spectacle showed an 'Ortus deliciarum',[42] a garden of delights with, at its highest point, the Virgin Mary represented by a beautiful girl dressed in blue with a surcoat covered with *fleurs-de-lis*. In her hand she held a palm indicating the victory she could bestow on rulers. She stood between two pillars, surely repre-senting the pillars of Hercules and the extent of the Roman Empire. The Virgin was shown with her usual attributes, the sun around her and the moon at her feet, symbolism drawn from the *Book of Revelation*, 12:1, which could be interpreted, as *L'Entrée* suggested, as 'la vision de lapocalipse'.[43] As the final spectacle in the mil-lenarian sequence, the image indicated that the old order was over and a new and blessed era had begun.

---

[38] Lecoq, 'Salamandre', p. 96.
[39] Henry Cornelius Agrippa, *Three Books of Occult Philosophy*, trans. J.F., (London, 1651), p. 9.
[40] Lecoq, 'Salamandre', p. 99.
[41] Virgil, *Eclogues*, IV, 37.
[42] *L'Entrée*, p.18.
[43] *Ibid*.

The decorations of the enclosed garden were lush with green and black grapes, pumpkins, roses and other flowers, which recalled Virgil's description of the un-trammeled vines and vegetation in the renewed Golden Age.[44] A lamb appeared from beneath the Virgin's feet and coming to the front of the scaffold, which was decorated with *fleurs-de-lis*, saluted the king. *L'Entrée* explained that the lamb pas-sing between the lilies stood for 'Rouen conduit et gouverné soubz la couronne de France' ['Rouen guided and ruled under the crown of France'].[45] Together with local and Norman concerns, the spectacle also functioned effectively to articulate the wider implications of the whole sequence of spectacles. The Virgin's garden was the traditional space apart and Paradise garden and also, as the lilies and the frisking lamb suggested, the realm of France. The pillars, taken as the bounds of the known world, turned the garden of France into a world garden, the garden of the new order. The palm of victory that the Virgin held might well signify heavenly victory over earthly anarchy. The palm might also suggest that Francis, like Christ entering Jerusalem, had come into his own.

Two fountains, attributes of the Virgin as 'fountain of living waters',[46] played in the garden emphasising its spiritual and physical fecundity. *L'Entrée* interpreted the fountains and garden in two ways, spiritual and political:

> par le jardin on peult entendre paradis. Aussi peult on entendre Nor-mandie arrousée de deux fontaines de Justice et Charité par lesquelles florit.

> [By the garden, paradise may be understood: but one might understand Normandy watered by the two fountains of justice and charity by which it functions.][47]

The combination of Justice and Charity is somewhat unusual, and an explana-tion can be sought in Dante's *De Monarchia* in which he argues that an absolute monarch combines justice and charity. He states that 'of all mortals, the Monarch can be the purest incarnation of Justice' and that 'since to live in peace . . . is the chief of human blessings, and since justice is the most powerful means towards it, charity gives force to justice so that the more powerful it is, the more force it will have'.[48] According to Dante, this power and force enables the monarch to estab-

---

44 Virgil, *Eclogues*, IV, 40–5.
45 *L'Entrée*, p.19.
46 See Ferguson, *Signs and Symbols*, p. 45, and Naomi Miller, *French Renaissance Fountains* (New York: London 1977), pp.17–20, on water as a symbol of cleansing and purifying, and on the fountain as the symbol of life and rebirth. On fountains as symbols of physical and spiritual fecundity, see T. Comito, *The Idea of the Garden in the Renaissance* (Brighton, 1979), pp. 89–90, and R. Strong, *The Renaissance Garden in England* (London, 1979), pp. 20–1. See also Miller, *French . . . Fountains*, pp.14–17, on temporary fountains in ceremon-ials.
47 *L'Entrée*, p.19.
48 Dante, *Monarchy*, p.17.

lish universal rule and universal peace. The fountains could be seen, therefore, as attributes of the Virgin and symbols of the purity of Norman law and charity. They could also be understood in national and supranational terms, as illustrating that France, depicted as a Paradise Garden, had the necessary qualifications for imperial rule.

This final spectacle served as the culmination of the sequence depicting the present and future role of Francis as king of France. Hope, Temperance and Perseverance had made their appearance in the first spectacle. Prudence had appeared in the fourth, and had been described in L'Entrée as one of the themes of the sixth. Justice and Charity appeared in this last spectacle and Faith might be taken as implied by the Virgin and the Lamb. Thus, by the seventh spectacle, the seven virtues had been articulated and shown to be attributes of both France and Francis. Time had moved with powerful symbolic significance throughout the Entry ceremonials. Time had rolled back to the Golden, Bronze, Silver and Iron ages of mythology and forward to the second Golden Age foretold in Virgil's fourth Eclogue. On the way, events from the recent past, such as Francis's victory at Marignano, had been celebrated and also commented upon. His reign had been cast in a classical/mythological mode which was flattering in its assessment of present achievements and future possibilities. There was a providential determinism in the clear connection made between the reign and the marvellous child of Virgil's Eclogue. The allegoric logic of the spectacles articulated the argument of Empire, and the final spectacle offered celestial and imperial images of an achieved splendour. Peace and empire, which emerged in the sixth spectacle, were surely combined in this garden world of France.

The imperial intimations patently present in the Entry ceremonials can be understood to represent two ideas of Empire. One, long established and widely held, was contained in the maxim that 'the King is Emperor in his Kingdom'.[49] It is possible that the imperial ideas merely referred to Francis' authority within the realm of France. However, as well as this nationally grounded concept, France had an equally long tradition of aspiration towards the throne of the Holy Roman Empire. Indeed, Michel François described Francis' candidacy of 1519 as wholly within 'une tradition reçue';[50] this was no vague aspiration for Francis I who, as early as 1516, had been approached by Franz von Sickingen with promise of support for his candidacy.[51] Further, as Anne-Marie Lecoq has argued in her recent study of

---

[49] On this, see André Bossuat's discussion on the tradition of the king as emperor in his kingdom ('The Maxim "The King is Emperor in his Kingdom". Its use in the Fifteenth century before the Parlement of Paris', The Recovery of France in the Fifteenth Century, ed. P. S. Lewis (London, 1971), pp.185–95, and J. J. Scarisbrick (Henry VIII (Harmondsworth edn., 1971), pp. 351–7) on Henry VIII's attitude to this.

[50] M. François, 'L'Idée d'empire en France à l'époque de Charles-Quint', Charles-Quint et son temps (C.N.R.S., Paris, 1959), p. 25.

[51] See Le Journal de Jean Barrillon, secrétaire du chancelier du Prat, 1515–1521, ed. P. de

Francis' reign,[52] imperial ambition was a powerful motivating force during the early years of his monarchy. It seems reasonable to suppose that the Rouennais élite, aware of the political situation and of traditional French imperial hopes, trusted that their vigorous and recently victorious king might achieve this ambition. It is not necessary to believe that they distinguished between the differing traditions very exactly for, as Donald Kelley has written, 'there is no point in denying the ambiguity and even duplicity of renaissance historical thought'.[53]

Universal peace was a feature of universal monarchy, indeed even its justification, as these ceremonials have demonstrated. And in 1517 universal peace was a key issue throughout Europe. The mood of the years immediately preceding the Field of Cloth of Gold was highly optimistic in regard to peaceful co-existence. This co-existence, as the second spectacle implied, involved the defeat of enemies such as the Turks and, three months after the Entry festivities at Rouen, Pope Leo X and the Sacred College called for a crusade against the Turks to be led by the Emperor Maximillian and Francis I. By 1518 France, England and the Empire were all ostensibly committed to a perpetual peace which involved dynastic marriage alliances. However, as Joy Russell has shown, the search for a universal peace at the conferences of Calais and Bruges in 1521 was conducted with difficulty and concluded with no positive results.[54] Perhaps, given the courtly and pacific message of the Rouen spectacles, the city appreciated the fact that in 1520 their financial contribution to the monarchy went towards the costs of the meeting between Francis I and Henry VIII at the Field of Cloth of Gold.[55] This meeting of 1520 was effectively the last meeting of a united Christendom. After that year hopes for a universal peace, such as those expressed at Rouen, were frail.

In the light of the trials and disappointments of the years ahead for France and the religious and territorial wars which were to characterise European politics in the course of the next hundred years, there is something poignant about the Rouen ceremonials' optimistic view of France's glorious and peaceful destiny. The ceremonials which articulated a vision of a new order were in fact the product of an old tradition in European politics. And although that tradition, so eloquently set forth in De Monarchia, was to influence the propaganda of the Habsburg Emperor and be incorporated into most court ceremonials, the age of universal monarchy, in so far as it ever existed, was already over. None the less, the Golden Age

---

Vaissière (2 vols., Paris, 1897–99), I, pp. 251–2 on Sickingen's visit to the court at Amboise.

[52] The present essay was prepared for printing prior to the publication of Anne-Marie Lecoq's François Ier Imaginaire (Paris, 1987). It has not been practicable to incorporate references to this important work in the text.

[53] D. Kelley, Foundations of Modern Historical Scholarship: Language, Law, and History in the French Renaissance (New York, 1970), p. 306.

[54] J. G. Russell, 'The Search for Universal Peace: the Conferences at Calais and Bruges in 1521', Bulletin of the Institute of Historical Research, xliv (1971), 162–93.

[55] R. Herval, Histoire de Rouen (2 vols, Paris, 1953), II, p. 31.

was to remain an important and adaptable part of the pageant-masters' vocabulary. The Entry into Rouen arranged for Francis' son, Henry II, in 1550 included amongst the tableaux the figure of Saturn with an inscription proclaiming 'Je suis l'age d'or.': 'I am the Golden Age.'[56] The analysis of the Rouen Entry of 1517 indicates how this could be so. Few topics could so well demonstrate humanist learning and Christian piety, glorify peace while paying tribute to war, or blend provincial with national aspiration. Whether or not an empire was immediately possible, it was never out of place to intimate how well an imperial crown would become a national monarch, nor to point out how effectively the monarch was 'Emperor in his kingdom'.

[56] McGowan, 'Forms and Themes', 224.

Looking for the Origins of the French Reformation

DAVID NICHOLLS

The artificial divide between 'late medieval' and 'early modern', conceived as a break occurring at some time in the later fifteenth century or at the turn of the sixteenth, despite the fact that it appears to be fading away in the teaching of general European history courses in higher education, still dogs our perceptions about French history between the Hundred Years War and the Wars of Religion. Reading and hearing about the fifteenth century reminds the historian of the early sixteenth of the contradictions of the later 'Renaissance' period, of how the self-confidence apparent in the political and cultural spheres co-existed with a haunting fear of civil strife. And the burgeoning historical interest in questions of culture and power, represented strongly among the papers in this volume, indicates some of the most fruitful ways of forging the necessary links in the historical chain. It should, therefore, not be inappropriate to include here an admittedly rather speculative paper on the origins of the Reformation, first, because the Protestant Reform represented a radical challenge to the dominant forms of cultural power, and, secondly, because the search for its 'origins' – understood in Marc Bloch's two senses as 'causes' and 'beginnings' – inevitably necessitates looking back into the fifteenth century. How far we look back is another matter. The Reformation in France has no obvious starting date or crucial 'big event', no nailing up of theses or Reformation Parliament. It grew by fits and starts, with dramatic events erupting to the surface of a gradual creeping up on the unsuspecting centres of power. But once the mental block of the medieval/modern division is lifted, we may hope to move closer to an understanding of the long-term processes at work.

This problem of the origins of the Reformation is notoriously 'une question mal posée'. When Lucien Febvre published his celebrated article with that title in 1929, his purpose was to free historical inquiry from what he saw as outdated diversions – the Reformation as the result of 'abuses' in the Church, and controversies, as much political as historical, about the 'French' nature of the Reform – and to replace these weary debates with discussion of those religious and social developments of the fifteenth century which contributed to the desire for a new form of religion suited to new social conditions and new spiritual needs.[1] Religious history, wrote Febvre, should be separated from the history of churches and integrated with the study of political, economic, social and cultural change, while 'specificity, priority and nationality' were 'words to be erased from historical vocabulary'.[2] In particular, attention should be given to the religion of 'the masses' and to the attitudes towards religion expressed by Christian humanism, seen by Febvre as representing the search by a conquering bourgeoisie of merchants, lawyers and officers for a form of religion appropriate to its new place in the social and political sun. Seeing 'superstition at the base, coldness at the top', this humanist bourgeoisie found in the vernacular Bible and the doctrine of justification by faith alone the necessary tools for a redefinition of the relationship between mankind and God, while throughout European society an 'immense appetite for the divine' manifested itself in various ways, leading to reform of one variety or another and ultimately to Protestant and Catholic Reformation.[3]

It cannot be said that all the dubious tendencies identified by Febvre have disappeared completely from the historiography – a confessional background still looms behind even some of the best recent work on the French Reformation – and important aspects of Febvre's own approach appear today as too vague and generalised to be of much use for a re-examination of the problem. His all-conquering bourgeoisie, for example, certainly needs careful dissection, and his insistence on an international context is no longer urgent: the desire to isolate what was specific to the Reformation in France no longer implies getting embroiled in political polemics about the 'Frenchness' or 'Germanness' of Protestantism. Nevertheless, for all the criticism that can be (and has been) levelled at him, much of what Febvre wrote remains pertinent. It is, after all, easier to criticize Febvre than to tackle a difficult question directly, but contemporary developments in religious history indicate new ways of exploring his questions.

First and foremost, there is the greatly increased knowledge of early French Protestantism, much of it provided by 'Anglo-Saxon', British and American historians, unaffected by the kind of confessional debate which Febvre so deplored. Secondly, confessional concerns have themselves been transformed. Committed Christians looking at the Reformation today are likely to be broadly liberal and ecumenical in approach, concerned not so much with arguments between Christians as with the meaning of Christianity, both in the Reformation era and in our own supposedly secular age. This anxiety demands an attempt to construct a comprehensive understanding of the history of Christianity, which, while it has its dangers – the Reformation seen as basically a big mistake – does help all histo-

---

[1] L. Febvre, 'Une question mal posée: les origines de la Réforme française et le problème des causes de la Réforme', in his *Au coeur religieux du XVIe siècle* (Paris, 1957), pp. 3–70. The article was first published in the *Revue historique*, clxi (1929), 1–73.

[2] *Ibid.*, p. 70.

[3] *Ibid.*, quotations at pp. 39, 37.

rians, including non-believers, to identify general socio-religious movements
going beyond differences between churches, and to avoid the inappropriate label-
ling of particular groups and individuals as necessarily 'Catholic' or 'Protestant'.

Thirdly, we may today adopt a more sophisticated attitude to the relationship
between 'religion' and 'society' than was once common in Reformation history.
By not viewing them as separate spheres or as representing incompatible approaches to the history of the Reformation, we can avoid the pieties of confession-
alism without falling into the traps of social or economic reductionism. This
entails a critical engagement with another tradition in the study of the French Reformation. If Febvre saw the Reformation as the expression of a rising bourgeoisie,
the other great early twentieth-century historian of the subject, Henri Hauser,
viewed it rather as the work of artisans excluded from the affairs of their guilds by
more restrictive governing oligarchies, and as provoked by a falling standard of
living, caused by inflation, among the urban *menu peuple*.[4] The Hauser tradition is
alive and well, as shown in the work of Henry Heller, who also pays due attention
to Protestantism within city oligarchies and tries to adapt the East German idea of
the Reformation, as the 'early bourgeois revolution', to French conditions.[5]

Yet it does raise serious problems. It is never entirely clear why economic revolt
should take on a Protestant religious form; the explanations as to why the majority
of artisans remained Catholic − illiteracy, 'parochialism', advanced age − are inadequate or dismissive; and the choice between Catholicism and magisterial Protestantism remains too clear-cut as a description of religious attitudes, particularly
within the bourgeoisie. Without denying the class basis of society or that class
conflict played a role in the early history of Protestantism, it is, I believe, necessary to be more attentive to recent work on popular religion, on the dialectical relationship between popular and high religion, and on the links between religion
and locality in order to explain why large minorities in all the urban classes became Protestant but, equally important, why most did not, and why only a tiny
minority of the peasantry adopted the new religion. Such work also helps us to re-
appraise the relationship between belief and behaviour in the religious life of the
laity. Humanists and Reformers alike saw 'bad' behaviour as the visible manifestation of 'bad' belief, whereas Febvre, in his desire to dispose of 'abuses' as a cause of
the Reformation, tended to make a very sharp distinction between them. Now
that historians take the magical and 'superstitious' elements in popular belief more
seriously, we can see that the Reformers were on to something important which

---

[4]   See in particular his Études sur la Réforme française (Paris, 1909), and, for his interpreta-
tion of socio-economic change during the Reformation period, Ouvriers du temps passé
(Paris, 1913), and Les débuts du capitalisme (Paris, 1931).
[5]   H. Heller, The Conquest of Poverty: the Calvinist Revolt in Sixteenth-Century France
(Leiden, 1986). See also idem, 'Les artisans au début de la Réforme: Hommage à Henri
Hauser', Les Réformes: Enracinement socio-culturel, ed. B. Chevalier and R. Sauzet (XXVe
Colloque International d'Études Humanistes, Tours, 1er–13 juillet 1982, Paris, 1985),
pp.137–49.

Febvre missed: the visible and concrete as signifiers of the invisible and of beliefs. This reforming insight, when translated into action, may serve to re-connect us with the Hauserian tradition, as religious reform became a part of the attempt to control and channel the religious and social 'disorder' of the powerless classes.

Various historiographical developments, then, help us to renew at least some points of Febvre's badly-posed question, though we cannot hope to cover all the ground in a short paper such as this. What we can do is to try and assess long-term processes between the fifteenth and sixteenth centuries, and weigh them against the influence of short-term events during the period of Protestant growth up to 1563. And a brief look at one city – Tours – may help to avoid too many vague generalisations and to keep Febvre's questions in our minds, as we see how reform and Reform came to the localities.

'Reform' was, of course, a ubiquitous notion in fifteenth-century France, especially in the second half of the century. Religious reform, however imprecisely defined, commanded widespread allegiance in the upper reaches of the secular and ecclesiastical authorities, from the king downwards, taking such familiar forms as the introduction of the strict Observance in the mendicant orders, or Charles VIII's assembly for the reform of the Church held at Tours in 1493. But it could take so many forms as to weaken the chances for any of them to be really effective, with the 'abuses', which Febvre said should be excluded from discussion of the origins of the Reformation, in the forefront of official minds. Everyone would at least pay lip-service to the ideas that discipline needed to be re-imposed in the houses of the regular clergy, and that the secular clergy, led by the example of their bishops, should lead lives worthy of their positions. Beyond this, however, no need was felt for a consensus, and plans for general reform lacked urgency, mainly because so many vested interests were at stake. Reformism, like Protestantism later, was concerned with the right ordering of religion, the establishment of 'correct' religious priorities, and the purification of the religion of both laity and clergy. But such re-ordering would inevitably have significant social consequences, especially if people did not want to be rightly ordered. Attention, then, should focus less on 'abuses' as such than on the consequences of attempts to eradicate them in specific localities, and this shift of perspective should help in re-assessing the relationship between reform and the subsequent success or failure of Protestantism.

The complexity of this last point is suggested by the possibility that France may have preceded other countries in attempting the kind of reforms which are supposed to have weakened the appeal of Protestantism. For example, in 1493 we find Ferdinand of Aragon writing to Louis d'Amboise, bishop of Albi, enquiring how he had proceeded in the reform of the regular clergy in his diocese.[6] D'Amboise, a 'prélat politique' if ever there was one, and a leading member of a powerful ecclesiastical and political clan, was not necessarily the right man to ask. In 1491

6   Y. Labande-Mailfert, *Charles VIII et son milieu (1470–1498)* (Paris, 1975), p. 518.

he had attempted to introduce the Observance into the local Franciscan house, but the consuls and townspeople of Albi had supported the unreformed Conventuals against the bishop and his reformers. This was not due to any great affection for the Conventuals, but arose from the long standing conflicts between bishop and municipality over their respective jurisdictional rights in the city. In attempting reform, d'Amboise was overriding municipal privileges, and, as a result, his supporters on the town council were thrown out and the rebels took over the town for five days in May 1491, forcing d'Amboise and his party to barricade themselves in the bishop's palace and defend themselves with artillery. The revolt lost support when the rebels tried to impose a tax to pay for presenting their case to the king; d'Amboise retired to the safer business of negotiating the marriage contract between Charles VIII and Anne of Brittany; and the case dragged on until 1493 before the *Parlement* of Toulouse where the bishop won, but an elaborate agreement left the respective areas of jurisdiction of bishop and municipality unchanged.[7] Significantly, among the complaints against d'Amboise presented by the city to the *Parlement* was the matter of an order issued by him in 1484 demanding that 'all those who dance, wear masks and play the fool during Carnival should be expelled from the town of Albi', an edict which had been cheerfully ignored by the townsfolk.[8] Defence of municipal rights by Albi's ruling oligarchy went hand in hand with defence of the ludic elements of 'popular' (or lay) culture against purificatory reforming zeal. Both the rights of town government and the nature of urban culture were at stake.

The Albi case, because it involved open revolt against the bishop, illustrates in a particularly stark form the underlying conflicts at work. Reform (and here a link with the Counter-Reformation may be made) involved increasing the power and authority of bishops against town councils, but also against ecclesiastical bodies such as abbeys, cathedral chapters and collegiate churches. Other less spectacular examples could be given extending from the mid-fifteenth into the sixteenth century, from Pierre de Longeuil at Auxerre between 1449 and 1479 and Jean Coeur, son of Jacques, at Bourges during the same period, to François and Antoine d'Estaing at Rodez and Angoulême after 1517.[9] To be truly effective, reforming impulses had to come from broader social bases, and these were not forthcoming before the arrival of Protestantism complicated matters further. In Albi, Protestantism seems to have gained only limited success, attracting a small group of mer-

---

7 A. Vidal, *Révolte des Albigeois contre l'évêque Louis d'Amboise* (Albi, 1892), *passim*.
8 *Ibid.*, pp. 60–1, 69–70.
9 See Abbé Lebeuf, *Mémoires concernant l'histoire ecclésiastique et civile d'Auxerre* (2 vols, Paris, 1743) I, pp. 526–53; G. Godineau, 'Statuts synodaux inédits du diocèse de Bourges promulgés par Jean Coeur en 1451', *Revue d'histoire de l'Église de France*, lxxii (1986), 49–66; C. Belmon, *Le bienheureux François d'Estaing, évêque de Rodez, 1460–1529* (Rodez: Albi, 1924); J.-C. Tillier, 'La pré-réforme catholique à Angoulême et les statuts synodaux d'Antoine d'Estaing', *Société Archéologique et Historique de la Charente: Mémoires pour l'année 1972*, pp. 259–316.

chants and a handful of artisans and lawyers, but none of the consuls.[10] Further research may change the picture, but sixteenth-century Albi appears as a traditionalist small city, which had probably never fully recovered from the demographic disasters of the fourteenth century, and where a united municipal élite felt secure in its privileges and its festivities, confirmed by the events of the 1490s, and where the local school, run by churchmen, faced no challenge from humanist education. We need to look more closely at towns where Reformed ideas found more fertile ground.

Within the colourful and lively but complex socio-religious life in a France recovering from the Hundred Years War we may discern the two broad movements of 'revivalism' and 'humanism', both of which were related to attempts by municipal élites to control local religious manifestations. A major part of fifteenth-century reform may be seen as an attempted 'revival', using fear of judgement to infuse new fervour into both laity and clergy through sermons, confession, private reading (for the literate) and images. The idea that Christians must use all their interior resources to gain salvation was forced upon the faithful by every available emotional means, and a new insistence on personal destiny, saving oneself through moral reform, superimposed a new emotional component upon the established collective forms of religious life, as expressed in confraternities or saints' cults, which were seen by turbulent reforming spirits as the focal points of 'superstition', or laxity and 'scandals'.

The most active and visible agents of the revival were the great virtuosi Franciscan preachers in the tradition of the Dominican Vincent Ferrer, and including such famous names as Olivier Maillard, Michel Menot, Jean Vitrier, and Thomas Illyricus. The mendicant orders, which had established a special place in urban life and gained a particular popularity in the wills of the laity, set themselves up, under the often hostile eyes of the secular clergy, as the purifiers of urban society, sweeping through the moral cesspits of the cities. Their preaching attracted large crowds and could take on the characteristics of a true revival.[11] During his circuit in the Midi in 1518–19, undertaken for preaching and also possibly in an attempt to win over the Franciscan province of Aquitaine for the Observance, Illyricus is said to have attracted 25,000 people to Advent and Lenten preaching at the future Protestant centre of Montauban, and similar numbers at Condom, Nérac, and

---

[10] See the table in J. Garrisson-Estèbe, *Protestants du Midi, 1559–1598* (Toulouse, 1980), pp.18–19.

[11] The most useful general works on the Franciscans and their preachers include H. Martin, *Les ordres mendiants en Bretagne, vers 1230 – vers 1530* (Paris, 1975); idem, 'La prédication et les masses au XVe siècle. Facteurs et limites d'une réussite', *Histoire vécue du peuple chrétien*, ed. J. Delumeau (2 vols, Toulouse, 1979), II, pp. 9–41; A. J. Krailsheimer, *Rabelais and the Franciscans* (Oxford, 1963); and M. Piton, 'L'idéal épiscopal selon les prédicateurs français de la fin du XVe siècle et du début du XVIe', *Revue d'histoire ecclésiastique*, lxi (1966), 77–118, 393–423. The facts and figures about the mendicant orders are in R. W. Emery, *The Friars in Medieval France* (New York: London, 1962).

Toulouse, where his sermons had to be moved from the Franciscan house into the open air to accommodate the crowds. The figures are undoubtedly exaggerated, but those who went to hear him got a good free show. The preacher would arrive on foot or riding a donkey, with, at Montauban, an entourage of three other Franciscans and two born-again former prostitutes. The sermons themselves, probably in some form of Italianate Occitan for southern audiences, combined a well-studied and rehearsed theatricality with a logical structure moving, albeit at times rather tortuously, from premise to conclusion. Using popular language, topical and local allusions, first-person delivery and oratorical tricks of the trade, they stressed the basic articles of the faith, the value of material and spiritual poverty, and the necessity for a worthy clergy, culminating in a Savonarola-style bonfire of vanities. At Toulouse, Illyricus persuaded the local card-makers to switch from making playing cards to producing cards portraying the Holy Name of Jesus, a devotion much associated with the Franciscans. In sermons and letters to élite groups (which were subsequently printed, but in Latin) Illyricus, like his fellow revivalists, stressed individual reform, using personal qualities to follow the path to holiness, and timidly suggested the reading of Scripture for personal edification and improvement. But the form of the discourse was suited to the audience, and the moral content of the sermons, attacking all classes, including the clergy, provided everyone with something with which to agree. For while all were flagellated for their corrupt morals, bad behaviour in church, and use of church buildings for profane purposes, the urban classes could approve of attacks on the nobility, all the laity could approve of denunciations of avaricious and hypocritical clergy, while all would be pleased by assaults on the chicanery of lawyers.[12] 'Superstition' and carnivalesque culture were the visible signs of immorality: Illyricus attacked all manner of 'superstitions'; Maillard condemned the drunken debauchery of carnival; and Menot condemned popular festivites for bringing shame and dishonour to girls in taverns, this last as part of the preachers' general anti-female obsessions.[13]

The virtuosi revivalists were invited to preach by town councils, but, as urban ruling groups gradually developed a taste for more learned sermonising, their weaknesses were exposed, in particular a kind of emotional overkill as their moralising grew increasingly wearisome and inadequate, the tendency of their metaphors to become clichés more marked, and their use of complex logical structures, learned in universities, became more obscure when combined with *exempla* far

[12] On Illyricus, see C. Daux, *Histoire de l'église de Montauban* (tome I in 12 fascicules, Montauban, 1878–81), fasc.11, pp. 6–10; R. M. Mauriac, 'Un réformateur catholique: Thomas Illyricus, F. M. O.', *Etudes franciscaines*, xlvi (1934), 329–47, 434–56, 584–604; xlvii (1935), 58–71; M.-F. Godfroy, 'Le prédicateur franciscain Thomas Illyricus à Toulouse (novembre 1518 – mai 1519)', *Annales du Midi*, xcvii (1985), 101–14.

[13] Mauriac, 'Un réformateur catholique', 598–600; R. Vaultier, *Le Folklore pendant la guerre de cent ans d'après les lettres de remission du Trésor des Chartes* (Paris, 1965), pp. 54–5; Krailsheimer, *Rabelais*, p. 57.

remote from contemporary life and events. To ask whether revivalism, when it did not die away as quickly as it flared up, could lead directly to people embracing Protestantism requires psychological speculation for which we do not possess direct evidence, but a couple of preliminary points are worthy of consideration. First, a possible continuum from the Franciscans to 'holy men' and wandering preachers during the Reformation, notably unorthodox Protestants in the 1550s and early 1560s; and secondly, Bernard Chevalier's suggestion that Protestant *prêches* – large open-air meetings held in any available open space outside town walls – built on the tradition of the gathering of large crowds by the Franciscans.[14] The difference, of course, is the appearance of dogmatic deviations. The Franciscans were fiercely orthodox, but they had shown the potential for religious enthusiasm based on moral reform, and raised themes which could be taken up by more radical spirits.

Humanism is more difficult to pin down than revivalism, being a question of attitudes as much as actions, but there are signs of its progress among urban élites, most clearly in the foundation of schools by municipal authorities, which help point the way.[15] For our purposes 'humanism' is a convenient term to describe an intellectual stance, probably stimulated by university education, developing into social attitudes and involving, among other things, a concern for the purification of religion, disapproval of 'disorders' and emotional excess in religious practice, and concern for the essentials of a Christian belief free from 'superstitious' and venal accretions. A link between humanism and Protestantism is a generally accepted idea, going back as far as Florimond de Raemond, but its precise nature has never been entirely clear. Humanist bishops, some occupying their sees right up to the beginning of the religious wars, are too numerous to list. They were likely to attempt religious reform (mostly with little success), to protect fellow humanists accused of heresy, and to exhibit curiosity about Protestant ideas (which could land them in trouble), but were, if anything, less likely than non-humanists finally to embrace Protestantism.[16] The so-called 'middle ground', which I would prefer to call the non-confessional ground, was still occupied by bishops such as Jean de Montluc of Valence and Antonio Caracciolo of Troyes, even in the 1550s.[17] Similarly, among the urban bourgeoisie no simple identification of humanism leading to Protestantism is possible. The most substantial link, I believe, is through the municipal colleges, and is particularly well documented in the case of Agen, and

[14] B. Chevalier, *Les bonnes villes de France du XIVe au XVIe siècle* (Paris, 1982), p. 260.

[15] Cf. P. Imbart de la Tour, *Les origines de la Réforme* (4 vols, Paris, 1904–35), II, pp. 349–58; F. Simone, *Il Rinascimento francese* (Turin, 1961), pp.114–40; and, for schools, G. Huppert, *Public Schools in Renaissance France* (Urbana: Chicago, 1984).

[16] See F. J. Baumgartner, 'Humanism and Heterodoxy in the French Episcopacy under Francis I', *Proceedings of the 8th Annual Meeting of the Western Society for French History, 1980* (1981), pp. 57–68.

[17] On Montluc, see Heller, *Conquest of Poverty*, pp. 225–33; on Caracciolo, see J. Roserot de Melin, *Antonio Caracciolo, évêque de Troyes, 1515–1570* (Paris, 1923).

also Bordeaux, which de Raemond attended.[18] Humanist teachers, possibly Protestant inclined to a greater or lesser degree, either introduced Reformed ideas directly to their students or else opened up the literary path towards new ideas. But neither a municipal college nor any other source of indigenous humanism was necessary for the growth of a strong Protestant movement, as a closer look at Tours should demonstrate.

Tours is particularly useful for testing any theory of a 'new class' behind humanism and Reformation. The conquest of municipal autonomy here had been accomplished without major conflicts with the clergy, and resulted in the consolidation of a strong and coherent urban ruling class. In the late fifteenth century a group of families, initially based in local commerce, money lending, and the ownership of urban property, had profited from the presence of the royal court in the Loire valley to make the big move into the financial service of the monarchy, and at the same time came to form the core of the ruling group in a city dominated by financial and legal officers rather than merchants. These clans – Briçonnet, Beaune, Burdelot, Berthelot, Fumée, Poncher, Ruzé, Gaillard, Bohier, Cottereau, Hurault, Babou – were all so inter-married as to form a kind of municipal mafia based on family connection. We immediately notice some familiar names, notably Briçonnet and Poncher, from the history of religious reform; but reform at Meaux or Paris, not in Tours. The acquisition of ecclesiastical benefices had been part of the power-seeking of the Tours mafia, and those of its members who entered the church whilst young became the carriers of humanism and the reform-minded element within the class.[19] Without pushing the point too far, religious reform appears in some cases as the last fling of families excluded from national political power after about 1517. Guillaume Briçonnet the elder, financier, diplomat and bishop of St Malo, who entered the Church on the death of his wife and became a cardinal within two years during and because of Charles VIII's invasion of Italy, is a classic example of the unscrupulous use of the Church for the pursuit of personal and family ambition. His son, Guillaume the younger, bishop of Lodève and then of Meaux, saw his political career terminated by 1517, took his first serious look at the diocese of Meaux two years after being made bishop, did not like what he saw, and is remembered as the leading reformist prelate of Francis I's reign and sponsor and protector of the 'Meaux group' of evangelicals, whose part in the early history of the Reformation has long been recognised.[20]

But this reformism elsewhere has little to do with Tours. There the arch-

---

[18] *Enquête sur les commencements du protestantisme en Agenais*, ed. M. O. Fallières and A. Durenges (Agen, 1913); Heller, *Conquest of Poverty*, ch. 3; E. Gaullieur, *Histoire du collège de Guyenne* (Paris, 1874), modified and corrected in R. Trinquet, *La jeunesse de Montaigne* (Paris, 1972), pp. 409–507.

[19] For the general background in Tours, see *Histoire de Tours*, ed. B. Chevalier (Toulouse, 1985), chs 3–5; and *idem, Tours, ville royale (1356–1520)* (Louvain: Paris, 1975).

[20] There is a parallel here with the careers of the d'Estaing brothers, both of whom were excluded from political power on the accession of Francis I.

bishops, with the exception of Hélie de Bourdeille between 1468 and 1484, were absentee grandees, and indigenous humanism was very weak. Popular piety seems to have been conventional enough, with the cult of St Martin as a particularly strong focal point, while the ruling élite was enthusiastic about revivalism but ignorant of humanism. The élite supported the revivalist preaching of the Observant Franciscans, who were attracted in the late fifteenth century by the proximity of the royal court; while François de Paule established his Minims at Le-Plessis-lès-Tours and Amboise, and became the spiritual director of at least part of the ruling class, stressing interior religion and personal austerity.[21] On the other hand, the town council successfully opposed the rather heavy-handed attempts by Olivier Maillard to impose the strict Observance upon the local Franciscans, despite the backing of the monarchy. As elsewhere in the 1480s and 1490s, and as we have seen in the events of 1491 at Albi, reform imposed from above, which could serve to increase or revive clerical power within the city, was opposed by the laity en masse, the fervour for individual moral reform shown by many lay people notwithstanding.[22] The rulers of Tours sponsored no companies of sots or fous, farces or carnival plays, but confined themselves to supporting preachers (as long as these stuck to sermonising) and moralising mystery plays. One has the impression of a newly-prominent élite desirous above all of social and religious tranquility, and impervious to the activist mentality of humanist reform. The printing press arrived in Tours in 1491, rather late for a city of such importance, and the élite owned few books. No municipal college existed until 1557 (again, very late), and the city had no Parlement or university and lay away from the great European trade routes.[23] But for urban oligarchs hoping for a quiet life, sources of trouble were building up – among the artisans below them, the lawyers alongside them, and in their own shifting ranks.

After the brief Huguenot occupation of Tours in 1562 a list of Protestant 'suspects' was drawn up. It included both large numbers of silk-workers and members of the élite, including about one third of the town councillors and many lawyers. Partial later studies indicate a Protestant presence in all classes, fortified by refugees from elsewhere, but with Huguenots tending to be better-off than the average.[24] The early history of Protestantism in Tours between the 1520s and 1540s shows the normal pattern of individuals, including churchmen, being attracted to

---

[21] Chevalier, Tours, ville royale, pp. 535–60; J. Guignard, 'Humanistes tourangeaux', Humanisme et Renaissance, vii (1940), 133–89.

[22] B. Chevalier, 'Olivier Maillard et la réforme des cordeliers (1482–1502)', Revue d'histoire de l'Église de France, lxv (1979), 25–39.

[23] The latter point distinguishes Tours from Lyon, the economic significance of which was crucial in making it the main French centre of cosmopolitan humanism under Italian influence.

[24] A. Dupin de Saint-André, Cinquantenaire de l'église réformée de Tours (Paris, 1887), appendix I; P. Aquilon, 'À Tours entre les "cent jours" et la Saint-Barthélémy. Les protestants de la paroisse Saint-Pierre-du-Boille', Les Réformes, ed. Chevalier and Sauzet, pp. 73–94.

evangelical ideas, with, by the mid-1540s, small clandestine groups meeting together in private, and Protestant artisans involved in acts of iconoclasm. The silk-workers and artisans of other luxury trades seem to be prototypical 'Hauserian' Protestants. Their trades were new, stimulated by the still frequent presence of the royal court in the Loire valley in the early sixteenth century, and had made fortunes for several rich merchants. By the 1540s, however, they were in an economically precarious position, and, as artisans, had never been allowed any taste of political power by a ruling group itself becoming smaller during the first half of the sixteenth century. Further up the social scale, Protestantism had gained its strongest footholds in the ever-growing office-holding class – all municipal officers were held to be suspect in 1562, as were eighteen members of the *bureau des finances* – and in the law. Seven *notaires*, twenty-four *avocats* and forty *procureurs* were listed, but the biggest concentration was in the new *présidial* court, founded in 1552, where the *Président* and seven other officials were Huguenots.[25] The evidence in Tours, as elsewhere, suggests that if we are looking for a 'new class' implicated in Protestantism, then we shall find it in the growing bureaucracies of the sixteenth century rather than in a thrusting bourgeoisie already prominent before the Reformation.

But if the Protestant movement in Tours appears as remarkably successful, considering the apparently unpromising context, it was far from united. On the eve of the religious wars the Huguenots constituted a squabbling minority searching for guidance. Divisions within Protestantism have traditionally been played down or ignored by Calvinist scholars, while the Hauserian tradition provides a partial explanation along class lines, with militant artisans, possibly led by members of the minor nobility, contrasted with more cautious bourgeois. Tours bears this out, but suggests that it was not the whole story. At no point, while Protestantism was still a growing movement, was it free of schisms based ultimately on an ambiguous attitude towards discipline, recognising its necessity while resisting its implications, and illustrating the imperfect nature of the Calvinist ascendancy in its search for an impossible unity. Disunity afflicted the church of Tours from its foundation in 1556 through to the end of the first religious war. The key figure in a sometimes confusing story, for which we are reliant on Calvinist sources, was Martin Piballeau, sieur de la Bédouère, a local petty nobleman, who first backed the unorthodox preacher, François de Beaupas, *dit* Chasseboeuf, but was opposed by a section of the congregation, who obtained two ministers from Geneva. The majority, however, followed La Bédouère and summoned from Poitiers another 'Genevan', Jacques L'Anglois, who, in turn, refused to preach. La Bédouère and L'Anglois journeyed to Geneva to plead their cause before the Company of Pastors, who admonished them and ordered L'Anglois to stay there for further instruction. When

---

[25] Heller, *Conquest of Poverty*, pp.117–20; Dupin de Saint-André, *loc. cit.*

the Genevans sent a new minister, a part of the church was never reconciled, and La Bédouère was excommunicated by the consistory.[26]

These events can only be properly understood in the context of the Reformation in the Loire valley, where the churches were particularly prone to schism, and the urban network allowed wandering preachers to go from town to town, regardless of the wishes of Geneva. The underdevelopment of education in Tours may have had something to do with this. In 1561 a group of 'unofficial' Protestants set up an 'Academy' in which, according to the Calvinist account, 'anyone, even women, was free to put forward whatever propositions he or she might choose'.[27] The Edict of January 1562, granting certain rights to Protestants, but under strict conditions, put an end to this effort, and the Protestants had no school in Tours until 1570. So the problem of discipline at Tours seems different from, for example, that at Poitiers, caused by a certain Lavau de Saint-Vertunian, a disciple of Sébastien Castellion,[28] suggesting that Calvinism had to deal both with alternative concepts of dogma and order and with a continuing doctrinal agnosticism among people wanting to become 'true Christians', without being sure what this meant. Disunity within the church combined with the events of the first religious war – a very brief Protestant occupation, followed by a firm Catholic reestablishment – to reduce the Huguenots of Tours to an embattled minority, whose relatively secure economic position served to make more conspicuous as potential targets of popular hostility. The example of Tours, then, indicates one possible outcome of the interplay between revivalism, humanism and heresy in a city with a strong revivalist tradition, but where humanism was imported by bureaucrats coming from elsewhere.

The search for the origins of the Reformation in France does nothing to deny the revolutionary character of organised Protestantism in its brutal overthrow of so many practices, which were signs of beliefs, and of a conception of relations between the human and the supernatural based on a complex series of mediations. But the circumstances of its arrival in different places show a set of significant variables working their way through both long-term processes and short-term events. The link between humanism and the Reformation remains problematic. Tours has given us an example of a powerful Protestant movement developing where native humanism was virtually non-existent, a case to be set alongside the many, predominantly south of the Loire, where the Reformation had its beginnings in the new municipal colleges.[29] Humanism did not lead inexorably to

---

[26] *Histoire ecclésiastique des églises réformées au royaume de France*, ed. G. Baum and E. Cunitz (3 vols, Paris, 1883–89), I, pp.127–9; R. M. Kingdon, *Geneva and the Coming of the Wars of Religion in France, 1555–1563* (Geneva, 1956), pp. 49–50.

[27] *Histoire ecclésiastique*, I, pp. 835–6.

[28] Heller, *Conquest of Poverty*, pp.199–200.

[29] *Ibid.*, p. 77, has a list of 26 colleges where evangelical ideas are known to have been disseminated before 1550, the majority of them south of the Loire, and with none in the Loire valley itself.

Protestantism, but humanist reformism continued alongside the new religion until the outbreak of civil war imposed often unpalatable choices. The concern for the right ordering of religion could not now be separated from doctrinal matters, forcing reformist bishops into what came to look like an ambiguous position and into forlorn attempts to create in their dioceses a form of religion neither papist nor Huguenot, inevitably running aground on the reefs of Calvinist intransigence and the necessity of creating a precisely-defined Catholicism in response to it. And the 'born-again' nature of Protestant moralism, even allowing for the variety of opinions and actions subsumed within it, was ultimately, in its emotional commitment and developing élitism, more revivalist than humanist.

The direct relationship with God upon which Protestantism was built depended on having power or the promise of power, or at the least on preserving one's condition in circumstances of economic and political insecurity. The purpose of life had to be more than survival, that is to say more than the purpose forced by the social order on the urban poor and the bulk of the peasantry. For the bourgeois Protestant, 'living a Christian life according to the Gospel' was an alternative form of luxury, avoiding the moral reproaches which came with power and riches, but leaving room for accusations of hypocrisy. Protestantism was a new form of the urban asceticism previously urged by revivalist preachers, but with the fundamental difference of being a permanent way of life. Protestants did not need bonfires of vanities because, theoretically at least, they lived without vanity. It was a rival, intellectualised form of expiation of the urban sins of avarice and usury, based on being individually reborn in Christ rather than relying on the intercession of saints and clergy for remission. But at the same time the urban oligarchies were in a dilemma: they had to defend municipal autonomy while preserving social order within the city and the myth of civic unity, a dilemma compounded by the growth of the financial and legal bureaucracies, and in some towns, as Heller's study of Valence shows graphically,[30] by the continuing combat against ecclesiastical rights within the city. They could not, therefore, consider the religious question separately from its social consequences. This could mean playing down religious divisions for the eyes of outsiders, while minorities of committed Protestants and intransigent anti-Protestants faced each other across a majority worrying more about order than theology, and including the 'Nicodemites' so vehemently denounced by Calvin. The political crisis and economic instability of the late 1550s strengthened commitment on both sides and imposed a 'coming out' on bourgeois Protestants. On the eve of the religious wars the majority may have been neither 'Catholic' nor Calvinist, but the Protestants made the running for a while, buoyed up by movements from below.

Peter Burke has identified five broad popular attitudes to social injustice in early-modern Europe – fatalist, moralist, traditionalist, radical, and millenarian[31]

---

[30] *Ibid.*, ch. 7.
[31] P. Burke, *Popular Culture in Early Modern Europe* (London, 1978), p.174.

– all of which are evident in the crises leading up to the outbreak of religious war. Protestantism provided a minority of artisans, most notably in the newer trades, and above all, perhaps, among those who had recently settled in a new city, with a solution that was moralist and radical, with hints of the millenarian. But for the majority in, say, Tours, was not St Martin, with his local connections, historical role as protector of the city, and place up above in the kingdom of God, a better safeguard against misfortune than was the unalloyed, intellectualised Gospel? And were not both of these surer than John Calvin and the Company of Pastors of Geneva? The further one gets from the centres of power – among those on the receiving end of urban avarice and usury – the more rational do fatalist and traditionalist responses appear. The centres of power and the powerless were both divided among themselves, with, in both instances, the 'newer' and more mobile attracted to radical solutions, but with a majority probably fitting no rigid characterisation, and bolstered in their uncertainty by a degree of undisguised *attentisme*.

Our search for some origins of the French Reformation confirms the vitality of both the Febvrian and Hauserian traditions, though possibly in different ways from those envisaged by their founders. An organising triad of locality, civil power, and the Church seems to point the way forward. Hauser pulls Febvre down to earth, but the Reformation is revealed as comprehensible only when the events of the early sixteenth century are placed in the context of a localised history going back at least into the fifteenth. And for the purposed of this colloquium the value of studying the period of French history from around 1450 to 1562 is confirmed.

NOTES ON CONTRIBUTORS

Christopher ALLMAND (Editor) is Reader in Medieval History at the University of Liverpool.

Kathleen DALY graduated at Oxford in 1978 and obtained her D.Phil. there in 1984. She has taught History at the University of Lancaster, and is currently a Lecturer in Medieval History at Lady Margaret Hall and St Hugh's College, Oxford. She has contributed articles on French medieval historiography and iconography to *Peritia*, *Bodleian Library Record*, and to the Congrès National des Sociétés Savantes.

Elizabeth DANBURY, a graduate of King's College, London, at present teaches in the department of History at the University of Liverpool, where she is Lecturer-in-Charge of the postgraduate course in Archive Administration.

Brian G. H. DITCHAM graduated at St Andrews in 1975. He moved to Edinburgh where, in 1979, he obtained his Ph.D. for a thesis on the role of foreign troops in the French royal armies from 1415 to 1475. He now works for the Department of Trade and Industry.

David NICHOLLS received his Ph.D. from the University of Birmingham, and has taught at the Universities of Leeds, Warwick, and Exeter. He has published several articles on sixteenth-century French social and religious history, and he is currently working on a book on the social history of the French Reformation.

Catherine REYNOLDS graduated at Oxford in 1973 and obtained her Ph.D. from the University of London in 1986 for a thesis on the Master of the Duke of Bedford. After nearly ten years at the University of Reading, she is now Lecturer in the History of Art at Westfield College, London. Her published work has mainly appeared in *The Burlington Magazine*.

Penny RICHARDS, Senior Lecturer in History, College of St Paul and St Mary, Cheltenham, wrote her thesis on the royal entries of Francis I, and is now working on Anne d'Esté. She had presented papers in England, Poland, and America, serves on the committee of the Society for the Study of French History, and is an active member of the Woman's Studies Group, 1600–1825.

Alison ROSIE graduated from Edinburgh in 1982. In 1983 she gained the Diploma in Archive Administration from the University College of Wales,

Aberystwyth, and that same year began research at Edinburgh on court spectacle in Anjou, Orléans, and Savoy in the fifteenth century. Since 1986 she has been on the staff of the Scottish Record Office, Edinburgh.

Guy THOMPSON graduated from Corpus Christi College, Oxford in 1979. His doctoral thesis on the Anglo-Burgundian régime in Paris 1420–1436 is to be published by the Oxford University Press in the 'Oxford Historical Monographs' series. He is now a solicitor specialising in commercial law.

INDEX

abbeys, 135

'Abrégé des Chroniques de France': see Fribois

'abuses', 131, 134

Aeolus, 120

Agen, college at, 138

Ages of man; see Bronze, Golden, Iron, Silver

Agincourt, battle of (1415), 3, 39

Agrippa of Nettesheim, 122n; his *Three Books of Occult Philosophy*, 126

Albi, 135–6; bishop of, see Amboise; consuls of, 135; disputed jurisdictions, 135; Franciscans at, 135; municipal privileges, 135; municipality, 135; reform at, 135–6, 140; school at, 136

Alençon, Jean, duke of, 27n

Alexandre, trumpeter, 68

Allinge, François d', seigneur de Servete, 65

Alnwick, William, bishop of Lincoln, 90–1

Alps, 62, 73

altar hangings, 39; pieces, 45; vessels, 46

Ambleton, Michael, 11

Amboise, 129n; Louis d', bishop of Albi, 134–5; Minims at, 140

Amedée VI, duke of Savoy, 58

Amedée VII, 66

Amedée VIII, 57–8, 62–3, 67, 71–2; his new order, 71, 73; see also Dupin, Felix V, *Statuta Sabaudia*

Amedée IX, 65

Amer, Pierre, 102–03

angels, 105n; heraldic, 83, 86–7, 90–1, 94–5

Angoulême, bishop of; see Estaing

Anjou: ambassadors of, 69; court of, 59; see also Isabelle, Margaret, René

Annalles . . . des Gaulles; see Gilles

Anne: of Brittany, 135; of Cyprus, see Louis, duke of Savoy. *See also* Bedford

anniversaries, 53

antelope, 91

Apelles, 45

Apocalypse, 67, 126

Aquitaine, 94

Aragon; *see* Ferdinand

Arbeau, Thoinet, 57, 59, 61; his *Orchesography*, 57

architecture, 38

archives, 101–04

Areopagus, 16

'argent batu', 61

'Armagnacs', 5, 8, 17, 19–20, 22, 27n, 28–9, 31–2; sash of, 48

armour, 87n

arms, coats of, 5, 45, 51, 53, 61, 63, 68, 76n, 80, 82–3, 86–7, 90–4, 97n, 105–06, 122; *see also* Bedford, Bristol, Burgundy, Dauphin, Edward III, Eleanor, Ferrante, Henry V, Henry VI, Margaret, Milan, Savoy, Stewart of Darnley, Talbot

army, mercenary, 3, 5n; *see also compagnies d'ordonnance*, English, France, Scotland

Arras: Congress of, 32; treaty of, 40

art, in politics, xi–xii, 41, 47–9, 75ff, 99ff, 117ff

Arthus, Wastre, 10

artillery, 32; *grenier* in Paris, 49; used at Albi, 135

artisans, 133, 136, 140–1, 144

artists, xii, 41, 46, 54, 61, 66–7, 75–6, 79–80, 82, 86n, 94, 97; *see also* embroiderers, goldbeaters, goldsmiths, illuminators, metalwork, musicians, painters, tapestry-makers; Bernard, Châtel, Estienne, Michiel, Robert

Astesano, Antonio, 17, 24, 33, 46

Astrea (Justice), 117, 121, 123

Athena, 122–3, 125

Athens, 16, 122

Atlas, 125

Aubigny; *see* Stewart

Aubigny-sur-Nère, 11

Augustan era, 124

Aurillac, 9

Auvergne, 6

Auxerre: Guillaume d', 28; Michelette d', 28n; Jeanne d' 28n; *see also* Longeuil

Auxon, Pierre d', 44